D0563152

One Thousand
And One
Night Stands

by *Ted Shawn*

with *Gray Poole*

ONE THOUSAND

AND ONE

NIGHT STANDS

New introduction by **Walter Terry**

A DA CAPO PAPERBACK

ST. PHILIPS COLLEGE LIBRARY

Library of Congress Cataloging in Publication Data

Shawn, Ted, 1891-1972.
    One thousand and one night stands.

    Reprint of the ed published by Doubleday,
Garden City, N.Y.
    1. Shawn, Ted, 1891-1972. 2. Choreographers —
United States — Biography. 3. Denishawn school
of dancing, New York. I. Poole, Gray Johnson,
joint author. II. Title.
    [GV1785.S5A3 1979]   792.8'092'4 [B]   78-20818
    ISBN 0-306-80095-0

S 5

-921
S537

ISBN 0-306-80095-0

First Paperback Edition 1979

This Da Capo Press paperback edition of *One Thousand and One
Night Stands* is an unabridged republication of the first
edition published by Doubleday & Company, Inc. in New York
in 1960. The present edition contains a new introduction by
Walter Terry and is reprinted by arrangement with the
original publisher.

Copyright © 1960 by Ted Shawn.

Introduction copyright © 1979 by Walter Terry.

Published by Da Capo Press, Inc.
A Subsidiary of Plenum Publishing Corporation
227 West 17th Street, New York, New York, 10011

All Rights Reserved

Manufactured in the United States of America

ST. PHILIPS COLLEGE LIBRARY

Introduction

N "Walter," said Ted Shawn, "I'm too close to it to know what's funny and what is not. Why don't you just run through what I have written and extract the anecdotes." The item he expected me to "run through" consisted of close to three-quarters of a million words of autobiographical material! It had begun when a publisher expressed interest in a collection of stories, anecdotes, and incidents to be called *One Thousand and One Night Stands* —a saga of the mishaps (and *haps!*) of a famous, world-traveled dancer who had been on the road for close to half a century.

In his own methodical way — yes, he was highly organized as well as being highly temperamental — Shawn thought that the best way to prepare such a book was to start at the begin-ning and write down everything. Once the monumental chro-

57779

nology was on paper, it would be child's play to lift the "hahas" from the manuscript, wouldn't it? No, it wouldn't. I tried. There was just no way to accomplish the surgery while doing my daily critic's duties for the *New York Herald Tribune* and writing a book of my own.

Shawn was miffed at me briefly but all turned out for the best. Gray Poole, a marvelous writer with a delicious sense of humor, a sharp wit, and an expert's knowledge of dance, took on the job. Moreover, she knew Ted Shawn personally, for her husband had been a dancer and both regarded him as a close friend as well as a dance star whose accomplishments they had long admired. Gray was just the one to do this light, frisky, and curiously informative memoir.

The book itself, *One Thousand and One Night Stands,* might seem to be pleasantly inconsequential. It is not. Anecdotal it may be, as intended, but its stories, vignettes, and jokes report on an era in the theater that is gone. It is, along with its ability to evoke chuckles, a history. Today's reader will laugh at tales of maharajahs — themselves a disappearing breed — but he will be brought up short, since we live in the midst of the greatest dance explosion in history, with Shawn's report of a high school principal who canceled a talk on dance, saying: "I have decided that it would be dangerous for our students to listen to a dancer." The year was 1922.

A new generation of dancers and dance fans may think of Ted Shawn simply as on old-timer or, if they are knowledgeable, as a pioneer in the field of American dance. It is too easily forgotten that Ruth St. Denis, Ted Shawn, and the Denishawn Dancers *were* American dance for fifteen years. They brought dance as art, as well as entertainment, not only to major cities but also to small towns, not just once but again and again. They also dared to believe that dance had educational values and they saw to it that their teachers and schools ranged from coast to coast. They broke box office records in concert halls, vaudeville houses, stadia; they made lots of money and spent every cent of it . . . on next season's dance productions.

Denishawn was unique in the annals of dance and it has never been equaled. Ted Shawn was also unique and his pioneering company of all-male dancers in the post-Denishawn era was and remains unparalleled in the chronicles of American dance. Shawn's (and Mrs. Poole's) *One Thousand and One Night Stands* does not pretend to be a definitive history of a remarkable dance age, but while you are laughing, tut-tutting, or murmuring "I don't believe it!", something of the magnitude of the achievements, the trials and the triumphs, of Ruth St. Denis, Ted Shawn, Martha Graham, and all the other dauntless dancers of not-so-long-ago will give you pause. For dance history was indeed made during those one thousand and one, two, three, four . . . . . night (day, week, month, year, decade) stands.

—WALTER TERRY

New York
November, 1978

Contents

CONTENTS

*One Thousand
And One
Night Stands*

●● ●●

1

Santa Fe Hop

Ever since my first and unprecedented tour of one-night stands, I have devoted myself to dancing as a profession. For more than forty-five years dance has been my life. An inevitable result of my professional perseverance as performer and teacher, writer and lecturer is that I now am listed in most catalogues given over to facts and figures of biography. The skeletal accounts of my statistical self are more or less accurate but they omit any reference to certain events that have made the years ever lively, often lovely for me.

I have yet to find any biographical statement about the Sunday I spent kissing Gloria Swanson by stop watch. Missing, too, is a note about the later occasion, when, to complete a sylvan costume, my bare torso was girdled with poison ivy. Absent from chronicles óf my achievements is the fact that I

ST. PHILIPS COLLEGE LIBRARY

once fashioned a costume helmet from a kitchen colander which I had first tried on for size in the basement of a five-and-ten-cent store.

Such disparate incidents surely cannot be matched by others alphabetized with me in volumes of who and why. Indeed, I myself should regret to have the sum total of my own life and work judged by such extraordinary goings on. However, my path as a pioneer dancer was milestoned by the bizarre and spectacular, the hilarious, the horrendous. Today it is as difficult to imagine as it would be to duplicate the trivia and travails, the sidelights, the highlights of theatrical trouping as it existed for years after I struck out as an itinerant performer.

On the morning of January 2, 1914, I dropped off the train at Gallup, New Mexico, where I was to play a one-night stand with a company that carried my own name. My imagination linked Shawn with Pavlova, St. Denis, and Hoffman, the few dance stars then intrepid enough to tour the United States. The fact that they played full week engagements, and those only in big cities, in no way lessened my youthful sense of identification with the greats of the dance world. I was in high spirits. Even before checking on the hall where we were to perform, I set out with sure strides of confidence to see the town.

Within a few minutes perspectives and my pace changed. The vast desert spreading to the horizon seemed to shrink in size as the men of the town began to loom giantlike against sand-colored Gallup. Cold sweat chilled my skin and an ice lump weighted my middle as I tallied the side arms holstered against slim hips. The faces under broad-brimmed felt were prototypes of the two-gun, grim-visaged movie stars of silent westerns.

How would the male citizenry react to a man garbed in a flame-colored chiton as I would be that night when I performed my Greek dance? I formulated a dreadful answer. Behind the footlights I would be at the mercy of any draw-happy cowpoke who chose to spatter lead on the stage while he yippied, "Dance in that red nightshirt, boy. Dance!"

In a fair fight with fists I was equipped to face any man, for I was big and rippling with muscle. But I was properly respectful of shot and shell, and at twenty-two, young enough to be frankly fearful of public ridicule.

With no heart for further exploration, I turned back toward the hotel. I contemplated a surreptitious examination of timetables to find out what trains were scheduled to leave in either direction that day. Confronted by the gaunt men of Gallup, I briefly considered forsaking dancing forever.

My sudden panic was not as unreasoned as it may seem. Less then two years before I had been subjected to argument and invective about the man who danced. And from people much more worldly and sophisticated than the rugged frontiersmen of Gallup.

A fraternity brother in Denver, frankly appalled by my announced intention of becoming a dancer, had closed an impassioned harangue with the flat statement, "But, Ted, *men* don't dance." In vain I countered that men performed ritual dances in many countries of the world, that he and I together had enjoyed performances by Mikhail Mordkin, partner of Pavlova, and by Theodore Kosloff of the Gertrude Hoffman Company. "Oh, those people," he dismissed them with a shrug. He admitted, though grudgingly, that dancing might be all right for aborigines and Russians, but he contended vehemently that it was hardly a suitable career for a red-blooded American male.

The classmate did not dissuade me nor did a more august former friend who lashed at me by written word after he had seen newspaper pictures of me with a dancing partner. The partner and I were to do a ballroom exhibition at a benefit performance, and a page feature of us was part of the advance promotion for the charity event. I was shown in a full dress suit, and she in a dress with skirt slit up one side. In a couple of the action photographs my partner's silk-stockinged leg was exposed well above a very shapely knee.

Today those pictures would be considered quaint, but the artistic exposure outraged Chancellor Henry Augustus Buchtel of the University of Denver. The chancellor had been my mentor and counselor before poor health forced me to leave college in my junior year. He was then a nominee for the bishop of his church while I was a pre-theology student and of the same denomination.

My efforts in campus dramatic productions had been applauded by the chancellor so I was both hurt and surprised by his letter of stern reproof. In his lengthy communication he regretted that I was no longer at the university because he was deprived of the pleasure of expelling me for complicity in such an exhibition as the newspaper publicized. As it was, the chancellor made clear, he considered that I had brought dishonor to my alma mater.

With such experiences in memory, is it any wonder that I was apprehensive about the reception of a Gallup audience?

Like many another professional, I originally had turned to dancing as physical therapy. The long illness that disrupted my education left me with a temporary paralysis of feet, legs, and thighs. During a slow, stumbling spring convalescence, I enrolled as a student at the Barnes Commercial School from which I was graduated into a summertime secretarial position with the Northwestern Mutual Life Insurance Company.

With a daytime job but without homework assignments or campus activities to keep me busy, I began to spend my evenings with a group of little theater amateurs. In vain I tried to take on small acting parts in their productions. The movements of my body still were so jerky and unpredictable that I could be suitably cast only as an inebriate. When it became painfully obvious even to me that I needed regular exercise to improve my co-ordination, I started to take ballet lessons.

That was the end and the beginning. I never went back to college and I have never stopped dancing.

My Denver teacher was Hazel Wallack, an accomplished, well-trained ballerina who left New York and a promising career with the Metropolitan Opera Ballet only because of illness in her Colorado family. Her dancing background was so sound that in later life I never had to unlearn the techniques she taught me.

Hazel was the third girl I asked to marry me but the first to whom I was formally engaged, complete with diamond ring. Cupid, however, did not triumph over Terpsichore. In time I found myself in artistic disagreement with Hazel, an unyielding exponent of the classical ballet. I was unwilling to limit myself either to traditional ballet or to any other single dance style. I yearned to experiment.

Without Hazel's blessing, I followed an insistent urge to broaden my dance experience and left Denver for Los Angeles. There I fully expected to be able to study with dance experts working in the booming motion-picture capital. My first weeks of disillusionment were made sorrowful by a broken engagement and return of the ring so lately a symbol of future happiness.

I was unable to find the teachers I sought in southern California but my experience was unexpectedly broadened by the great ballroom dance craze. "Everybody's Doing It" was a popular hit and theme song for a dancing public eager to learn the steps of the bunny hug, the grizzly bear, and the turkey trot, as well as those of the more sedate dances: the tango, the one-step, the maxixe.

Caught up in the sweeping movement, I gave ballroom exhibitions with Norma Gould, who ran a ballet school for children. She was as little interested as I in a ballroom dancing career but neither she nor I could resist the easy money which helped to support our separate dance studios, our serious dance projects.

For more than a year I kept a marathon pace which, in retrospect, leaves even me breathless. During the day I worked as stenographer to the auditor of the City Water Department of Los Angeles. By arranging for a fifteen-minute lunch period when I gulped a malted, I was able to close my ledger at four-fifteen. From the office I dashed to the Angelus Hotel where Norma and I had organized a series of successful dances, the Tango Teas.

Following the *thé dansant*, I gobbled a snack before rushing to my rented studio to teach the first of three consecutive ballroom classes of an hour each. The last class finished at ten, and by ten-five I was changing speedily into white tie and tails. Shortly afterward I stepped into a spotlight at the Alexandria Hotel where Norma and I danced nightly for the after-theater set.

The split-second schedule of weekdays was accelerated during week ends. On Saturday afternoons and Sundays I choreographed and practiced my own solo dances, and taught "classic and interpretive dancing," the high-flown phrase then descriptive of any dancing other than tap, ballroom, acrobatic, or ballet. With Norma, I created duets for programs we gave for clubs and other organizations in the area. We pooled pupils to form a modest supporting company which gave me my first chance to experiment with group choreography.

During my second summer in Los Angeles I made a movie for the Thomas A. Edison Company. At Long Beach studios we shot scenes for *The Dance of the Ages* based on a sketchy scenario idea I submitted to the company. I wrote a thread-thin dance history beginning in the Stone Age, progressing through the glorious ages of Egypt, Greece, and Rome into Medieval Europe, and ending with contemporary dance of the United States. The ambitious undertaking, slated for production during my two-week vacation and finished on schedule, featured Norma and me with our dancing group.

Everybody in California was pioneering in business or the arts. The movies, themselves experimental, were exciting to imaginations geared to accept the creative process wherever it mushroomed. No serious-minded innovator was sneered at or ridiculed and, for more than a year, I worked with freedom and encouragement.

Money accumulated rapidly in my bank account during this boom period, but I began to feel that I was only marking time. My ambition was to be a great dance star, an artist in my profession, a goal that I could not approach until I stopped teaching and gave up ballroom exhibitions. I needed intensive training in various styles and techniques with exacting teachers. And I was convinced at long last that the classes, the courses, and the people from whom I could learn were all in New York three thousand miles away.

Just when my thoughts were more often on the future than on my work, I heard a rumor that the Santa Fe Railroad was recruiting entertainers to play at employee recreation centers along its line. On the chance that I might get to New York fare-free with my nest egg intact for lesson fees, I called on Mr. S. E. Busser who engaged the Santa Fe talent.

The Santa Fe previously had engaged only single artists, a singer, a violinist, or a diseuse, but Mr. Busser liked the novelty of a proposed program by a small dance group. He signed us to play nineteen performances for the Santa Fe in return for round-trip tickets for each member of our company of six. Though eventually we did reach New York, I will never know why we didn't quit the tour even before the first performance at Gallup.

En route to Gallup we preened as we read and reread the program notes prepared by the Santa Fe for our performance:

THE SHAWN-GOULD COMPANY
OF INTERPRETIVE DANCERS

Dancing as an interpretive art—Appearance of Ted Shawn and Norma Gould, assisted by Adelaide Munn and Otis Williams in the rendition of classical and historical works of the Masters, accompanied by a Virtuoso Pianiste and Violiniste and Soloist.

Ted Shawn	Dancer and Manager
Norma Gould	Dancer
Adelaide Munn	Dancer
Otis Williams	Dancer
Blanche Ebert	Pianiste
Brahm Von der Berg	Soprano soloist, Violiniste

Announcement

In the past few months the names of Ted Shawn and Norma Gould have become household words in Los Angeles and Southern California. Their appearance and work have been hailed with delight by the educated and refined, and the results of their entertainments, from a classical and literary standpoint, have been very satisfactory. Miss Munn and Mr. Williams have become members of the company in order to make the interpretations more complete and to direct the dramatic ensemble. Each of these dancers has attained eminence in the profession. Some people may object to an entertain-

ment of this character because it is dancing; but
please do not commit an error here. It is a portrayal
of perfect development by the most exacting labor
and much self-denial. It is the drama acted and
illustrated by music and the graceful movement in
artistic forms of the human body guided by pure
hearts and active brains. It is an attempt to per-
sonify history. It is an effort to make a past age
live in the present. It is a pleasure to introduce such
artists to our employees. I subjoin a few points to set
your thinking and accentuate your participation.
Dances of Henry VIII
Diana and Endymion
The Cycle—Winter, Spring, Summer, Autumn
Don't Miss the Shawn-Gould Company of Interpretive Dancers.

Surely we were not to blame for expecting that everything
would be arranged for our comfort and pleasure. Were we not
being presented as artists without peer? On arrival, we found
that no arrangements had been made for a group, and that
Gallup was geared to the solo recitalist. After my shortened
stroll through the town, I disconsolately met the rest of the
company and together we visited the recreation building where
my spirits took another dive. By noon we had decided that
the conditions under which we were expected to perform were
the worst in the world. Actually they were only the worst on
the Santa Fe circuit. Before many years passed I often had
played under greater handicaps in big theaters and small, in
hamlet and metropolis.

At the time we were enraged at the Santa Fe. The stage
on which we were to dance was simply a tiny platform at
the end of a lounge where off-duty employees read or played
checkers or shot pool. The performance area was impossibly

small for any of our dance numbers. No provision was made for theatrical lighting and there was no front curtain.

The men's dressing room was an emptied swimming pool, cold as an old-fashioned ice chest in the New Mexican night. Costumes had to be carried down into the pool where our make-up table, a rickety monstrosity, was lighted with a single bulb dangling from a long extension cord. Icy rungs of metal almost tore the flesh from my bare feet as I climbed the ladder to make my first entrance, shivering from cold and shaking from the presentiment of trouble from the audience.

On stage we had to dodge and dip our heads to avoid light brackets that jutted out from the walls. We had to improvise our choreography with shortened steps to keep from toppling off the postage-stamp stage. The whole experience was a nightmare of apprehension and discomfort. I remember nothing of the audience response.

I only know that we finished the performance without a shot being fired. The entire company safely and thankfully rolled away from Gallup on a midnight Pullman. We had eighteen more one-night stands to play before we used our last train stub, the one marked NEW YORK.

2

Too Late?

Our tickets read "Los Angeles to New York," but our immediate destination was New Canaan, Connecticut, where we had been encouraged to study by Bliss Carman, the famous Canadian poet.

Our pilgrimage was the result of correspondence between me and Mr. Carman after I had read an article, "The Making of a Personality," in which Carman expressed opinions about the dance that brought into focus some of my own uncrystallized thoughts. Excited by his prose, beautiful, concise, and explicit, I sent him a letter of appreciation and inquiry. He answered quickly, suggesting that if his stated ideals and ideas of dance had such appeal for me, I might want to study with Mrs. Mary Perry King, his collaborator in dance expression. I shared my Carman correspondence with Norma Gould and

Addie Munn and they, too, decided to go to New Canaan.

I have a diploma to prove that "The Uni-Trinian School of Personal Harmonizing and Self-Development" did once exist. Its classes were held at Sunshine House, home of Mrs. King, the school's manager, treasurer, teacher, and artistic director.

Bliss Carman, an old friend of Mrs. King and her doctor husband, was at the studio every day making himself useful in little ways and going off alone into quiet corners to write poetry. He was a devoted disciple of Mrs. King, designer of "Uni-Trinian shoes" with the semicircular soles that gave the poet a hobby-horse gait. The curious shoe construction required him to step heel down first, then rock forward to the toe, and rock forward again from the heel of the other shoe. Mr. Carman was a tall man with spare frame topped by a shock of sandy hair and he looked quite like a nodding sunflower as he walked about in his original rock 'n' rolls.

I never understood the purpose of the shoe design but it was no more weird than other less tangible inventions of Mrs. King's.

Our six-day-a-week schedule with her was intensive. We went to Sunshine House every morning at nine. There we stretched, exercised, and practiced sweeping arm motions in various tempos and rhythms until noon when we lunched with Mrs. King. After lunch we exercised again and practiced dances choreographed by Mrs. King. By five or six, at the latest, we were dismissed for the day.

Many years later, I learned that the exercises, movements, and gestures that we practiced and studied were pure Delsarte. That term, however, was never mentioned by Mrs. King and we thought, in our ignorance, that the system was her own. I found through later study that she did indeed teach thorough and inclusive Delsarte but then restricted it to a limited framework of elementary dance patterns.

Her own application of Delsartian principles was bizarre;

I know that now. Even then I was aware that her choreography was lifeless, unimaginative, and exceedingly amateurish. The only notations of her choreography were sketchy ones made by the accompanist on the piano music. One day Mrs. King went over to the piano and dum-dummed a bar or two to recall a section of a dance. "Lift left foot. Lift right foot." She broke off her chant and screamed at the accompanist, "Why, you've got both my feet off the ground at the same time." We three students from California thought that laughter-control during such studio incidents might be classed as "Uni-Trinian Self-Development."

Before we knew Bliss Carman and Mrs. King, they had collaborated on two productions, *Daughters of the Dawn* and *Earth Deities,* using the spoken word of his poetry as accompaniment for dance movement. Mrs. King continued the recitation and dance method with the three of us which was all very well for Norma and Addie but hardly suitable for me. Mrs. King's work had been almost exclusively with girls and she not only had never choreographed for a male dancer, she had no instinctive feeling for what was suitable to masculine movement as theme material for a man.

When I found that I was expected to dance while Mrs. King recited, "The wind went combing through the grass, the lithe young daisies swayed and bowed," I rebelled. I would have been embarrassed even to have Mr. Carman wander into the studio while I was combing, swaying, and bowing. Perhaps those were his own lines but, if so, they do not appear in either the "Daughters" or the "Deities" volumes which I still have in my library.

Our month in New Canaan was about over when Mrs. King announced that she had a brilliant idea. She wanted to put Norma and me in vaudeville with a dance sketch she had originated: "The scene is Central Park. An Irish nursemaid (Norma) and an Irish-American policeman (Shawn) meet and break into a Kerry dance. And then——"

Before Mrs. King could bring her sketch to a close, I undiplomatically burst out that I had not come three thousand miles nor spent some hundreds of dollars with her to end up as an Irish policeman in vaudeville.

Mrs. King glowered at me, "And what else are you going to do? You're too big for a classic dancer. You started to dance ten or more years too late ever to acquire a ballet technique. You are mildly good-looking but you'll never stop traffic on Broadway. Just exactly what do you think you can do?"

In a flash I replied, "Mrs. King, I shall become a great and internationally famous dancer with a style and technique of my own." She looked at me wide-eyed for one second and then flopped back on her couch screeching with uncontrolled laughter.

Right here let's make it clear that Mrs. King had some truth on her side. I was big for a dancer. I stood a full six feet and my frame was large. It was a struggle to keep my weight in control. For twenty years I varied only five pounds during tour season but to keep down to 180 pounds, I always dieted and sometimes fasted for as much as three consecutive days.

The press has been concerned about my weight, in print and out, for forty years. "Haven't you lost weight (gained weight) since I last interviewed you?" are questions I must have answered a hundred times. And I always have lost or gained because calories and I keep up a running battle.

My height, in the beginning, was more asset than drawback. The willowy Hazel Wallack rushed my early training so she would have a partner tall enough for her. Norma, also more than average height, was delighted to find a partner who complemented her as a team.

I was perfectly frank to admit the limitations of my size,

to accept the evaluation of my looks, but I could not forgive
Mrs. King's ridicule of my ambition. Put it down as an admitted flaw in my character that for twenty-five years afterward, Mrs. King received copies of my best press notices,
mailed by me, from London and Berlin, Tokyo and Calcutta,
Bombay and Boston. I never eased up on the barrage of rave
reviews of Shawn although, in later years, Mrs. King and I
did become friends. No friendly feeling warmed me, however,
as we left New Canaan and its Uni-Trinian School.

The grudge was temporarily dismissed from my mind in
New York where I concentrated on the study of many forms
of dancing. I was determined to stay as long as my savings
lasted and wherever possible augmented my bank account with
fees from performances. Friends made it possible for Norma
and me to appear now and again in New York recitals. At the
MacDowell Club we appeared on one program with two well-
known dancers, Lydia Lopokova and Eduard Makalif, and
were no end set up to receive equal applause with those established performers.

After we had given a few New York performances, I was
approached by young dancers who wanted to study the techniques that were my own and which they could get from no
one else. Since every dollar earned meant that I could stay
longer to study, I rented a studio by the hour, and took on a
number of private lesson pupils.

For practical purposes I perfected the latest ballroom steps
as soon as we went to New York. After that I applied myself
to the ballet techniques of Russia, France, and Italy. I attended classes in Spanish dancing taught by a true flamenco,
and worked on pantomime with someone who had been with
Max Reinhardt in Germany. I lacked only instruction in
oriental dance, and yearned to study that with St. Denis, un-
challenged star in the field.

One of my own pupils, Marielle Moeller, casually mentioned one day that she was going to a St. Denis studio party. I asked if she would tell Ruth St. Denis that I had unbounded admiration for her as an artist, that I was eager to study with her, and could pay well for lessons.

With a caution uncharacteristic of Ruth as I knew her later, she sent Brother St. Denis to see me before she would make an appointment. This man, billed on dance programs as René, was always *Brother* to friends, family, and business associates. He and I chatted pleasantly, if idly, on the day that he came to look me over and, as he left, he assured me that I would hear from his sister. A few days later I held in my hand a treasured paper—an invitation to tea from Ruth St. Denis.

···

3

I Meet the Idol

When I stepped into the New York studio of Ruth St. Denis one spring day in 1914, I had no premonition that the course of my life was about to be redirected.

I was an ardent fan of St. Denis and had been since first I saw her dance in Denver during her 1911 tour. Her performance, her grace, her ethereal beauty had thrilled me. The impact of her broad approach to the dance had strengthened my own determination not ever to be trapped by one limited style of dancing.

On the afternoon of my first appointment with St. Denis, I waited impatiently for her to join me, hoping that she would accept me as a pupil. Pictures of her in many roles lined the walls of the huge room at the front of her five-story house off Riverside Drive. I paced about looking in vain for a photograph of the dancer in street clothes. For the first time I was curious about St. Denis the woman, the human being. Through the years I had carried in my mind the flowing image of the performer. I had visualized again and again the raven-haired nautch girl whose feet were more supple than most hands, whose hands were the most expressive in the world, whose walk was a ballet in itself.

The real St. Denis was quite different, I knew. Although I had never seen her off stage, friends had told me that she bore little resemblance to the Hindu and Egyptian goddesses she brought to life across the footlights. I had heard that for the street she dressed casually in prim, tailored suits, and wore hats lacking in chic pulled over her prematurely white hair. No such person was pictured in the studio photographs that at all corroborated my memory of the sensuous exotic beauty which was St. Denis's theatrical self.

My reverie was interrupted by a thumping and clop-clopping on the stairs high up in the house. Rudely brought to myself, I thought, "Not even a cook or an old aunt should stomp about like that in the home of Ruth St. Denis." The weighted footsteps came nearer, the studio door swung open, and Ruth herself entered. I'm positive that my jaw literally sagged.

My immediate shock was at once magically dispelled and forgotten as the radiant personality of St. Denis engulfed me. Her dynamic charm never fails to cast a spell over the person on whom she chooses to use it. I was no exception.

On sight we began to talk. The conversation we started then was continuous through our years of touring and has been interrupted only at semicolons by geographical separations. That day in the spring of 1914, we talked from teatime until Ruth asked me to stay for dinner, through dinner until well after midnight when I asked what time we might meet later in the morning of the same day.

At Ruth's request I returned with costumes. Her pianist

accompanied me as I performed three dances beginning with the pseudo-Greek number which had given me the shakes in Gallup. That was followed with a spirited Slavic dance based solely on my own vague notion of how Slavs might dance. My climactic offering was the *Dagger Dance* in which I portrayed a young Aztec who elected to die by his own hand rather than to accept his doom as a living sacrifice.

During the dance I worked myself up to the moment of plunging the knife into my heart and the resultant very violent dramatic death. I was quickly revived in the St. Denis studio by Ruth's cries of delight. She lavished me with praise asserting that I was the finest man dancer in America, worlds beyond anything she had seen up to that time.

Buoyed by such flattery I returned to the studio on Eighty-ninth Street again the next day expecting Ruth to give me her decision about my lessons in oriental dancing. Instead I was called into the office of Brother St. Denis, then business manager for his sister, who asked me to join the St. Denis company as Ruth's dancing partner.

Dazed, amazed, and shaken, I managed to gasp an enthusiastic "Yes." There was no time to savor my good fortune because we went at once into rehearsals for a brief spring tour. An already frantic pace was complicated at the very last minute by a change in personnel that made it necessary for me to rehearse even en route to our first date at Paducah, Kentucky. I found myself with a substitute ballroom partner, Hilda Beyer, who previously in Ruth's company had appeared only in background parts and as local color in the oriental numbers. She was a sculptor's model, beautiful and instinctively graceful, but untrained as a dancer.

I have never worked so hard in my life as while teaching performance routines to Hilda on three days' notice. We literally tangoed and maxixed up and down the aisles of the Paducah-bound day coach. Soot and sound pouring through the open windows presented special problems for us in our extraordinary rehearsal hall. Our feet crunched on coal dust layers, and our arms and hands were black from the grimy plush seats against which we had to brace ourselves when the train swayed round a bend. My vocal chords were overworked by loudly ta-ta-ta-taing the music so Hilda could hear me above the clack-clack of the wheels. As we rocked south the only easy step to perform was the key movement of the hesitation waltz which was produced automatically by the jerking train.

We went directly from the railway station to the parlor of our ante-bellum hotel where we rehearsed with conventional music until theater time. On stage during performance I kept the ballroom numbers going like a terpsichorean ventriloquist. Through controlled and motionless lips, I gave *sotto voce* instructions to Hilda: "Go right, five steps and turn. Now you leave me and swing back—one, two, three, four."

The success of my deception was evidenced by the morning newspaper of April 14. It read: "Miss Hilda Beyer danced divinely the 'Blue Danube' and various ballroom dances. She was ably supported by Mr. Ted Shawn." How ably the reviewer obviously had not even guessed.

I was unnerved by our opening night in Paducah with its stress for me and an on-stage accident that might have terminated the St. Denis tour, perhaps even the St. Denis career.

Ruth's big number that spring was a combination of three of her established successes: *Incense, The Cobras,* and *Rahda.* The scene for the latter was a temple with a shrine in which a bronze goddess was enthroned. The Hindus of Ruth's company, as priests of the temple, came on stage carrying incense, lighted tapers, and small bells for a worship ritual. Their High Priest opened the grille doors of the shrine and reached up to sound a bell which was supposed to be the signal for Ruth, the goddess, to come slowly to life.

In Paducah, careless stagehands insecurely installed the entire shrine apparatus, so the goddess nearly left life, and quickly. When the High Priest reached up, beam with bell crashed onto the head of St. Denis whose skull fortunately was protected by the metal crown of the goddess costume.

The rest of the company, old hands at touring, accepted the stage mishaps as routine. I was a novice. Having toured only along the Santa Fe trail, I knew little of the misadventures, the inconveniences of one-night stands. I eventually accepted touring conditions with fatalism, if not with equanimity, but that spring I was in revolt a great deal of the time. I resented the false impression the public held of the glamour of the life of the dancer, of any performing artist. The truth was that the public had no way of knowing what difficulties confronted us en route, at the theater, in performance.

How could audiences have known about our lives? They entered a well-lighted lobby, presented a ticket to a doorman, walked down a carpeted aisle to a comfortable seat in a theater or auditorium. When the curtain parted we performed in beautiful costumes and glamorizing make-up. Our intent was to entertain, to enchant. The audience surely was not to blame that we succeeded so well that they thought of us as other-worldly people even when we were off stage. Hadn't I myself had the same impression of Ruth St. Denis? And I was a professional.

Our trek through Kentucky, Tennessee, Georgia, North and South Carolina, Virginia and West Virginia was typical of many full-season tours to come. I could not have known then that the normal elements of dance touring were capsuled for me during that six weeks on the southern circuit. The high spots and low, the good points and bad were balanced on our schedule.

My indignation about backstage conditions hit a peak in the tiny community of Jackson, Tennessee, where I circled the theater building several times without finding a stage door. And no wonder. It was a bulkhead sort of cellar entrance through which coal had been dumped. Entering, I slipped and slid ankle-deep in loose coal, until I finally reached a smooth floor in a pitch-dark basement.

The theater had not been opened for months and when the lights were turned on in the dressing rooms it was revoltingly evident that the building had not been cleaned in years. Filth was over everything in a disgusting, odoriferous accumulation animated by scampering rats, skittering cockroaches, and spinning spiders. I was enraged that any artist should be asked to prepare for performance in a place so foul-smelling, dirty, and dank.

Minnie Maddern Fiske, a seasoned trouper, once listened to my complaints about backstage conditions and then dismissed them by saying, "All theater newcomers have the same reactions." She recalled standing at the box office of a theater where her company was to play a one-night stand when a new youngster in the company came up in tears. She sniffled, "I've been around the block four times now and I simply can't find any stage door. Mrs. Fiske, do you know where it is?"

"Certainly, my child," Mrs. Fiske replied soothingly; "it's down the next alley and up a drain." The girl, of course, was more confused than ever by Mrs. Fiske's ironic generalization about the inaccessibility of any and all stage doors.

During the early days of my first tour, there was nothing that I wouldn't have believed about theaters and their entrances and accommodations. But in fairness I must say that here and there, even on that tour, we did play a few old grand opera houses where we occupied stage-level dressing rooms that were moderately clean and equipped with running water.

Violent contrasts marked our lives backstage, on stage, and off stage. In Asheville, North Carolina, we were entertained at a magnificent party given by a charming friend of Ruth's, Miss Grace Allen, who wintered at that resort community. Her guests from the social world included the Duchesse de Chaulnes on whom I centered my attention. The Duchesse, formerly a Miss Shonts of New York, was as American as I, but I was thrilled to meet and partner a real, live, honest-to-goodness duchess.

We left Asheville on a train that pulled away about five in the morning, a fairly normal, if ghastly, hour for the departure of touring companies. We stopped about noon for a layover of several hours at Spartanburg, South Carolina. In that charming town, Ruth and I set out for a walk through a beautiful residential area where mansions were set far back on landscaped lawns. We had just sat down under a flowering shrub to rest and chat quietly when an irate servant dog-trotted from a huge house to order us off the grass. Once more I had to reconcile myself to the extremes of our life. There we were being chased off a lawn like irresponsible vagrants while the very night before we had been honored as respected artists at a distinguished party.

At such parties we feasted on the traditional luscious food of the South. But fine southern food was served only in private homes and at a very few large hotels; elsewhere in the South the meals and the service were equally awful. After a few weeks on tour we were reduced to a limited diet of milk toast and boiled eggs, and even the latter were not always safe bets.

I shall never forget the morning when, after a long, long wait, I was served with three eggs. In surprise, I pointed out that I had ordered only two eggs. The waiter agreed, "Yes, suh, I knows that but I figured as how one of those eggs might fail you." Understandably reluctant to chance any of the eggs after that remark, I asked if he could get me something else in a rush since I had a train to catch. He shook his head slowly and answered, "No, suh. It was a *strain* to get you what I got!"

It was a strain for us to cope with the food and other handicaps of touring. The pianist-conductor of our company had a particularly nightmarish time that spring when our orchestra was recruited from each community where we danced. Sometimes the musicians were accustomed to playing together as a local orchestra; more often they were individual amateurs banded together just for our performance. I remember a group that included the drugstore clerk, the veterinarian, the insurance agent, the blacksmith. Our pickup orchestras ranged from quite good through adequate to hoe-down horrors.

In one little town a smooth rehearsal was shattered by a trombone passage. The notes came loud and sour. Our conductor just rapped for silence and, pointing to the trombone player, said firmly, "Out." In a minute or two another ear-splitting note blasted from the trombone. Stopping again the conductor said with polite control, "What I meant was that you had better not play this number. I'm afraid it is too difficult for you."

The trombone player looked up from his music and said blandly, "I'm mayor of this town. Either I play or there won't be any show." Then he added threateningly, "I hear it's a leg show, anyway." At that the theater manager dashed from the back of the house, bleating. "Let him play, let him play. The house is sold out!"

A flute solo provided music for the title-section of Ruth's dance, *The Cobras*. Ruth, sitting crosslegged on a platform placed downstage center, made snakes of her hands and arms. She wore hunk-sized emeralds on the index and little finger of each hand, her nails were painted blood red. The red fingertips, by the way, were a sensation predating by about twenty years the casual acceptance of nail polish as a respectable addition to a lady's grooming.

While the flautist performed, the St. Denis arms coiled and writhed like cobras, the spectacular hands moved with hypnotic rhythm, then one struck out like a viper attacking a victim. The effect, heightened by mesmerizing lighting, was so realistic that one could almost hear the reptile hiss. And one night the audience did.

No local flute player, good or bad, was available, so the town violinist was sawing away at the cobra solo with squeaking results. Ruth, on her little platform, was only about three or four feet from the conductor and, while her arms were twisting and her hands stabbing all about her, she whispered with enough force to be heard by several rows of the audience, "Stop that violinist, he's terrible. . . . Well, I can't help it if it is a solo, stop him." After a brief pause she ordered with sibilant violence, "Then play it on the piano but, for God's sake, stop him. I can't bear it any longer."

It was possible to have music problems even with professionals as I discovered later that season when I was dancing at Ravinia Park with the Chicago Symphony. I had created a dance to the "Rondo Capriccioso" of Saint-Saëns faithfully following the tempo of a Mischa Elman recording. When it came time for Ravinia Park rehearsals, the concertmeister, a bullheaded German, said, "I know that 'Rondo' backwards. We will not need to rehearse." I begged for at least a run-through but he was adamant, repeating over and over that he "played it right" and all I would have to do was dance it right. Being young and inexperienced I let him get away with his high-handed lack of co-operation, and went on without rehearsal before an audience of three thousand.

The tempo of the orchestra was so slow that I had to move like a man under water. I pushed, lifted, and struggled with the music until I could get down front close enough to call to the conductor, "Faster, faster." There was no change in the deadly tempo that was not a bit like my recording.

After the performance I rushed to the conductor with tears in my eyes and a catch in my voice, storming, "You ruined my dance." He looked me up and down, then snorted, "Well, if I had played it your way, I would have ruined the music and that would have been far worse." I let that debatable opinion pass since it was already too late to prevent the fiasco of my performance.

I sometimes marvel that we ever built a dance audience, but we did, in spite of the drawbacks, handicaps, and misunderstandings that blocked our way. There was no such thing as an informed dance audience when we began our tours of the United States.

The general public didn't know what to make of us. We were a "road company" obviously, but nobody sang, nobody spoke lines. Those people accustomed to the stereotyped entertainment of melodrama and comedy were disappointed by our numbers designed for neither the sob nor the guffaw. Bigtime-Charlies who misinterpreted the pictures of our advance posters booed when they realized we weren't putting on a hootchy-kootchy, Little Egypt sort of show. The front-row boys paid to see legs in action not legends unfold.

Only a few informed people out front knew what to expect of us, how to look at a dance performance. We, in turn, could count on no consistent reaction from across the footlights, and knew for certain only one thing about audiences —they were totally unpredictable.

The first St. Denis-Shawn duet was a dramatic North African number, featured on the spring tour program. The curtain rose on a quiet desert scene with a Bedouin tent of striped camel's-hair silhouetted against a brilliant wide sky. Ruth, in a soft and feminine costume of maize, coral, and turquoise, performed her interpretation of the dance of an almeh. At the finish of her solo, she sank down at the tent entrance to await the coming of her lord and master.

In this role I entered, burnoose flying and white turban twisted high. Brandishing a curved sword, I executed a dashing vigorous dance full of leaps and turns accented by pounding feet. I was a veritable whirlwind or movement and, to the accompaniment of rolling drums and clashing cymbals, worked to a terrific climax of spiral leaps ending center front in a heroic pose with scimitar held high above my head.

The Paducah audience reacted to this frenzied finale with excited applause that re-echoed wherever we performed the number. Certain that the dance was a sure-fire success, we accepted as routine the immediate ovations it received after each performance. Then an audience rocked me with an unprecedented reaction. In Topeka, Kansas, after we had performed the number for months, the Bedouin finale was followed by the longest silence I have ever endured in the theater. There I was, scimitar held in triumph, waiting for the usual salvo of applause. Nothing happened. I waited in position so long that I thought my arm muscles would snap. From the pitch-black vastness of the auditorium there was not a sound, not a rustle of movement. Tension was becoming unbearable for me when, from the abyss, a voice exploded with feeling, "Jesus!"

I told that story long afterward to a group of theatrical friends, including Ethel Barrymore, who did not join in the general laughter. Very seriously, she nodded her head and said with quiet conviction, "And a very great tribute, too."

Only a stage veteran evaluates an audience reaction with such certainty. It's the experienced performer who knows when tense silence is approbation, when applause is perfunctory, when "bravos" are subsidized. Sounds from beyond the apron are undecipherable to the neophyte, or they were to me. I ended the spring tour still trying to interpret the sounds that came over the footlights in wafts or waves, as thunder or lightly.

4

Without This Ring

Ruth St. Denis and I were married on August 13, 1914. That statistical statement, while quite true, is completely misleading in its simplicity. The courtship which preceded that mid-August day was stormy on several counts, and our marriage license was obtained under the most ludicrous of circumstances. We exchanged vows in a ceremony tinged by cloak-and-dagger overtones, and our honeymoon trip, far from being idyllic, was in fact a strenuous and frustrating road tour of one-night stands.

It is quite likely that we might never have been married at all if Mother St. Denis had not made a mistake. Throughout Ruth's professional life, Mother had traveled with her as the duenna, companion, counselor, and protector who shooed suitors from the stage door and routed Romeos from the dance company. Her vigilance had been so effective that hordes of infatuated men, with intentions ranging from honorable to infamous, had been discouraged from pursuing Ruth. Mother quite honestly believed that there was no room in Ruth's life for romance, that Ruth should give her all only to art.

No one will ever know why Mother decided to skip the short southern tour the spring I joined the company. Whatever her reason, she regretted the decision at the top of her lungs when she learned that Ruth and I had fallen in love and were planning to be married. Mother, not one to give up without a fight, battled first Ruth, and then me. By the time Mother came around to saying, "Yes, and my blessings," Ruth again was chorusing, "No, no, no!" as she had when first I proposed.

It never entered my head when the tour began that Ruth St. Denis and I could possibly have any relationship but the professional one. I was not yet twenty-three, and she, at thirty-four, was already an acclaimed artist, a fascinating woman established in her career. I vaguely fancied myself as a sort of acolyte to an unobtainable high priestess who might be worshiped from afar.

The relationship which developed into such a wrangle about love and marriage began quite innocently. Ruth turned to me for companionship for the simple reason that, in Mother's absence, she needed someone to talk with, to, and at. Conversation was ever much more important to Ruth than food or drink.

As we traveled, our conversation progressed from the abstract to the particular, from the impersonal to the intimate. It was inevitable that this should have been so because we talked constantly, during tedious train hops between engagement towns, after performances, and while waiting for curtains to go up. We talk-walked by moonlight along riverbanks, by sunlight under fragrant flowering trees. Although sometimes we ran out of breath, we never lacked for subject. Both of us had read avidly and extensively, so we shared and compared books as well as ideas, beliefs, theories, hopes.

The subject of religion and art as compatible forces was of vital interest to us. Ruth had made a study of the religions of the world, and had translated some rituals into dance. I had gone even further in my imagination, and eventually I felt free to ask Ruth's opinion of my concepts.

I was far too serious-minded in those days to repeat to Ruth a family story which indicated that in childhood I gave lisp-service to the religious life. Doting aunts claimed that on my fifth birthday when asked that inane career question so often put to small fry, I answered without hesitation, "Most of the week, I'll be an actor but on Sunday and Wednesday nights, I'll be a preacher."

The expression of ministerial aspirations was regarded as a joke in the family. My parents' own religious life was relaxed and casual, and no member of either family had ever been pulpit-minded. It was conceded that my ambition to be an actor was quite natural and inherited. Mother, who had been Mary Lee Booth, was distantly related to the theatrical Booth brothers, Edwin, the distinguished actor, and John Wilkes, the actor-assassin. Closer relatives, thespians at heart, acted in amateur productions, and I often was cast in toddler roles in church and school plays directed by my mother.

She had been a high school principal and even after her marriage kept many outside interests. Somehow she found time to write book reviews and also was the daring author of articles about such controversial personalities as Ibsen and Wagner, then spoken of as advanced moderns. My father, Ellsworth Shawn, was a newspaper editor and, like Mother, an avocational reader who made books a part of my life.

Mother was a lifelong friend of Annie Fellows Johnston, author of the *Little Colonel* books, who sent me an auto-

graphed copy of each volume in the series. In appreciation
I decided to go to a book-title costume party as a Little Colonel, a symbolic character. I was not the heroine of Mrs. Johnston's stories but a Lilliputian officer wearing a braided uniform
complete with a high stiff collar in which I was wretchedly
uncomfortable. My mother begged, "Please, Teddy, put on a
low soft collar so you can enjoy yourself at the party." With
the righteousness of a martyr, I refused to compromise, "No,
mamma. Anything to be pretty."

Child and man, the Booth in me has cheerfully endured
torture for theatrical effect. I have spent weary hours applying colored body make-up that itched when I sweated under
hot stage lights; my temples have been painfully squeezed
by tight headdresses of metal that had to be viselike in order
to stay on while I danced.

On several occasions I have inadvertently learned that my
suffering has not been in vain. One night in a dispersing
audience crowd, I heard a female voice say, "Look, there goes
Ted Shawn." A second voice asked eagerly, "Where?" Ap-
parently the first woman pointed me out because again I heard
the second voice, its tone dishearteningly changed, "That's
Shawn? Well, all I can say is, distance certainly lends enchantment."

I could have told her that not only distance but hard work
and a determination to do "anything to look pretty" contributed to the enchantment. Make-up, stage lights, and exciting
costumes combined to glamorize even a man who had been a
bookkeeper and looked the part, who had wanted to be a minister and appeared to be the type.

My determination to be a preacher was bolstered by tragedies
of my childhood. When I was eleven years old my mother and
my older and only brother, Arnold, died within a few months
of each other, and I turned to books for comfort. I always
had been a great reader but in my loneliness I became an addict,

reading two and three books a day. I estimated once that I had read five thousand books by the time I was fifteen.

The winter I was a high school junior, my father went to Denver to become chief editorial writer of the *Rocky Mountain News* and the Denver *Times*, leaving me in Kansas City to finish out the second term. Family friends boarded me and I bicycled thirty blocks to school with Wes Stout, a great pal. Years later a magazine writer, who wanted to do a *Saturday Evening Post* article about me, was turned down by Wesley Stout, the *Post's* managing editor, who explained, "Sorry, but I don't see any story in Ted. You see, we went to high school together."

We didn't graduate from the same school because I received my high school diploma from the Denver University Preparatory School, which I attended after I joined my father and stepmother in Colorado. Our Denver home was diagonally across the street from a Methodist church with a dynamic pastor, Dr. Christian F. Reisner, whom we had known in Kansas. Dr. Reisner and I were firm friends and I might now be a preacher if he had not accepted a call from a New York church. During a long quarantine and solitary hospitalization, I changed my mind about entering the ministry, but Dr. Reisner was just the man who might have changed it back had he still been in Denver.

My family made no effort to influence my thinking in the matter because they never quite understood why my resolve to be a minister, instead of diminishing, had strengthened as I grew up. They were more puzzled by my determination to go to divinity school than opposed to the idea, and when finally I decided against a life devoted to the church, they neither rejoiced nor grieved.

Shortly after I began to study dancing, I recognized the broad possibilities for religious, even for church, dancing. Prayer and dance didn't seem incompatible to me then and through the years the two have fused in my personal life, in works choreographed for church performances. My first faltering but specific ideas for choreographies based on religious dance themes were discussed with Ruth on that fateful spring tour of 1914.

After we had talked for hundreds of miles about religion and art, I felt that Ruth would be sympathetic to other intimate confidences. I yearned to discuss my broken engagement and the perfidious Hazel Wallack who not only had written me off in a curt letter but had sent back the engagement ring, Return Receipt Requested.

In bitterness I wrote voluminous verses to purge myself of the anguish of my shattered romance. Still dramatizing the experience, I dug up the doggerel that I presumptuously called poetry, and read passages to Ruth who wept. It occurs to me now that she may have been crying over the bad construction but at the time I was certain that her tears welled over the sad sentiments.

Long discussions about love led me to dreams of love and I found myself daring to think of the great artist, St. Denis, as Ruth a woman, a desirable female. With the confidence of youth, I formally proposed to Ruth while we were having dinner at a harbor-view room on the roof of a Norfolk hotel.

My proposal was the beginning of wecks of despair. Ruth said "No" over and over again for a number of reasons including the difference in our ages. I persisted and persuaded until she said "Yes" and then Mother campaigned against our marriage. My final interview with Mother lasted without a break for six third-degree hours. She raged, ridiculed, appealed to my common sense, turned pathetic, whimpered and laughed, through a dramatic performance of enviable range.

I countered each mood and statement with the sincere reiteration that Ruth and I loved each other, that we intended to be married, preferably with Mother's consent. At the ending of the grueling session, it was Mother who capitulated, saying, "Ruthie, I still do not think that marriage is wise for you but I respect your young man, so if you must, marry him. But I warn you, he's no weakling."

The immediate result of Mother's consent was that once more Ruth became indecisive and plans were off and on for several weeks. One bright morning when she was in a "Yes" mood, Ruth stuck her head in the rehearsal studio and called, "Come on. Let's go down to the City Hall and get this over with."

We stepped into line at the Marriage License Bureau behind a Jezebel dressed flamboyantly for her big day. In contrast Ruth, having put on the first thing she saw in her closet, looked seedy in her unpressed suit of cheap blue serge. The illiterate and confused "Jez" stuttered vague statistics about three former husbands while we impatiently shifted from foot to foot. Long lines on either side of us moved up steadily, but we marked time behind the woman trying desperately to align matters so she could marry prospective husband number four who stood meekly beside her. Her memory lapses concerning the status of husbands one, two, and three, interminably delayed the signing of necessary documents with our legal names, Ruth Dennis and Edwin Myers Shawn.

We slipped out of the bureau without having been recognized by friend or fan which was just as well because Ruth insisted that our marriage be kept a well-guarded, sacred secret. Mother St. Denis concurred with enthusiasm because she felt that Ruth's appeal and drawing attraction might be affected if her public thought of her as a married woman. The arrangement did not upset me as it would a bridegroom of today because forty and more years ago stars of stage and the movies and the arts did not admit to happy domestic lives. Only within the past couple of decades have they been able to publicize legal bliss, to prophesy blessed events.

Attune with my epoch, I curbed my exuberance and settled for a hush-hush wedding with no guests but Brother St. Denis and his wife, Emily, as witnesses required by law. A minister friend, sworn to secrecy, prepared for us a special ceremony leaving out the word "obey" which Ruth refused to say, and omitting reference to the ring which Ruth couldn't wear then and wouldn't wear ever. Even after she herself gave away the marriage secret in an expansive moment, Ruth refused to put on a wedding band, dubbing it a "symbol of bondage."

With our last "I do" still echoing in the preacher's parlor, we dashed back to rehearsal for the tour scheduled to begin within a fortnight. Until the very day of departure we slaved, dancing for hours, sewing costumes, packing trunks, painting props, stitching backdrops. Finally we boarded the first train on an itinerary that took us north into Canada where we met unavoidable trouble head on.

The day of our engagement in Montreal, the Princess Pat Regiment of World War I paraded through the streets en route to embarkation for France. Although no one could have known that the group would nearly be wiped out on a distant battleground, gloom descended on the city and at His Majesty's Theatre that night we played to no more than a dozen people. Throughout Canada, feeling its first impact of war, our audiences were so small that finally we were without funds to get us to the next town. By telephoning to theaters where we were booked for the week following, we discovered that our house was sold out at Port Huron, Michigan, and a co-operative management there wired our advance of the gross receipts so we could continue the tour.

Ruth and I were working and traveling under a telling strain. Some numbers of the program were still in daily rehearsal, audiences were poor, traveling conditions were worse than usual because of wartime restrictions, and, in addition, we had to keep from giving away the fact that we were married even to members of the company.

We had been on the road for several weeks when we played my home town. Misguidedly I anticipated a favorite-son welcome from Kansas City and favorable press notices from the Kansas City *Star* with which my father had been associated for many years.

No flag-waving celebration marked my return. On the contrary, my former school chums and onetime neighbors seemed to react with the attitude, "Look at Teddy Shawn. What does he think he's got up as?" The *Star*'s review, the first unfavorable one I had ever received, was written with a petty viciousness that was unforgivable.

Hurt by the unexpected treatment, I warily greeted a woman reporter who had asked to interview us. She was so pleasant and sympathetic that I reluctantly excused myself after the formal interview to go to the theater for a costume check. I left the reporter with Ruth who was so taken by the woman's charm that she talked freely and, as she thought, off the record about a number of matters, including our secret marriage.

The news was out and I was outraged by what followed. Kansas City papers of the next morning carried banner announcements of our marriage and the word was flashed around the country. When our clipping service began to send us copies of news stories and photographs which appeared coast to coast, I was indignant at the recurrence of the half-truth statement: "Ruth St. Denis Marries Ted Shawn—the Most Beautiful Man in the World."

By telegraph service or at some newspaper desk, my name had been confused with that of Paul Swan, a performer who did bill himself as "the most beautiful man in the world," a claim no other man ever wanted and to which I certainly was not entitled. It took me years to live down the stigma of that mistaken identity and I had a really dreadful time for the rest of the honeymoon tour. Every audience waited defensively to see whether I lived up to what had been erroneously claimed for me. Interviews invariably were prefaced either by the question, "How does it feel to be the most beautiful man in the world?" or by the statement, "Gosh, I don't think you're so beautiful."

I didn't look like the Devil either but I certainly went through Hell that spring. The last weeks of the tour were spent along the West Coast where we planned to open a dancing school in Los Angeles. En route we played most of the major cities of the Northwest including Portland where, quite by chance, our corporate name originated.

....

5

Denishawn on the Lawn

I should like to claim that either Ruth or I had thought up the word Denishawn which so long was used to designate our schools and our performing company. In all honesty, I am forced to confess that we pulled Denishawn straight out of a hat where it was jounced about with other entries in a contest promoted by a publicity-wise theater manager of Portland, Oregon.

A prize of eight box seats was offered to the person submitting the most suitable name for a new and supposedly untitled dance that we programed for our Portland engagement. Our new number that we had been calling simply the *St. Denis Mazurka* was a ballroom exhibition dance. Every touring dance company had to program at least one such number because of the continuing popularity of ballroom dancing.

Even the Russian company presented the *Pavlova Gavotte* as a concession to American audiences.

It was the Portland theater manager's idea that a dance-name contest would help his box office and we had no compunctions about changing the name of a ballroom duet. The contest entries poured in and we read over the submitted slips. Ruth and I with the manager, as a jury of three, discarded trite titles by the score before we came to our unanimous choice: the *Denishawn Rose Mazurka*.

The manager was happy with the title because it honored Portland, City of Roses, and we were excited by the invention of a corporate name for us. If Mrs. Margaret Ayer of Portland, who was the prize winner, used her box seats she didn't come backstage to see us. We never met her and often wondered if she ever knew that her fortuitous elision ultimately attained international fame.

The word "Denishawn" was much publicized shortly after the Portland contest when we opened our dance school in Los Angeles. Feature writers, swarming over our terraced lawn, embellished human-interest stories about a bevy of Denishawn beauties dancing on the greensward. Reporters rushed to us at the first hint of a flash news event like the escape of a peacock and its pursuit through suburbia by Denishawn's co-director clad only in bathing trunks.

Photographers snapped their shutters indoors and out at the Sixth Street place we leased for our home and school. The house, large enough for our living needs, had one extra downstairs room suitable for a private-lesson studio. Class lessons were given outdoors in a setting that was romantic but on a floor expertly sanded. Our own painful experiences had taught us that barefoot dancing on a lawn, pleasing as it may be to the eyes of an audience, is trying to the soles of performers. The practice-performing platform, set on a terrace within our walled garden, protected our students' feet from such lawn hazards as toe-nipping bugs, itch-producing weeds, bruise-making pebbles.

At the end of the 40- by 80-foot floor, a huge practice mirror was placed under its own gabled roof. A summerhouse of sorts sheltered the studio piano from the elements, chiefly southern California's brilliant sun. Towering eucalyptus trees shaded the terrace, and a small swimming pool cooled the students after strenuous forenoon sessions.

Despite certain pictures caught by the clicking cameras of newsmen who haunted our hillside, all was not exotic, glamorous, and mysterious at Denishawn. Ruth and I were in fact day laborers who worked morning, noon, afternoon, and, minus overtime pay, through quite a few evenings. I started the teaching day by supervising the students' exercises in stretching, limbering, breathing. We went on to pure ballet, then to free movements; and midmorning, Ruth took over the class for instruction in oriental dance and the techniques which were uniquely her own. Together we introduced and experimented with the dance innovations and movements that in time were identified as Denishawn style.

Class students worked for three morning hours, dipped in the pool, and stayed on for a simple lunch that consisted usually of fruit juice and a casserole, Spanish rice or a succulent stew, served with a wholesome dark bread. The light lunch and an informal talk on the dance were included in the lesson fee of one dollar which each student dropped into a cigar box on arrival every morning. Fees for private lessons were based on a more professional scale. By teaching in two places, one of us in the house studio, the other on the terrace platform, we were able to take on a fair number of individual pupils.

The success of our brand-new summer school made us prodigal when our first wedding anniversary rolled around on August 13. Ruth, in deference to my feeling that one of us should wear a wedding ring, gave me a gold band on which a beautiful Australian black opal was severely mounted. My present to her was a live peacock.

Mine was a symbolic gift in honor of Ruth's sensational triumphs with the *Legend of the Peacock*, a dance new in the repertoire that year. On stage Ruth was the fantastic fowl incarnate as she strutted with the distinctive peacock walk, arched and stretched her neck in perfect imitation of the preening bird. The costume skirt, fashioned of green lamé, fanned out like a peacock tail in full spread, and sparkled and glistened with bright decorations forming the colorful eyes.

Twice while the peacock dance was in creation, Ruth had me in a state of collapse, once from laughter, the second time from shock. One morning Brother St. Denis, beckoning me from outside the studio where Ruth was rehearsing, whispered, "Psst, Ted. Come here. Don't be frightened. I'm sure that Ruth's harmless but see what you think." Somewhat mystified I peered over his shoulder and swallowed a guffaw as I backed away from a sight I shall never forget.

Ruth, her white hair screwed into a tight bun, was wearing a hideous brown wool sweater pulled up to her chin and drooped down over the gorgeous green metal-cloth peacock skirt. The *Legend*'s star, expertly maneuvering the peacock tail and rehearsing the motions with earnest concentration, seemed unaware of the incongruity of her ensemble, unperturbed by the unfinished state of the costume.

When the costume top and the headdress were all but completed Ruth set out to find the proper ornament for the peacock crest. She searched fruitlessly and with increasing desperation. By luck or misfortune, the ornament came to roost in our own studio on the head of a tea guest who wore, with an impeccably tailored suit, a Paris hat of black straw topped with a feather crest.

Ruth took one look at the hat and, without a proper greeting of welcome, exclaimed, "That's the very thing." She snatched the hat from the guest's head, snipped off the ornament, returned the mutilated chapeau, and disappeared toward the costume room where the sewing woman was at work. The guest and I stared at each other too stunned to speak, I to apologize, she to protest. Ruth, undaunted, dashed back with the finished headdress, bubbling ingenuously, "Isn't this wonderful? . . . Look!"

The artificial crest was wonderful and did look exactly like the one that stuck straight up from the head of the real live anniversary peacock, bird of a species about which I knew very little. I had no idea that peacocks could fly or that they made the air hideous with their cry, two facts that were very quickly brought to my attention.

When class was dismissed at noon on the day following our anniversary, thirty students went screaming with anticipation to the far end of the garden where I had housed the peacock in a chicken-wire cage without a top. The handsome fellow took one look at the advancing horde of Amazons and rose, screeching, straight up and out of the garden.

Bare-torsoed, I rushed out of the Denishawn gate and dashed through the neighborhood determined to capture the feathered beauty in which I had so recently invested a sizable bankroll. The peacock was lazy in flight and I was gaining on him when he shifted course and flapped to a rooftop perch. I pressed the doorbell of the house and waited. When the door was opened, I gasped, "Madam, may I get my peacock off your roof?"

The lady's aplomb was remarkable, particularly for 1915. With no indication that it was unusual for her to receive such a request from a half-naked man, she opened the door wide, saying, "Follow me." I crawled through an attic window and inched along the roof until my fingers brushed the peacock's tail. I clutched. He zoomed away to the sill of a window next door. A woman sitting inside the open window screamed and dropped back out of sight as a sewing basket, spools of thread, and multicolored ribbons shot up into the air, scaring the peacock. He floated down into a chicken yard from which presently there came a terrible cackle.

Throughout the early afternoon, I paced the peacock's erratic flight of swoops and downs. He was placidly sitting on his fourth roof when Ruth in a taxi tracked me by way of the enthusiastic crowd gathered to watch the chase. I took advantage of the peacock's rest period by using the cab as a dressing room to don shirt, slacks, and sandals which Ruth had bundled hobo-style.

At sunset the peacock and I with a few faithful followers were many weary miles from Denishawn. My words "I give up" were drowned out by a youngster who yelled, "Mister, one buck and I'll get that peacock for you." He had a deal, and went inside a house and to the roof where he managed to grab the tail of the tiring fowl. Boy and bird slid uncontrolled down the roof to an upstairs porch from which we rescued them with ease.

I took the peacock home and roofed his cage, unaware that I also should have prepared a muzzle for him.

We needed a Maxim silencer for him on a summer evening when our students and some invited guests gathered in the garden for an operalogue by Havrah Hubbard, reading a condensed version of *Andrea Chénier*, and a pianist playing excerpts from the Giordano score. The effect of voice with music was soothing in the soft summer dusk until Hubbard, who read with dramatic feeling, reached a climactic point in the story and shouted with violence, "Death. Death. Death." Each word was echoed from the back of the garden by a peacock cry so cacophonous that *Andrea Chénier* was almost cut off in its prime.

Our bird, featured in a dance I choreographed for a Cecil

B. De Mille picture, thrilled a little extra girl who had never before seen a peacock. She was first breathless with excitement at the sight of its widespread fan and then crushed by the sound of its accompanying cry, harsh and strident. Almost in tears, the youngster turned to me and asked piteously, "Can't God do nothin' perfect?"

Our imperfect bird often was posed with the famous movie vamp, Louise Glaum, who created a sensation every time she arrived to be photographed in her siren uniform: a slinky dress with spangles; a turban, intricately twisted; and pearls in ropes by the mile. Louise sometimes had to lie out on the grass for five, ten, or even twenty minutes while the photographer and I subdued the peacock for her to pet. While many resultant prints showed Louise looking wickedly languorous, the peacock appropriately haughty, the preliminary posing was more often sportive than seductive.

Louise, who took private lessons from me, simply could not stretch at the *barre* without help because of a pair of the most curious, inflexible knees. Before each lesson I tried to painlessly straighten the Glaum legs but invariably I passed the crucial point and Louise let forth screams more piercing than any peacock's cry.

Our Denishawn neighbors, extremely tolerant of the nocturnal sounds from our grounds, were unceasingly fascinated by the daylight sights within our garden. We heard, though the rumor was never confirmed, that rents on all apartments facing our property were raised after the school opened. We were aware that we never lacked for audience, that interested spectators regularly filled every window with a view of the garden, the pool, the dance platform.

Any apartment tenant with prying binoculars could easily recognize the silent movie-stars and stage personalities who practiced and posed at Denishawn. Mabel Normand and Blanche Sweet, silent movie stars like Louise Glaum, took regular private lessons from me; Ruth Chatterton, young sensation of *Daddy Long Legs,* was a theater friend interested primarily in expressive and dramatic movement; and Lenore Ulric, getting ready for a Belasco show, had me choreograph her dances for the production.

Roszika Dolly, one of the famous Dolly Sisters of Broadway musicals, was in Hollywood that summer doing a movie with Lillian Gish, heroine of countless silent films. By arrangement with their studio both of the stars came to learn dances representing their separate characters in the picture which was called *The Lily and the Rose.* Lillian, blond and fragile, was the pure element in a man's life, of course, and Roszika, dark and sultry, the evil element. I worked out a stately and formal minuet-like dance for Lillian. Ruth produced a provocative oriental-houri number for Rosy, as she was known to her friends.

Lillian and Rosy continued to take private lessons through the summer and against my better judgment Rosy talked me into doing the most unsuitable dance for her. After seeing a rehearsal of *Crescent Moon,* one of several dances I choreographed for Ina Claire, Rosy insisted that she must have a similar number. I knew that what was right for Ina, willowy and controlled, was all wrong for the fiery, energetic Rosy. And so did Rosy. She worked hard on the steps, had a sumptuous costume made for the number, and then one day took a good look at herself in the practice mirror and chuckled, "If I ever did this dance on Broadway, they'd say, 'Well, look at Rosy, *she's* having a good time.'" No audience ever did see that dance in any variation because Rosy knew exactly what she could do well and what she shouldn't try.

We were the kind of people about whom Rosy fretted. She admitted quite frankly that she "might not be a great artist" but she knew from experience that she was a "great business woman." All summer she shook her head over our slapdash bookkeeping, our day-to-day extravagances, and the consistent generous gestures that she could afford and we couldn't. For our wedding anniversary, Rosy sent us more flowers than we had in our garden and a pair of birds, not feathered pets that might escape or squawk, but superb specimens of the art of the taxidermist. These stuffed birds were doves, pure white, symbolic both of wedded bliss and of our innocence in matters of money and management.

Rosy never found out that even while she was clucking over us, we were making the most impracticable plans for enlarging our fall tour company. The financial success of the school impelled us to splurge without considering the fine distinction between solvency and affluence. It would be too easy to point the finger of accusation at Ruth whose disregard for money might always have been interpreted as extravagance. In this instance, Brother St. Denis and I were not without blame. Money in hand was money to be spent —on costumes, on production, on new numbers, on musical arrangements. We operated on a theory that was long on art and short on cents.

With no thought for the relationship of intake and output, we arbitrarily chose to broaden the scope of our programing with a supporting group of eight, recruited from our student body. With meticulous deliberation from the artistic point of view we made our selection of eight talented girls: Margaret Loomis, Ada Forman, Carol Dempster, Florence Andrews, Sadie Vanderhof, Claire Niles, Yvonne Sinnard, and Chula Monzon. We weighed and considered individual ability and versatility and then made certain that we had chosen dancers who would complement each other visually and technically.

The varied program we devised was in line with the school's credo which stated formally our dedication to the flexibility of dance forms. We made it clear that we intended to experiment with dance techniques of the past, to recognize dance movements of all ages and lands, and to adapt new dance styles as they emerged. We could not have foreseen that our creative achievements would leave an indelible imprint on the history of American dance.

We stressed the individual in all our teaching, in the dances we choreographed for actresses, for other dancers, for our own students. The last thing we wanted to produce was a facsimile row of pupils who would be robot imitators of St. Denis and Shawn. Our role as we saw it was to provide the stimulus, knowledge, and experience essential to the development of dance artists, and to give encouragement to the imaginative performer.

When six of the first Denishawn group of eight achieved fame, we were convinced that our artistic direction was properly aimed and our teaching method valid. In preparation for the first tour we worked with the girls as individuals, and each of the six successful ones went on to professional maturity in a different and unique way.

Ada Forman left the Denishawn Company to be a featured dancer with the Greenwich Village Follies, a move that I wouldn't have believed possible when I first saw her. No dance pupil ever looked less promising than Ada, one of our older students, who had red hair, a beanpole body, and no distinguishing facial feature. She seemed to get nothing from a private lesson but pages of notes, and then at some future lesson she would perform the notated material with flawless technique and finished style.

Ada seemed hopeless to Ruth and Brother but I persevered and, after I idly remarked that she reminded me of a flat Javanese puppet, I choreographed a puppet dance for her. When Ruth saw the dance, she nodded and mused, "With a lot of make-up I might do something with that girl." After paint, powder, and eyebrow pencil had turned Ada into a mysterious Eastern type, we dared to show the finished transformation to Brother. He frankly preferred females of more conventional good looks but, after the metamorphosis of Ada, he agreed that she was right for the company.

Nobody had to do make-up tricks to Carol Dempster who was so beautiful off stage that theater make-up tended to reduce rather than heighten her beauty. For her I choreographed *Valse Directoire*, a number so popular that I danced it for several seasons with a succession of partners, including Ruth. When we did the waltz it was called *Josephine and Hippolyte* and with her costume Ruth wore authentic, historic jewels given by Napoleon to the real Josephine; those gems were a wedding anniversary gift from me to Ruth.

Carol, my first partner in the long-lived waltz, left dancing for motion-picture acting and so did Margaret Loomis, whose father owned the Angelus Hotel where Norma Gould and I managed our Tango Teas. Carol was in the classic *Broken Blossoms* and other outstanding pictures directed by D. W. Griffith. Margaret, so long a student of mine, was leading lady for Wallace Reid, and appeared in many movies with Sessue Hayakawa during his silent movie career that so long antedated *The Bridge on the River Kwai*.

Florence Andrews's success on the stage equaled that of Carol and Margaret in the movies. When Florence had toured with us for a couple of seasons, I created a dozen dances for her, financed costuming and a publicity campaign for a nightclub act which I also booked. Her name was uninteresting and since Denishawn by then was nationally famous, I suggested that she call herself Florence of Denishawn. She did until a program printing error made Florence O'Denishawn of her. At the height of her success in night clubs, Florence was spotted by the famous comedian, Raymond Hitchcock, who started her toward Broadway by signing her for *Hitchy-Koo*. Later she was in the *Music Box Revue* and the *Ziegfeld Follies*, and continued with an active and successful professional career.

Sadie Vanderhof was already an accomplished ballet dancer when she signed up at Denishawn School to widen her style, range, and dance vocabulary. With the stage name Vanda Hoff, she starred in Brother St. Denis's dance drama *The Dancing Girl of Delhi* which had a successful vaudeville run. Paul Whiteman proposed to Vanda and she left the stage for marriage.

We choreographed off-beat dances to suit the originality of style which Claire Niles showed from the very beginning. A brunette with gamin charm, Claire later was the leading dancer of the Ruth St. Denis Concert Dancers, in which Doris Humphreys first attracted notice. Claire also left dancing to be married, and then long afterward took part in religious ritual dance programs given at Ruth's New York studio.

With solos planned for eight girls, it was necessary to reduce the number of oriental dances on our program, and Ruth kept on only one Hindu, Mogul Khan, who was married to her maid, Mary. Both of them were in the traveling group, of course. Mogul was to double as local color on stage and as my dresser backstage. With Brother as manager, an accompanist, Mary and Mogul, eight girls, and us, we were a company of fourteen.

Organizing a new company is hard work for the conscientious, and an expense to the pernickety. Hard work we didn't mind because we were full of energy. Expense we didn't worry about until too late. We were much too busy seeing that the Denishawn Dancers were up to standard to give even the most elementary consideration to budgetary affairs: the cost of travel for our company, the expense of costuming such a sizable group, the balancing of a fixed payroll against expected income from contract engagements. Our day of reckoning was to come at the end of the tour with a plunge from peak performances to finances at rock bottom.

6

••

—And on the Go

♥ Our vaudeville turn began at the top, in New York's Palace, a coup unprecedented in the history of the two-a-days. Most performers endlessly toured the circuits, ever hoping to be billed at the Palace, goal of their daydreams. Many never made it. When we did, we were too inexperienced to be impressed. We were just grateful for the job. Our booking was set up and the contract signed by Brother St. Denis who pushed our luck to get us out of a desperate jam. After a zigzag fall tour from Los Angeles, we were in New York broke and even in debt.

Along our route we experienced artistic triumphs, honors without profit to us. Theater managers made money on enthusiastic audiences who filled capacity houses while we collected percentages that barely covered expenses. The Deni-

shawn company, so recklessly assembled, was simply too big
to be supported by a tour of one-night stands in small-town
theaters. Salaries and train tickets took every cent of each
week's receipts. Overdue bills that caught up with us in the
East, found us with wallets flat and purses empty.

A limited engagement of dance matinees at the Hudson
Theater was our last date, and beyond was a perfectly blank
calendar. The eager young Denishawn dancers, after thrilling
to audience applause, adapting easily to rigors of the road,
and basking in the light of spots, met their first disillusionment in New York. So soon and so far from home they were
confronted by the uncertainty inherent in a dancing career.
We and they faced a dreary Christmas and a bleak New Year's.

Brother St. Denis, the miracle worker who changed dark
to bright, hustled around New York and brought all sorts of
vaudeville management people to our Hudson matinees. Even
he was surprised when the biggest fish took the hook. We
were signed for one early January week at the Palace and
stayed for two, another coup, the only star ever before held
over having been the great French actress, Madame Sarah
Bernhardt. During our first week the box office turned away
five thousand people, and in the middle of our second hit
week, Brother pressed his advantage and signed us for fifty-
six weeks of vaudeville touring. The contract spaced our engagements at sixteen weeks and forty weeks with a summer
layoff for teaching.

Vaudeville was a strange experience and harrowing even
to headliners like us who traveled the first-rate circuits. Management representatives, from agents and bookers in New
York to local theater managers and regional spies, were the
most sadistic, ghoulish, and horrible people encountered in
a long professional life.

They operated on a fiendish system calculated to break the
spirit of the performer, to undermine the morale of a troupe.

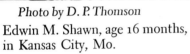
Photo by D. P. Thomson

Edwin M. Shawn, age 16 months, in Kansas City, Mo.

Pre-theology student at the University of Denver

With Hazel Wallack, my first teacher and dancing partner. The shocking pose rocked the University's Chancellor

Photo by Rembrandt

Norma Gould and I started the first "Tango Teas" in Los Angeles at the Angelus Hotel in 1912.

In 1914 the Topeka audience responded with stunned silence to my solo in this first St. Denis-Shawn duet.

Photo by
Moffett,
Culver Service

*Photo from
Culver Service*

Duet from St. Denis-Shawn *Egyptian Ballet* which we performed
more than 2500 times.

Tillers of the Soil was premièred at Berkeley, Calif., where we were
the first dance artists to appear at the Greek Theatre.

Photo by Hixon-Connelly, Culver Service

Photo from Culver Service

Snapped while on K.P. duty
right after enlistment in
World War I.

N. Y. Public Library Dance Collection
Denishawn Collection

Invocation to the Thunderbird was in my solo repertoire from 1918
until the early 1950s.

Photo by Witzel, Culver Service

Partnering Martha Graham in a duet from a Spanish suite. Martha was
my pupil and protégée for the first eight years of her dancing career.

Photo by Soichi Sunami

Spear Dance-Japanesque with authentic wig made for me in Japan.

Gnossienne, my solo on a Cretan theme, was an international favorite.

N.Y. Public Library
Dance Collection
Denishawn Collection
Photo by Nickolas Muray

American folk material for the dance–concert stage was first introduced to audiences through my *Five American Dances*. The suite predated other such folk theme dances by 20 years. Ernestine Day was the Mexican girl, left, and Anne Douglas, a dance hall girl, right.

N.Y. Public Library
Dance Collection
Denishawn Collection
Photo by White

The Eagle Dance from my ballet *Feather of the Dawn*. Drawings made from this photograph, with Urdu text, were shown in bazaars of India during our Orient tour.

Death of Adonis was the first plastic dance ever choreographed by a serious artist. Its première was delayed by a rehearsal-spy's report that the dance was "obscene."

Photo by Townsend

Photo by Nickolas Muray

A solo from *The Vision of the Aissoua*, the ballet I created after my return from North Africa. I bought authentic costumes and many props while in Algiers.

N. Y. Public Library Dance Collection
Denishawn Collection

The Denishawn Dancers posed for A *Street in Spain* scene in Santa Barbara, Calif. Ruth and I are lower right.

Portrait study of Ruth and me taken in Tokyo, 1925.

N.Y. Public Library
Dance Collection
Denishawn Collection
Photo by Hirano

The Cosmic Dance of Siva which I created in India.

I capsuled *Momiji-Gari*, a Japanese dance-drama for our repertoire. I am shown, left, as the Demon and, right, as Lady Sarashima.

Photo by Hirano

Photo by Eric M. Sanford

Prometheus Bound

Frohsinn

N.Y. Public Library Dance
Collection, Denishawn Collection
Photo by Charlotte Rudolph

Photo by Constantine

Mevlevi Dervish

Orpheus-Dionysus
with Margarete Wallmann

N.Y. Public Library Dance
Collection, Denishawn Collection

Shawn and His Men Dancers enroute to London, 1935.
Left to right, upper picture: Foster Fitz-Simons, Frank Overlees, Shawn, Barton Mumaw, Jess Meeker; lower picture, Fred Hearn, Wilbur McCormack, Ned Coupland, Dennis Landers, William Howell.

N. Y. Public Library Dance Collection
Denishawn Collection

N. Y. Public Library
Dance Collection
Denishawn Collection
Photo by John Lindquist

A solo from the *Kinetic Molpai*. This pose has become a personal trade-mark. It has served as motif for drawings and jewelry.

Photo by John Lindquist

As the Emperor Montezuma in *Noche Triste de Montezuma* from *O! Libertad!* that I choreographed as a full evening production for the men dancers.

Shawn and His Men Dancers performed virile dances that combined grace with athletic prowess. Above, a rehearsal in the Studio at Jacob's Pillow. Below, the group in flight over the grounds of The Pillow was performing the *Air Section* of *The Dance of the Ages*.

Photos by John Lindquist

Photo by John Lindquist

Shawn and His Men Dancers shown in their last performance, May 1940.

Proudly wearing the Cross of Dannebrog conferred on me in 1957 by the King of Denmark.

Photo by Mydtskov

Reports to New York offices were sent by local managers and by the spies, members of a low tribe. They timed applause and counted the number of bows taken by a single performer or by a whole troupe; tallied daily box-office receipts against each act's record; carefully checked to be sure that acts were not changed by a shortening of routine, by substitution of shabby costumes for new.

House managers, niggling masters of invective, kept in practice with relentless nagging, gratuitous insults. Variations of their familiar chants were "This act ain't flashy enough—put more gold cloth and rhinestones in it." Or, "Pep it up. This act's dyin' on its feet. It stinks."

Abuse of talent was part of a deliberate psychological scheme to make performers nervous and edgy about being rebooked for the next season. Too often the unscrupulous tricks worked and the timid, the cowed, the fearful signed for lower salaries at contract renewal time. It was unpleasant to be surrounded by the degraded characters who preyed on conscientious troupers.

Most performers regarded vaudeville as a profitable enterprise and thought it was good business to knock themselves out for audiences while saving for early retirement on chicken farm or cattle ranch, at the sea or in the mountains. The animal trainers, pantomimists, magicians, acrobats, equestrians, and other hard-working specialty talents were simply friendly folk who yearned to get far away from grease paint and variety.

We worked hard and yearned to return to full-length dance programs. Our act was a dance program squeezed into a time slot always less than half an hour from which we often lost precious minutes trying to get across to a confounded public. Those who spent hard-earned quarters to watch a seal twirl a trumpet were not always receptive to the dances of Denishawn. Against odds we made friends for the art of the dance, sparked applause by our sweat and sincerity. We gave our best at every performance and promptly forgot each one when the theater door slammed behind us. The big bang that closed the Orpheum Theatre door at the end of our spring tour echoed in the streets of Los Angeles. We were home free—free of vaudeville until autumn, free to dance, to teach, to slave through summer.

Our summer school advertising in national magazines resulted in a registration so large that we patently could no longer conduct affairs with the casualness deplored by Rosy Dolly. The cigar box till was replaced with a cash register. Ledgers, lesson charts, double entry books, and bank accounts were managed by Mrs. Edwina Hamilton, who put the school on a conventional business basis and, for years afterward, ran its office with quiet efficiency. She was the keeper of the keys to studio and practice halls, to safe-deposit boxes and food lockers.

Another addition to the summer staff was Louis Horst who came to us as studio pianist and arranger, and, as pianist-conductor, toured with us for eight years.

His was not the only piano played for long hours that first summer he was with us. We took on extra practice pianists, assistant teachers, and dance lecturers. One of the latter was an accredited teacher of eurythmics, the system of rhythm and bodily movement devised by Jaques-Dalcroze, and another was Mrs. Richard Hovey, onetime student of Françoise Delsarte.

Mrs. Hovey herself was the teacher of Mrs. Mary Perry King, who passed on to us the lessons learned without ever crediting either the original source or Mrs. Hovey. Although scornful of Mrs. King's choreography, I had accepted her techniques as original until Mrs. Hovey walked into my life.

Backstage while chatting with friends one afternoon, I noticed the remarkable approach of a slight and elderly lady who had the walk and bearing of a general on parade. She marched up to me and, with no preliminaries, said, "Young man, once during today's matinee you walked across the stage like a god. As for the rest of what you did—*rot!*"

That unconventional introduction led to a lifelong friendship, and to her lectures. She was nearly seventy, a handsome woman who appeared for lessons in long draperies of silver-gray that contrasted effectively with her hair that was white as a spring snowdrop.

Mrs. Hovey not only taught the principles of Delsarte for the last thirty-five years of her life, but she further developed the movement which is closer to dancing than the system of Dalcroze. She experimented with Delsartian expressions and rhythms, and was an inspiring teacher. From our 1915 meeting until Mrs. Hovey's death, I took private lessons from her. In 1916 I attended her lectures whenever I was able to duck Denishawn extracurricular activities like sewing and dyeing.

We had looked forward to a relaxed summer with days of comparative leisure pleasantly blending into each other. It did not materialize. We anticipated a light teaching load, planned to give a few lectures to the whole student body, and to spend quiet hours experimenting with and thinking about new dances for the fall vaudeville tour. Before school opened we knew that the summer ahead would be made up of frantic days and hectic nights. Our rosy plans were exploded by a complimentary bombshell.

Ruth was invited to be the first dance artist ever to perform at the University of California's Greek Theatre. The board of trustees let down the bars to admit dancers, a commendable action, unfortunately timed. Their vote to reverse a long-standing policy barring dancers was followed by a second approving Ruth as the star for a summer production at the famous outdoor amphitheater at Berkeley. We were overjoyed by the invitation, snowed under by Ruth's acceptance.

Together Ruth and I planned an ambitious dance pageant that depicted first the customs and then the afterlife concepts of three ancient lands: Egypt, India, and Greece. We researched the periods of history, sketched the story line, choreographed all dances from solos to crowd scenes. For the Greek Theatre's enormous stage we had to plan on a grand scale for life-sized mobs and outsized effects.

With a small-sized budget we had no choice but to substitute people for properties. We assembled a cast that totaled 170, which to us seemed a prodigious number. Extras were recruited from the university's summer school; dancers were auditioned in the Los Angeles area and selected from our own pupil roster. A corps of forty dancers rehearsed through the early summer at Denishawn, and then were transported up the coast for music rehearsals with the San Francisco Symphony Orchestra and the university's chorus.

Ruth and I designed the pageant costumes which were made by the Denishawn sewing crew with help from us in every minute we could spare from teaching and rehearsal schedules. The most tedious costumes to turn out were waves to be worn by the whole company representing the waters of the Nile.

We planned to achieve the effect by completely covering each figure, crown to toe-tip, with a voluminous veil of water greens. The veils were made from hundreds of yards of cheesecloth, a lightweight fabric that's quite tidy when duster size, but unwieldy by the bolt length. After veils were measured and cut, I took the material and personally dyed each of the 170 waves, first tying the cheesecloth here and there to make the rippling water pattern. I all but turned green from dyeing.

My hours spent in dunk-and-dip were rewarded by effective results. The pageant opened dramatically with a chorus singing off stage while the scene brightened with green lights. The human river flowed forward downstage along a ramp into the orchestra circle and then the tide turned and the water receded, the green lights slowly fading.

When the cast exited, Ruth and I were kneeling center stage, our heads bowed. We represented the first peasant man and woman, simply clad and humble. A spotlight flooded us and we slowly stood to face a rising sun. Ten thousand spectators set up a crescendo of clapping that resounded like thunder from the surrounding hills. In that remarkable moment, we two, standing alone on the vast stage, felt at once isolated and exalted.

In the dance that followed, *Tillers of the Soil*, we stylized elementary actions of plowing, reaping, spearing fish, tending sheep. We took that number into our repertoire where it remained as one of our own favorites. Its austere simplicity was universally memorable and persons who might not have seen *Tillers* for ten years could minutely describe it to me. And often did.

Our *Tillers* costumes were modest and the cast's Nile costumes sufficiently all-enveloping that we anticipated no public complaint about nudity in the pageant. Audiences of 1916 were apt to be shocked by the sight of bare flesh, even if revealed by an authentic costume, and the Greek Theatre's director, Professor William Dallam Armes, a dance enthusiast and fan of ours, specifically asked that we be a little conservative with our pageant costumes. He explained quite frankly that while he had not been shocked by certain scanty costumes he had seen us wear in performance, he was not certain that the trustees would approve of similar exposure.

Taking no chance on "unpleasant repercussions" about costumes, Dr. Armes monitored the pageant's dress rehearsals, and, from his front-row seat, he called out one evening, "Ruth! Ted! I know that those three girls have something on under those chiffon scarves but from where I sit, it doesn't look as if they did. Can't you make their underthings more apparent?"

Ruth's own lack of covering was quite apparent for one brief moment on opening night. Midway of the East Indian section, when she was to perform suttee across my lifeless body that was stretched out on its funeral pyre, Ruth rushed on stage to complete the scene and with beautiful arm movements unwrapped her sari. As usual she flung the undraped fabric back over her shoulder and then realized to her complete astonishment that she was nude from the waist up. Backstage she had been so busy with the costumes of extras, retying a dhoti here, correctly draping a skirt fold there, that she neglected to put on her own choli, the brassière-like bodice worn by Hindu women. Looking down at her bare breast, Ruth said aloud and quite audibly, at least to me, "Oh, dear, dear. Professor Armes will never stand for this!" While I tried to keep the stiff composure of a corpse, she redraped her sari with a hand quicker than the eye of any trustee.

The pageant's great success at Berkeley was repeated when we presented it outdoors in San Diego and indoors at the Los Angeles Shrine Auditorium. Everywhere the hit number was the *Pyrrhic Dance*, the first number I ever choreographed for an all-male ensemble. Pyrrhic dances which date from ancient Greece, originally were part of military training and symbols of victory. My interpretation was not a revival of the Greek classic form but an attempt to capture the spirit of the original.

Sixteen men dancers, leaping and jumping with power, muscles, and virile strength, created an impact that thrilled the pageant's audiences and won paragraphs of newspaper praise. Many years elapsed before I formed my own group of men dancers but after the reception of the *Pyrrhic Dance* I always had in the back of my mind plans, choreographies, and dance themes suitable for men dancers.

No male group danced in the abridged version of the pag-

eant that we took on our vaudeville tour in the fall of 1916.
We condensed the pageant for several reasons, all of them
time. We had none. Our summer schedule with its rehearsals
and performances at the Greek Theatre, four hundred miles
from Denishawn, left not a minute for working out new routines for the vaudeville act. We dared not think of our fate if
the vaudeville spies caught us doing old routines in costumes
that had been over the circuit before.

Somebody had an inspiration that saved our face, perhaps
even our contract. We packed the pageant costumes in our
tour trunks, cut the pageant story to an outline, practiced
dances shortened from the original elaborate choreography.
For a pageant-in-miniature we lacked only proper setting and
that was materialized by a few deft touches of a paint brush
against a backdrop curtain which could be lighted to look like
the Greek Theatre.

Against that backdrop we danced out the second part of
our fifty-six-week contract so eagerly signed in January 1916.
We performed twice a day, matinee and evening, for a total
of twelve times a week for forty weary weeks. An advantage
of the full-week engagement over the one-night stand was
that of being settled in one place for six days. No matter what
our accommodations, they seemed luxurious when we slept
in the same bed for six nights in a row, and ate delicious meals,
home-cooked.

We fell into the cooking habit during the earlier vaudeville
tour. Bored with hotel food, we decided one morning to fix
ourselves an Irish stew and set the mixed ingredients on the
sterno stove which we always carried as part of what we called
our tea-kitchen equipment. The stew wasn't finished at matinee time, so we wrapped the saucepan in a blanket and locked
the bundle in a bureau drawer, expecting that by our inven-
tive fireless cooker system supper would be ready when we got
back from the theater.

We returned to the hotel, an unpretentious New Orleans
hostelry, to be greeted in the lobby by an odor of onion
that grew stronger as we neared our room. Under our door
we found a management reminder that cooking was not permitted in the guests' rooms; we checked out at once, covering
our chagrin with loud defensive complaints against the hotel.

That New Orleans stew was responsible for a change in
our touring tactics. For the rest of the season we rented light
housekeeping rooms within walking distance of the vaudeville
theaters, and settled to a blissful domestic life of marketing,
cooking, and dishwashing. Our homes-away-from-home were
also sewing centers where we repaired costumes and even designed and made new ones.

On tour we planned new dances and shopped for costume
materials and accessories. We walked miles up and down the
aisles of five-and-ten-cent stores as we browsed or looked in-
tently for some specific item. Sales girls at jewelry counters
were suspicious of Ruth who looked like a storybook school-
marm and acted like a dime-novel madam. What was the
girl behind the counter to think when a sedate white-haired
lady, wearing a prim tailored suit and plain felt hat, began
to paw through junk gems, trying on the flashiest of rings,
earrings, and pins? The only girl who ever called a manager
yelled, "Counter Seven," when right in the middle of Wool-
worth's, Ruth circled her brow with several baby bracelets
intertwined. How was the girl to know that the customer was
designing an authentic *ouled naïl* headdress?

My own similar experience might well have landed me in
a strait jacket. I needed to replace a Siamese headdress of
gold cloth and jewels sewed on buckram that wilted from my
perspiration, lost shape with repeated packing. I got the bright
idea that I might use for the base a kitchen colander, a semi-
spherical metal bowl with perforations. Decorations could be

sewed through the holes on a foundation that would never wear out.

I wandered around a kitchenware department trying on colanders and saying to the sales girl, "Don't you have a colander, size seven and a quarter? None of these fit." Just in time I found the right size and escaped to the toy department where I bought a tin horn to make the spire-shaped top of the royal headgear. With tin shears, a couple of filigree metal lampshades and long needles, I produced a crown that survived many seasons of one-night stands.

While we were touring, Mrs. Hamilton was moving Denishawn School into larger quarters across from Westlake Park. Westlake School for Girls having moved to suburban Los Angeles, we rented their buildings which gave us more room for teaching and adequate space to board our out-of-town students. Behind one large building there was a tennis court which we floored with fine sanded wood, and shaded with a canvas tent top. Bleachers to seat more than two hundred were erected at one end of the stage where we planned to give regular performances of the first Dance Theatre. Fire laws and building restrictions prevented us from making the theater even more elaborate on plans that we discussed with Norman Bel Geddes, then at the beginning of his career as designer.

That was my summer for choreography. I did the first dances to the Inventions and Fugues of Bach primarily to train dancers to analyze, understand, and respond to one part of contrapuntal music. The dances were devised to Two and Three Part Inventions and a Four Voice Fugue, with parts learned and danced separately until each part or voice was perfectly rehearsed by its group. Then the groups danced together, each as a visual counterpoint of the separate audible counterpoints of the music.

New pupils that summer included Doris Humphreys and the fifteen-year-old Mary Hay who later starred with and

married Richard Barthelmess of silent movie fame. Mary,
daughter of Brigadier General Caldwell, was short, chunky,
snub-nosed, and vehement. She gave me the student nickname
which has clung through the years when she said, "*Papa*, I
hate those skippy dances. Do a really fierce one—just for me."
I choreographed for her an Indian dance set to "The Red Man"
music from John Philip Sousa's suite "Dwellers in the Western
World." That dance, *Invocation to the Thunderbird*, suited
me and Douglas Fairbanks, Sr., urged me to put it into my own
repertoire where it was immensely popular with audiences for
two decades. Several of my solo dances were originally designed
for individual students or as class exercises.

Gnossienne was a dance in flat, two-dimensional style
movement that didn't come off when the class tried to do it
for Ruth who dropped by the practice studio. I jumped in
and did the exercise, solo. To music by Erik Satie, I represented
a priest of ancient Crete going through a ritual at the altar
of the snake-goddess. When I finished I turned to the class
and then to Ruth, saying, "There. That's the way it's supposed to look." And that's the way it was done by me for
the next thirty years.

Religious dances formed into a program in 1917 had been
in the works for a couple of years, and in my mind for even
longer. From the beginning, I intended to present my religious
dance ideas through familiar Christian themes and began my
choreographies with the Twenty-Third Psalm. That was to be
one of three *Dances of David* (*The Boy*, *The Shepherd*, *The
King*), and in the David costume I also did a dance dramati-
zation of the well-known church solo, *The Palms* by Fauré.
My work continuously expanded until, in 1917, I was ready
with an entire Christian church service in dance form.

Dr. Henry Frank of the First Interdenominational Church
of San Francisco invited me to perform my service in dance
at his church. That minister with broad vision opened the

evening program with a half-hour history on the relationship
of dance and religion, and then without a word spoken or
sung, I performed. The string section of the San Francisco
Symphony Orchestra provided my accompaniment for the
program:

> Prayer (Music-Kammenoi Ostrow)
> Doxology and Gloria
> The Twenty-third Psalm
> Sermon: "Ye shall know the Truth and the
>   Truth shall make you free."
>   (Symbolic-Dramatic dance to
>   Rachmaninoff C-Sharp Minor Prelude)
> Hymn: Beulah Land
> Benediction: God be with you till we meet again

A jammed auditorium resulted from amazing amounts of
advance publicity. I expected respect from the audience but I
was needlessly apprehensive about the reviews that unani-
mously treated the dance service with dignity and seriousness.
With the religious dance program successfully completed, I
faced an even more serious engagement—with the United
States Army.

Personal affairs were settled with dramatic finality: my will
was signed and witnessed, and all arrangements made for the
posthumous publication of my manuscript-book about Ruth's
career as a dancer, a creative artist. Good-bys at Denishawn
were emotional as I left the school and said farewell to dancing, perhaps forever.

•••

7

This Was the Army

N I enlisted for World War I service with an ambulance unit, naïvely expecting that, within six weeks, I would be trained and in the thick of overseas action. Six weeks later I was in the thick of action centered around Camp Kearney in southern California.

At camp I breezed through the first part of the physical examination because I was in topflight condition: muscles toned, heart strong, lungs powerful, which was a good thing as it turned out. When the punching and thumping part of the physical was all but over, I ran smack into my first army obstacle—the test for color blindness. The test-sergeant was the fictional prototype, oldish, hard-boiled, illiterate. His rote question was "What color's dat?" as he indicated a swatch of wool.

For reasons best known to army authorities, the wool samples were not distinguishable colors bright, pure, and clear, but subtly blended, muted and soft. I was experienced in shading colors for sets and costumes and with the smug assurance of youth gave meticulous designations to the samples. I managed to get out "Taupe. Lime. London smoke," when the sergeant exploded, "Look, soldier, just answer red, yellow, blue, brown, gray—see?" I saw, conformed, and passed with colors flying.

My second stumbling block was set up by the press which refused to let me slip into the ranks with anonymity. Reporters and photographers rushed into camp for interviews, to take newsreels, and still photographs, to make headlines of my enlistment. For the first and only time in my life I had more publicity than I wanted.

The press photographers took conventional enough pictures of me in the army-issued uniform, but their editors chose to print shots of Soldier Shawn next to portraits of Dancer Shawn, selecting invariably the most sensational costume pictures that could be dug out of the newspaper morgue. Newspaper cartoonists sketched me out with pen and ink. After my hair had been sheared to regulation length, the resultant 1917 "butch" and my thick wavy hair, styled long for theatrical purposes, were featured in a before-and-after cartoon titled "TED—SHORN." Another cartoon paired me with Art Acord, silent movie western star, who joined up when I did. We were shown carrying a stretcher; Acord, at the back, identified by his chaps and ten-gallon hat, and I, holding up the front of the stretcher, done up in a leopard skin. Three wide-eyed Boches, with hair standing on end and helmets in mid-air, were saying, "Ach, Gott!"

My press notices drew mixed reactions from the members of the platoon. Some were totally indifferent to the clippings well circulated in mess hall and barracks. A few of the shy boys from down-on-the-farm areas eyed me with perplexity as if wondering what sort of freak I was. The quipsters barraged me with jeers, jokes, and jollity which I had to accept with good nature and wide grins. In time the stories slacked off, and so did the ribbing but by then I had been pigeonholed as available talent by the brass at headquarters. For the duration I performed at official command, not by public demand. I was often called out of rank to go to dance or to speak for a war cause, off-base duty hardly designed to endear me to barrack buddies left behind on K.P.

I was impelled to wage my personal battle for the cause of the male dancer. Nobody asked me to defend my profession, but I was determined to prove to every soldier with whom I served that a man could be a dancer and still hold his own with the toughest recruit, the most experienced N.C.O. I threw myself into every work detail to which I was assigned. I took more than my share of stretcher training on the drill field, and went through rigorous duets with the mop, the brush, and the potato peeler.

Like everybody else I hated to skin spuds and to spike cigarette butts on a policing detail, but I preferred those onerous duties to bond drive assignments. I can't imagine by what process of logic I was chosen to be a "four-minute speaker" to sell Liberty Bonds in San Diego. My professional experience until then had been limited to dance performances in character with appropriate costume and make-up, and I found it disconcerting to appear as myself. Although more fully clothed in my ill-fitting soldier suit than in most dance costumes, I felt naked and unprotected when I went out cold before San Diego audiences, night after night, several times each night. I forget how long the bond drives lasted or how many I participated in but I recall that every four-minute appearance was torture.

War charity programs I didn't mind. I performed as a

professional in my own field, and often the benefits were the occasions for reunion with old friends from the stage. I remember going eagerly to Los Angeles to appear with Madame Ernestine Schumann-Heink whom I worshiped as artist before I knew her as friend. When I turned up in uniform for rehearsal, the huge Valkyrian diva rushed to me with tears in her eyes. Engulfing me with powerful arms, she clasped my head to her ample bosom and wept bitterly, "My boy, my boy. You, too!" The war was a conflict of personal tragedy to Schumann-Heink, a German-born American citizen, who had one son in the United States Army and another serving with the Kaiser's forces.

Through professional friends I arranged entertainments for the twenty thousand men stationed at Kearney. We presented vaudeville performers, acting companies, and musicians, including Mischa Elman, the violinist, and Carrie Jacobs Bond, the composer. Her song, "A Perfect Day," then was so frequently performed that I saw a Hungarian diplomat rise when an orchestra played it at a dinner party given in his honor. The distinguished visitor stood at rigid attention through the last note obviously in the misapprehension that the popular song was our national anthem.

Ruth, who was bringing a group of Denishawn dancers down for a show, confused me in advance with a five-word telegram that read, "Can you furnish baby sprites?" After consultation with my committee of arrangements, I wired back, "Army able to furnish a lot of things but is fresh out of baby sprites." Telegraph keys had made "sprites" from "spots." Ruth had been inquiring about baby spots, small spotlights for special lighting effects.

I made army friends through work with the entertainment projects, and was accepted as a fellow-sufferer by the men in my own platoon. We griped together about chow, stupid orders, and nitwit regulations, and took regular week-end passes as our due. I was lucky enough to be able to go home for week ends. The rest of the men in my unit had to find ways to conquer boredom. Whether they managed or not, they came back to camp with tall tales about brawls with gobs in San Diego, and dates with dames, oh boy! I always entered into the camaraderie with my own brand of deception, a knowing look and the set line, "What a week end! Me, too, oh boy!"

Boredom was hardly my problem. I worked every week end. At noon each Saturday I caught a train that took most of the afternoon to get from San Diego to Los Angeles, less than 150 miles up the coast. Since I used the inevitable travel hours to catch up on my reading, the trip never dragged for me, no matter what the delays. With luck at the whistle stops, I was at Denishawn in time for dinner, for the luxury of a home-cooked meal.

Saturday nights and Sundays, I gave private dancing lessons, never fewer than seven and often as many as ten. When the teaching schedule permitted, I wedged in some of the school's paper work before I hopped the Sunday evening train back to Kearney.

There was no need for me to go the pace of a seven-day workweek; I personally wanted to make the most of every hour while we waited for shipping orders. Army life had shaken down to a bearable routine, and I was relaxed in my relationships with members of the unit, grateful to be able to work regularly in my own dance studio. In short, I was content.

But my captain was not. He summoned me for a serious talk prefaced by a preamble on the Army's need for officers, and climaxed by his conclusion that my abilities, executive experience, and education combined to make me ideal officer material. With wasted breath I pointed out that I was getting along fine as an enlisted man and wanted to be with the ambulance unit when it went overseas. He promptly insinuated that refusal to take officers' training was tantamount to shirking my duty, then explicitly outlined the procedure I would follow in applying for the necessary training. An examination was part one of that procedure and I ignominiously decided that I would deliberately fail the exam.

At the appointed time hundreds of candidates queued in a line that shortened rapidly as one man after another disappeared through a mess hall door. There was no way to find out what to expect inside because nobody came back. At last my turn came. I stepped into the huge hall and found myself facing seventy officers of various ranks. My name was called out and at once questions came at me from different sections of the room: "What was your mother's maiden name?" "What's your favorite vegetable?" "What children's diseases have you had?" For five minutes I answered such disparate interrogations and then was motioned out through an exit door. The preliminaries over, I asked where I was to go for the examination. I had just taken it, they said. And passed.

I was assigned to the Fourth Officers' Training School, an infantry unit made up of regular army men with experience ranging from months to years. Without exception these seasoned soldiers considered a man dancer to be some creature that might be found in the mud under a boulder. I heard one sergeant say to another, "Over there, that Shawn. Ya know how he makes a living? He waltzes around a stage waving a scarf. And he thinks he's going to make the grade and get a commission!" Raucous laughter drowned out the second sergeant's answer.

The challenge had to be met. I had wanted no part of officers' training but, once in, I was grimly determined to get through. Failure to earn the commission would bring disgrace not only to me but to my profession as well. Sick at heart, I started to study, to march, to shine and shoot my way through the three-month sentence.

The morning I reported for duty, I was handed a grease-covered rifle and told to stand retreat with it that very evening. Under my breath I muttered that I hoped nobody would expect me to put the rifle up and down, for I didn't even know the names of the various movements in the *Manual of Arms*, much less how to execute them. Hours later the lethal weapon was wiped clean and, thanks to a kindhearted tentmate, I faked my way through retreat. After supper I took up the *Manual of Arms* and didn't put it down until I had it memorized. My diligence paid off ten days later when in an elimination test on the *Manual* I placed seventh in the test group of two hundred. I never did learn to shoot the rifle and by the time I faced a target at Camp Fremont, I felt that I'd be lucky to hit the hills beyond the rifle range.

Our last day at the range, the major came out for inspection with his staff of officer-instructors. They stood behind each man, watched him fire a round, and then checked his score. The major stepped behind me, the target went up, I closed my eyes, said a prayer, fired my five shots, and held my breath. Only when I heard the major say casually, "Shawn fires well, doesn't he?" did I dare to open my eyes, lift my head, and look at the score: two bull's-eyes, and three shots in the first circle around the bull's-eye.

The officers' training grind numbed mind and muscle. By perseverance I overcame the hostility and derision to which I was at first subjected, but each successive training day I had to tackle projects and problems for which I had no aptitude, under conditions antipathetic to my taste and temperament.

Physically we went on the double from reveille to retreat and even then our workday was far from over. After dinner we were herded into an empty mess hall where we studied ballistics, trajectories, and trigonometry tables. All of us had trouble keeping heavy-lidded eyes open but any candidate who dozed in spite of himself was washed out and shipped back to his old outfit the next day.

The final ordeal was known as the benzine drill because it cleaned out so many candidates. Without warning a man would be called out of rank and told to take charge of the company under certain problem-conditions. A formation or maneuver had to be carried out by the minimum number of commands, in a voice that was dynamic and commanding. My day came and I was thankful for both powerful lungs and the bond drive speaking experiences. I didn't recognize the boom that was my own voice giving minimal orders for the problem-formation, halting the company smartly before a final military salute. I accepted my gold bars, privately convinced that a brigadier general's silver star would have been more adequate compensation for my efforts in training.

My 224 fellow officers, survivors of the original 750 candidates, were in a mood for celebration and asked me to take charge of the graduation dinner dance. With pleasure I chose the Fairmount Hotel in nearby San Francisco as the location, selected my favorite foods for the menu, and asked as entertainer, a great star performer: my own wife.

I stage-managed Ruth's number, duplicating a sensational entrance Ruth had made when she danced at a Chicago ball given by Mrs. Potter Palmer. A drum roll signaled for the parting of the portieres at one end of the ballroom. Ruth, regally perched on a palanquin carried by four magnificently torsoed Negroes, was followed by slave dancers waving giant fans of peacock feathers. The breath-taking procession circled the ballroom, the palanquin was lowered, and Ruth went into her famous nautch dance. Surely no other class of shavetails ever had such spectacular and inappropriate entertainment for their graduation banquet.

By the time I was a second lieutenant, my ambulance unit was in France and I was ordered back to Kearney to join the Thirty-second Infantry's Company I, then being activated. My troubles were not over. A captain and I were the first officers to report to the unit and, after four days, he went A.W.O.L. with army funds, leaving me in command of the growing company.

Our top sergeant was a grizzled multistriper who had been in the Army for six years when I was born, and I turned to him the minute I heard our captain had decamped. "Sergeant, this is your company for the emergency," I said. "I know how to go through all the motions—where to stand, how many paces to take here and there. I won't shame you in public but you're going to have to tell me what orders to give to keep the men busy until we have a new captain." Luck was with me in that crisis. The sergeant was the fatherly type who patiently coached me, guided me, saved my face.

When the company finally was assembled, I set about to make soldiers of the draftees, and to give myself experience in commanding and directing those in my charge. If lives were to be in my hands later in France, I wanted the men to have confidence in me, and me to have faith in myself.

Training suddenly was immobilized by the flu epidemic of '18. Leaves were canceled. We wore white masks whenever we were away from our own barracks. Congregating indoors was prohibited, which meant that even the camp movie was closed. With all recreational activity on base curtailed, lack of even simple diversions made the healthy men restless and bored. In the emergency I asked for and was given permission to invite Ruth down to give an outdoor dance program. By long distance she said, "Yes," and came to Kearney for three of the most frustrating days of my army life.

Headquarters' flu orders required that any outsider visiting on base be quarantineed under guard. Ruth, no exception, was escorted everywhere by an M.P. who dutifully saw to it that my wife and I were separated at all times by the regulation distance of twenty feet.

On three successive chilly nights, Ruth danced in an orchestra shell that faced the parade grounds where thousands of masked men huddled in overcoats to watch the performance. From my front-row seat, I noticed that Ruth shivered occasionally, and I couldn't tell whether her chills were from an onslaught of flu or momentary terror at the sight of a mass of spooks stretched out, out, out in the dark night before her. When I turned around in my seat, I too shuddered involuntarily at the sight of the weird audience of shapeless figures with ghost-white gauze rendering their faces featureless.

The last morning Ruth was on the post, my colonel paraded the regiment in her honor. She stood with her M.P. guard, twenty feet from the colonel, while platoon after platoon, including mine, passed in review. When the parade was over the colonel called to Ruth, "How did you like that?" She beamed behind her mask, "Oh, I thought *he* was grand!"

Ruth left for her fall tour right after her visit to Kearney, and we went back to drilling as best we could with the epidemic still raging even in camp. It was rumored that as soon as the quarantine was lifted we would be off to France.

Then came November 11, 1918. We heard that Armistice Day was an occasion of hysterical excitement and unrestrained celebration in cities. Camp was strangely quiet. Subsequent days dragged by as we all faced personal reorientation in a time of dispiriting uncertainty. My doldrums were interrupted by a telephone call from Hollywood. The voice at the other end of the wire was that of C. B. De Mille with whom I had been friends for several years. We knew each other socially and I had choreographed dances for a number of his pictures. He told me that he was doing a Gloria Swanson picture with vision-scenes of Wealth, Pleasure, and Love. "We've shot Wealth and Pleasure," C.B. explained, "but I can't do the Vision of Love without you."

"That's very flattering," I answered; "however, I'm still

an officer and, by Act of Congress, a gentleman, and I doubt that I'd be allowed to appear in a movie."

"We'll get around all that." De Mille thought fast. "You always are free from Saturday noon until Sunday night, aren't you? We can shoot the scene in four hours on Sunday. We won't shoot you in close-up or use your name so you'll be protected from the Army and also you won't be jeopardizing future star status. Your fee will be five hundred dollars for the four hours on set."

The following Sunday afternoon I replaced my uniform with a few autumn leaves, strategically placed, and stepped onto the studio set. The scene was a woodland glade with a pool, mossy trees, a waterfall, and a grotto graced with a statue of Pan. Centered in the pool was a flattopped rock big enough for me to lie on full length. A vine, heavy with bunches of grapes, was festooned above and across the rock.

The action was to open with me sitting on the rock playing the pipes of Pan, the first and only time I ever performed on that ancient instrument. Gloria Swanson, in her first feature-length film, would enter in the background. A snapped twig would attract my attention and I would turn, see the beauty, and dash in pursuit. After a spirited chase, I would throw her down on the rock, reach up for a bunch of grapes and squeeze the fruit into her mouth. At last I would fling myself down and kiss the lovely creature. The kiss, C.B. warned me, was to be held to a full count of twenty-eight while the camera cranked.

I was to rehearse the grape-squeezing sequence with a stand-in who came on set wearing a long overcoat and a hair-covering beret. The grape skins, bunched on a rack for rehearsal, were filled with sponges that had been soaked in grapejuice. The stand-in stretched out in the alluring pose Miss Swanson was to take later, and I selected a large bunch and squeezed. The eyes of the stand-in were two purple pools of grapejuice. Lavendar liquid poured out of her ears, and she choked on the generous ten-cent-sized portion of juice which hit the intended target, her mouth.

After the girl had been mopped dry, I tried again with smaller sponge-filled grape skins. More mopping followed each try. Finally I asked C.B. if we could try real grapes. He answered, "Yes, we can, but those sponge grapes have been prepared at great expense." We performed a spongedectomy and I proved my point: real grapes worked perfectly. Nature had provided grapes with just the right amount of juice for performing even in a motion picture lavishly produced by De Mille.

We were ready for the take. Gloria Swanson stepped into the scene and I took chase. We went through the routine and I kissed her while C.B. deliberately counted to twenty-eight. When I released Miss Swanson, she sighed, "Ooh, that was nice." I whispered, "What was nice, the grapejuice?"

When the third take was completed, C.B. said, "I wish, Ted, that I could pay you a regular salary to stay in the studio and teach all of my actors how to kiss!"

"My pleasure," I answered. I collected my five hundred dollars and was back in uniform and out of the studio within the four-hour time period that De Mille had said the scene would require.

A few weeks later I received my honorable discharge, banked my army severance pay, and headed East to see my wife. My travel expenses and our celebration sprees were paid for with cash received for kissing Gloria Swanson three times to the count of twenty-eight each.

8

At Sixes and Sevens

Everyone who exchanges an army uniform for civvies finds that there's more to the transition than tailoring. Like other men I had my own special problems: I was overweight, tight-muscled, and unemployed. It took me several months to diet off pounds gained on the Army's dull diet of starch, a great deal longer to retrain muscles misused in infantry drill, and no time at all to be involved in too many projects.

I really did intend to take a well-earned vacation during my first summer out of uniform. There seemed to be no real reason why I shouldn't. With Denishawn School closed and the pages of my professional engagement book blank, I could have loafed until fall. I didn't because hard work always hounds me the way hard luck dogs the unfortunate.

That summer Ruth had an acting job that took us to north-

ern California, to a charming guest house on an estate in
Piedmont close to Berkeley and the Greek Theatre. There
Ruth was cast in a dramatic speaking part, the title role of
Miriam, Sister of Moses, a play written by her old friend,
Constance Smedley. Max Armfield, the artist and husband
of Constance, was the designer of costumes and sets for
Miriam, and I was signed as choreographer and ballet director.
I willingly took on the dual responsibilities since both would
end on opening night.

Even before Greek Theatre rehearsals started, I practiced
daily at the estate where we leased our little house, and where
I also rented the huge garage as studio. Its spaciousness led
me to trouble. I half-heartedly let it be known in the community that I would be willing to teach a small summer class,
and students swarmed out of the hills to sign up for the
course. My bank account bulged and the lesson fees, like all
unexpected funds, tempted me to extravagance. I bought a
Packard, secondhand but handsome, and even hired a man
to chauffeur Ruth on the Berkeley round trips that she would
continue for the run of the play. Optimistically, I looked forward to the luxury of being driven around the Bay area during
our free time. For all the leisure I managed that summer I
might as well have owned and driven a jalopy.

Rehearsals for the play were going well and my duties about
over when the actor playing Moses flew into a hot rage and
quit cold. Ruth, Constance, and Sam Hume, the director,
decided quite arbitrarily that I should step into the Moses
role. I refused with a barrage of excuses, all sound: teaching
was keeping me unexpectedly busy. The ballet directing took
up too much of my time. And I was no actor. That final
argument seemed irrefutable to me whose only acting experience had been at the amateur level and in the long ago.
Though I knew better than to take a speaking part in a
cast with professionals, I was sacrificed to the cause of ex-

pediency. The trio, Ruth, Sam, and Constance, pressured and I reluctantly donned the mantle of Moses, a garment I wore uneasily.

Even with organ-pipe beard that fell waist-length over the prophet's voluminous white robe, I looked more like eighteen than eighty. Actually no actor over twenty should have played that octogenarian role in the Greek Theatre. I was required to dash like a track star through an exhausting number of back-stage sprints. After one scene I had to gather up my robes, clutch my teetering turban, and race up a spiral staircase inside the concrete wall that backed the stage. Just in time and breathless, I reached a precarious height and position where I was spotlighted with the Ten Commandments. After panting condemnation to the masses, I raised the tablets and with fury hurled them at the mob below. The dramatic effect was lost when, instead of shattering like the Biblical command-ments, my tablets of wood bounced resoundingly on the Greek Theatre stage.

Ruth was a sensational success as Miriam in spite of an-other bout with her first-night jinx. The Greek Theatre was a gift to the University of California and a marble plaque, which faces the audience and may not be covered at any time, honors the donor in incised green letters: *The Greek Theatre, a Gift of William Randolph Hearst.*

On the opening night of *Miriam*, Ruth slipped on a dra-matic line, "And I shall make visible the heart's corruption." With a sweeping gesture that by chance ended with a flourish directly toward the plaque, she intoned, "And I shall make visible the *hearst* corruption." The audience was convulsed with laughter that it made no effort to suppress.

More laughter rang through other hills of northern Cali-fornia when I worked on several summer productions of the famous Bohemian Club to which I was elected a member after the war. Charles Caldwell Dobie proposed me for membership in the extraordinary group and my association with the club was one of the most interesting and uncomplicated of the postwar years.

The club's Bohemian Grove plays were elaborate spectacles budgeted at an average of $10,000 for a single summer night's performance at the encampment. Club members wrote the book and the music, choreographed and danced in the ballet numbers, and staged and acted in the annual production that often was more than a year in preparation.

The Bohemians were outstanding men of intelligence, wit, charm, and ability but they were hard to cast as dashing Lotharios and seductive belles. Many of the club members led sedentary lives and some exercised only by moving from one board chairman seat to another. They actively rode hobbies but of a kind that required no more strenuous movement than that of the hand over a check for a masterpiece, a subsidy for the opera, for a ticket to a leisurely world cruise. Members included prominent San Franciscans, *bons vivants* all, artists, writers, musicians and lawyers, doctors and executives of big corporations.

Through the Bohemian Club I met Herbert Hoover, Nicholas Longworth and became fast friends with the author Charles G. Norris and his wife, Kathleen Norris, the novelist.

It was difficult to cast chorus lines for dance numbers because the composite Bohemian was paunchy, double-chinned, and balding. For one summer's show, *St. John of Nippomuk*, I managed to assemble a fresh-faced group of boys and "girls" for a folk dance that they performed with spirit. At dress rehearsal inspection I noted that one "chorine" bulged peculiarly at the hip. Rudely lifting the costume skirt, I removed a fifth of Scotch from the dancer's drawers. Dress rehearsals always were ordeals because the Grove was chilly after dark and performers prudently fortified themselves against the cold.

A young Bohemian member, Lawrence Tibbett, sang the

title role of *St. Francis,* one of the three Grove productions for which I choreographed the ballet. The St. Francis finale was a scene depicting the saint's ascension to heaven with a procession of dancing angels who were to wear little more than white wings. The costume sketches were magnificent and I begged the casting committee to choose archangelic bodies that were fit to be seen nude. When club member-angels turned up for first rehearsal, I could see through tweed, herringbone, and serge that we had our work cut out for us. During costume fittings, the tight harness required to support heavy wings dug into soft executive flesh and great dumplings of tycoon fat bulged above and below the heaven-bound apparatus.

On dress rehearsal night the angels took their places up a hillside where they could be cued for their appearance as if from heaven. In wings that provided no warmth, the men shivered through unavoidable rehearsal delays until a chilled runner rushed down to me chattering, "If you d-d-don't send a c-c-couple of bottles of liquor up that hill, you soon won't have a g-g-goddamed angel left!"

I was sympathetic to potential deserters, for I too had turned blue in airy costumes worn while dancing in Grove ballet numbers. On only one night that I remember was there no complaint about the cold. I was ready for bed when the sound of glorious piano music rang through the grounds. I pulled on clothes, grabbed a blanket, and started through the door to a little platform where members performed informally. Shadowy figures were converging on the place which was lighted by an all-night bonfire. Two hundred members silently huddled to listen to the music played by Paderewski. For an hour and a half he played, then he dropped his hands, sighed, and left the platform, striking out along one of the woodland paths. When he was out of sight, the Bohemian members dispersed as silently as we had gathered.

The club's informal productions were called *High Jinks* evenings and I performed at a number of those well-named occasions. During the time of my active membership, several of the club's famous artist-members put me on canvas, and Joe Mora sculptured a bronze figure of me as Demon Bird from Charles Dobie's *Ilya of Murom,* a Grove extravaganza. Dobie, with the Grove's director, Reginald Travers, who also ran the Players' Club, took me out of the bulrushes and once again made me Moses in a Dobie play written for Ruth on a plot of hers. This time I was a success as Moses at twenty.

My San Francisco church service given prewar resulted in a strange experience postwar. I was approached by a young minister, Charles Brandon Booth, son of the Salvation Army Booths, who wanted to found a new kind of church, a circuit organization that would serve seven communities on different days of the week.

He believed in the fusion of religion with all the arts including the dance, and asked my co-operation for a tour of church services that would be concerts with dance ritual and a ten-minute sermon. No salaries were to be paid during an experimental tour of southern California, but Booth expected that freewill silver offerings would pay traveling expenses for the group. In addition to the two of us it included three girl dancers, a singer, a pianist, and a harpist.

The harpist was distressed literally to tears each time she saw her beloved instrument strapped to the Overland which was one of the automobiles in our two-car cavalcade. I was less emotional about my dancing groundcloth that, in transit, was roped around the Overland's radiator.

Vague arrangements had been made for our appearance in about a dozen towns but after two nights on the road, we found ourselves in an epidemic territory where public gatherings were prohibited and schools and churches closed. Resourcefully Booth turned our automobiles north and, after scouting ahead himself, flagged us down at any town free of epidemic. We finished our unorthodox tour with the minister setting off for a town, making hasty arrangements if possible, and then standing out on the main highway route waiting for us to come along. We would drive to the edge of a town having no idea where or whether we would perform there until we spotted the Reverend Mr. Booth, his arms flapping like a semaphore. Braking, we would hear him say, "We appear here at Parish Hall tonight," and then we unpacked. For whatever widespread reason, epidemic or apathy, Mr. Booth was never able to establish his circuit-church.

Ironically I broke even on the unsuccessful church tour but about the same time went deep into the red with a publishing venture that was a triumph artistically. Through John Howell, the San Francisco book publisher and dealer from whom I bought my rare dance and costume volumes, and Albert Bender, art patron and connoisseur, I was able to interest John Henry Nash in *Ruth St. Denis, Pioneer and Prophet,* for which I had assembled manuscript material before I went into the Army.

My guide and friend, who saw me through the reading of proofs for that first book, was Bertha Damon, author years later of the best-selling *Grandma Called It Carnal* and *A Sense of Humus*. Bertha, a patient guide, often has looked over my shoulder while I poured out notes and theories, anecdotes and philosophies.

Nash was a master printer and eccentric who accepted only those books that he really wanted to do. I had been warned that once he decided to print a book the author had no further word on the subject. It came as no surprise to me that I had no say in the publication arrangements. I was told that my book would be in two volumes, one for text and the other for illustrations. The limited edition of 350 copies, numbered and signed, was to be sold for $25, or so Nash thought.

We mailed Nash's handsome prospectus about Ruth to potential buyers with an encouraging return of two hundred advance sale orders at the $25 price. But the printer's bill was for a cost of more than $35 a set, so I took a personal loss on each of the advance two hundred orders. The edition was sold out long ago, and the last few secondhand copies, collector's items, have sold for as much as $90.

The $2000 loss on the book was nothing to what was ahead but I was no clairvoyant and threw myself into two absorbing projects: my own school in Los Angeles and the production of vaudeville numbers.

When Alexander Pantages, vaudeville theater owner of the West, commissioned me to produce a spectacular dance act for his own circuit, I was ready with a subject: the story of Julnar from the *Arabian Nights*. At every rereading of the tales of Scheherazade, my imagination had been excited by the briefly mentioned Julnar, daughter of the Emperor of all the kingdoms underneath the sea. I envisioned her as a beautiful princess pursued by an earth prince who explored submarine depths to woo her.

I wove my interpretations of a fragile tale into a three-act dance drama with a cast of seventeen people, one a narrator. It had been my conviction that people often failed to understand dance themes because they neglected to read program notes. With Julnar's vaudeville audiences I took no chances, but introduced a storyteller, the first ever used by a professional dance company. The vaudeville audiences who attended Julnar performances had no choice but to sit, look, and listen.

The dance drama opened with a stylized oriental exterior, a drop curtain with a big central window that was a transparency through which the audience could see Scheherazade. She reclined on a divan, wine and fruit in hand, and told the story of the first act to an invisible Shah. The introduction was followed by a black-out during which the divan on rubber tires was rolled off stage and the window drop pulled up. The story was danced full stage and each scene was followed by another black-out and continuation by Scheherazade of the tale that served as prologue for each dance.

Julnar of the Sea opened at the Pantages Theatre in Los Angeles with Lillian Powell in the title role and Louis Horst as pianist-conductor. It toured the circuit for more than twelve hundred continuous performances and was a success with press and audiences.

With *Julnar* launched, I turned my attention to a dance drama for Martha Graham, who had been a private pupil and protégée of mine for a number of years. She had first signed up as a Denishawn class pupil in 1915 when she was shy, plumpish, and older than most of the students. For two years Martha applied herself in class without distinction but with a diligence that was just short of dedication, and then one day I saw the miracle happen. I was teaching a new number, *Serenata Morisca*, to thirty students and suddenly saw Martha performing the dance as I had despaired of ever seeing any pupil dance it. After the class, I had a serious talk with Martha and explained that she had a long way to go before she would be a great dancer but if she would promise to work, I would give her the private lessons that I knew her family could ill afford.

From then on Martha was my student and was so well trained in Denishawn techniques that she taught classes of business girls at night. Postwar I wanted Martha as assistant teacher at the Ted Shawn Dance Studio I opened on Grand Avenue in Los Angeles but she was more eager to perform than teach.

Since I was hopeful of staging another successful vaudeville act for the circuit, I enthusiastically designed a dance drama for Martha. It was *Xochitl*, the first contemporary dance production based on an Aztec theme. Its original music was by Homer Grunn, whose American Indian compositions I had long admired. Francisco Cornejo, a Mexican artist who was an authority on Aztec, Toltec, and Mayan civilizations, designed the sets and costumes. The latter were hand-embroidered with colored wools, and some of the robes of satin and gold cloth were overlaid with small feathers. Expensive plumes of exotic birds were fashioned into sensational headdresses. Act One was danced before a single drop and the other on a full stage set with many papier-mâché props. The story told of Xochitl (the flower) taking a bowl of pulque to the emperor who, inflamed by the strong liquor and her beauty, jumped from his throne and pursued the innocent. When Xochitl's father was about to plunge a knife into the emperor, she stopped the blow, and there followed a happy, legal ending complete with court wedding.

Martha was perfect in the role that made the most of her exotic features and allowed her body freedom of movements that ranged from tigerish and primitive to passionate and regal. Robert Gorham, a tall handsome student, went off on tour as the emperor but, after he broke a foot bone, was replaced by Charles Weidman.

While the dance drama toured I worked on several vaudeville acts that were simple *divertissements*, and at last found time to produce a straight ballet again. I chose a Greek theme and set my ballet, *The Mysteries of Dionysus*, to the music of Massenet's opera, *Bacchus*. We thought that the dancer doing Bacchus was miscast, so I replaced him. That was no help. The *Mysteries* lasted only for a four-week tour of California vaudeville houses, and we were lucky to get even those bookings. The commercial flop later was a great hit with Berkeley audiences when I included *The Mysteries of Dionysus* on a dance program that I did with a small company of my own at the Greek Theatre.

By the time *Xochitl* returned from the circuit, I was negotiating for a concert tour with Harry Hall, who came to me representing himself as agent, manager, and impresario. He had managed Ellen Beach Yaw, a well-established coloratura, and other lesser performers with whom I should have checked before I accepted Hall's terms.

He was willing to go out for twenty per cent of the receipts and without an advance for his own traveling expenses on the original booking trip. The arrangements should have roused my suspicion but I accepted them because I needed what little money I had for costumes and scenery for the concert production.

Producing for vaudeville had been an unprofitable experience. *Julnar* made money and so did one or two smaller acts. *Xochitl* broke even but I lost money on the rest of my productions. My cash on hand was earned the hard way—by teaching.

After Hall and I agreed on terms, he went out to sign us up with theater managers. Eventually he mailed me contracts that seemed sound, and totaled $28,000 for a ten-week tour. After one look at that paper profit, I was off on a spending spree. I arranged for my New York solo debut that I had always wanted to be at the most prestigious place, the Metropolitan Opera House. By mail I leased the Met for a single evening date at the end of our tour. In those days Tuesday was dark night at the Met and the house was available for a $600 rental fee, which I paid before we left Los Angeles.

Encouraged by the printed words of our contract and the round number in expected gross, I began to arrange a three-section program: Church Service; Music Visualizations; and Romantic, Barbaric, and Pictorial Dances. That last section had as its fitting finale, a condensed version of *Xochitl* with me as Emperor and Charles Weidman as the father.

The Music Visualizations, a term we used as replacement for the sloppy and inaccurate term "interpretive," included my *Gnossienne* and three other solos by me. Martha, Betty May, and Dorothea Bowen did a *Contrapuntal Dance* to music of Scarlatti, and the Bach Two and Three Part Inventions. Betty May had a solo with MacDowell music. I created a light comedy number with Martha as an old mammy, Betty May and Dorothea as pickaninnies, using for accompaniment Nathaniel Dett's "Juba Dance." That was the first dance use made of Dett's lively tune now so hackneyed.

Before we left on our formal tour, we played a few dates in southern California towns including Santa Barbara where Martha's mother and sisters lived. Martha quite properly was excited at the prospect of having her family see her in a dance concert with solos of her own and duets with me, her teacher. We were a never-to-be-forgotten sensation that night but hardly as Martha had anticipated.

Our big Spanish duet was programed after my flamenco series. At the end of my solo group that night I landed with a deep lunge accompanied by the sound of a loud report. My skintight black trousers had split with an explosion that could have been heard on the street and hastily I backed off stage. Martha stood crestfallen in the wings, so obviously disappointed by the thought of our canceled duet that I covered the wide open space with my *sombrero sevillano* and explained the situation to the audience which roared for the duet, split and all. While Martha did a solo number I closed the trouser gap with every safety pin available in the dressing rooms. I can't remember how our duet was received but the Santa Barbara reviewer admitted in print that the prayer of a lifetime was answered when "incredibly tight Spanish trousers burst wide open during last night's performance."

We finished our short local tour with scenery and costumes paid for but without money for rail fare to our first contract date. Hall had booked us into Duluth, Minnesota, an expensive jump from Los Angeles for me and the little company:

Martha, Charles, Betty May, and Dorothea Bowen, Louis Horst, and Sid Winton, our longtime stage manager.

I borrowed money for travel expenses to Minnesota. At Duluth and again at Virginia, Minnesota, we were well received and promptly paid by reputable local management. I should have been pleased with the way things were going but an uneasy feeling nagged at me. Some of the managers up ahead were not answering my letters, and our next engagement was for a week in St. Paul, then known as the theater grave-yard, so many shows died there.

The St. Paul engagement was disastrous as I had feared and at the end of it we heard shocking news from June Hamilton Rhodes, who as a favor had gone ahead as press agent and advance representative. She had found that one block of five towns was worthless. Harry Hall had pressured a clerk in a tobacco warehouse into sending me a signed contract. With Hall gone, the little clerk got cold feet, and never even tried to fulfill any part of his agreement.

We wrote off that fiasco but tried to locate Hall through his wife's California address. The last word I ever heard from him was a return wire that read: "Worry is a dishonest God. Hall."

June jumped ahead of us again and tried to wildcat the show to fill in the open dates. She managed to pick up one or two small percentage dates and then went to Texas to investigate another contract that seemed shaky. Only two performances had been booked by a Dallas concert bureau that had signed us for twelve in Texas, Oklahoma, and Louisiana. The bureau asked for an extension to make good on its con-tract and we agreed only because that contract was my last hope of breaking even.

Through correspondence with the Met I discovered that its management would neither refund my money nor give me an alternate date if I were forced to cancel my Tuesday night.

In Dallas then I was faced with forfeiting the rental fee in New York or passing up the possible proceeds from the Texas contract. I took a long chance and let the Met have my hard-earned $600.

Eventually we played the full twelve engagements set up by the Dallas bureau but collected less than one third of full contract for the booking. I sued the bureau and received a judgment but not a dollar because the organization went into bankruptcy.

One of the bureau's contract cities was Shreveport, Louisiana, where we were booked for matinee and evening performances. Some miles out of town our train was boarded by the Commissioner of Public Safety who begged me to withdraw the church service from our program. He explained that a delegation of some two hundred ministers and church elders had marched on city hall demanding that my sacrilegious and blasphemous dancing be prohibited.

The city attorney after thumbing through legal tomes said that there was nothing to prevent the performance from starting but, if it were found to be obscene, it could be stopped by ringing down the curtain. The two hundred followers of the gentle Nazarene made it clear that if I were allowed to proceed, they would first tear down the opera house, and then tar and feather me before riding me out of town on a rail.

That unholy threat raised the dander of the chief of police who cautioned the clergy, "You start anything like that and I'll treat you just like any other lawbreakers and put you behind bars!"

The commissioner, shaking along with us on the local train, admitted to me that officially he could not stop me from giving the performance, but he begged that in the interest of peace and public safety, I please voluntarily withdraw the church service from our program.

That was impossible. And I explained why. The church

service part of our program had been well received in many cities and several states. Frequently clergymen had come backstage to express their personal appreciation of the beauty, dignity, and reverential treatment of the religious themes. Withdrawal of the section would indicate that there was something wrong with it and, if trouble arose again, I would be in a weakened position. I was regretful but definite.

That day I lunched with a Shreveport friend who said, "Well, you're certainly brave. They lynch people down here on the slightest provocation. Why, just the other day, they got all het up about something and plain had to lynch somebody. It was all over when it turned out that they'd lynched the wrong man entirely."

The full police force of Shreveport was at the theater when I arrived. Uniformed men were stationed in the lobby, at the stage door, on stage by my dressing-room door, and even outside my dressing-room window. By twos other members of the force were scattered throughout the auditorium. In spite of an impassioned appeal for boycott from the ministers of one religious sect, we played to a packed house.

I admit quite frankly that I faced the first curtain with some trepidation. We danced the church services to an audience that was completely silent. When the section's final curtain fell the hush was drowned by waves of applause from the audience who brought me back for innumerable curtain calls. After the house lights went on for the first intermission, I was startled by new applause that puzzled me until I discovered that it was for the mayor and other city officials who were starting backstage. They congratulated me first for courage and then for the beauty of the church service performance.

A few days later we danced at the University of Oklahoma at Norman and afterward I received a letter from an official of that institution who condemned our "lascivious, Oriental dances." I never could get him to specify which dances could be qualified by either adjective.

In a Dallas hotel, at the end of the contract and out of money, I faced one of the worst dilemmas of my theatrical career. The map indicated that the distances to Los Angeles and to New York were about equal and equally costly to reach. Which should I try for? New York, I decided. But how would we get there?

Out of desperation came inspiration and I wired my Aunt Kathryn that I had to have $2000 within twenty-four hours to avoid total disaster. I waited out the hours by counting the minutes until I read the four beautiful words of her answering telegram: "Money on the way."

●●

9

Patterns for the Future

N An S.R.O. sign hung next to the box-office wicket at the Apollo when I dropped by the theater lobby before my first concert appearance in New York. It was incredible to me that the house should be sold out. I never before had given a solo performance in New York and hadn't appeared there at all since the prewar vaudeville engagement. Bemused I strolled backstage to make up. The concert date had been set on short notice and promoted with limited funds; yet the whole house was sold for cash with bona fide press tickets the only paper. I was dumfounded by the fact that I was going to make money on my gamble with the last of the borrowed $2000.

That night, more significant than I could guess, was extraordinary even on the surface. The packed house gave me a real ovation and, after the performance, my dressing room was

filled with celebrities. No backstage visitor surprised me more
than Dr. Arnold Genthe, in genial mood. I had known the
eminent photographer only as hypercritical and could hardly
believe that he was saying to me, "It's very difficult nowadays
to add anything really new to the vocabulary of the dance but
I think you have done it with your *Gnossienne*. It's a genuine
contribution."

Compliments and congratulations pleased me but I thrilled
to the evening's coup, a contract offer from Daniel Mayer, the
internationally known impresario who managed Paderewski,
Pavlova, and similarly shining stars. Mr. Mayer didn't wait for
the program's finale but came back at the first intermission
to say that he would be "honored" to have me under his
management. The next morning at his office I signed a tour
contract and a month later the persuasive Daniel Mayer signed
Ruth, too. She and I were guest stars of a festival at Greens-
burg, Pennsylvania, where by prearrangement Mr. Mayer outlined his plans for us. They included two advance tours, one
a spring trip through the South and the second, six weeks in
England; and the grand tour of the United States to begin
as originally scheduled in the fall. The six greatest years of
Denishawn history resulted from that business conference in
western Pennsylvania.

With ink dried on the contracts, Ruth returned to California, and I went back to New York where I had opened a
Denishawn School in a combination apartment and studio
on the roof of the Chatsworth on Riverside Drive.

The last months of winter somehow vanished like melting
snow while I taught and studied, played and worked. Four or
five weeks were spent in producing experimental motion pictures for an inventor-promoter who came to me with a novel
idea for filming dance subjects. He had developed an ingenious
method for synchronizing music of movie theater orchestra
with dancing in motion pictures. His idea was to have dancers

perform in a film studio to the accompaniment of a real orchestra directed by a conductor who would be camera-shot using a white baton against a black stage front. Orchestration for the film would be sent to each local movie theater where its live orchestra would follow the baton of the filmed conductor.

My part in the enterprise was to direct and provide dancers and the dances, and to supply costumes, on a royalty basis with a percentage from the film showings. With Martha, Charles, Marjorie Peterson, and Lillian Powell, we made eight or ten dance film shorts that were quite stunning. The synchronization of live orchestra with filmed conductor was a successful system soon outmoded by the perfection of sound films. The dancers luckily were paid their fees, about $10 a day. Only the royalty speculation system failed and for my efforts and work on the films, I have yet to receive even 10 cents.

Denishawn School was building with a steady increase of pupils, including some celebrities like Mae Murray with the sensationally beautiful legs, and Mrs. Lydig (Julia) Hoyt, a society matron with acting ambitions. I myself turned student during this time and took flamenco lessons with Ortéga, a Spanish dancer with authentic background and experience.

After hours I went to the theater, to concerts, to parties, and made friends that have lasted to this day. I posed as a favor to a prewar friend, Allan Clark, the sculptor, and I also loaned him studio space because he and his art photographer wife were too close to being penniless to afford either model or studio. I introduced Allan to Amelita Galli-Curci and she commissioned her portrait head and two dancing figures that started him toward his outstanding success.

Galli-Curci and Homer Samuels, her husband, were old friends with whom I often dined, and whenever she sang at the Metropolitan I attended her opera performance with

Homer. There were other fascinating evenings that winter with Rose O'Neill, the poet-artist whose kewpie drawings made her famous and rich; with Dhan Gopal Mukerji, the Hindu author and lecturer; with poet Witter Bynner, and the costume designer, Grace Ripley.

It was "Rip" who introduced me to Mrs. Guy Currier of Boston, and quite indirectly started me on the long road to Jacob's Pillow, my summer dance theater and school which had its Silver Jubilee Year in 1957, and continues to flourish with the passing years. At the time of our meeting, Mrs. Currier was about to launch a summer theater project on an eighty-acre site near Peterboro, New Hampshire. Plans were drawn for a drama school with a campus of faculty cottages, student cabins, practice studios, and dining halls, and for a perfectly equipped open-air theater designed by Stuart Walker.

I could not promise Mrs. Currier to be in continuous residence as head of her dance department because it was already evident that heavy enrollment of Denishawn summer courses would require me to be in New York for part of each week. We worked out an arrangement that I could manage and she approved. I was to have an assistant teacher and an accompanist, both full time, at Mariarden, Mrs. Currier's place, where I would teach for two and a half days at the end of each week.

Spring was a busy time with preparations for summer classes in town and country, with students finishing the term at Denishawn, with arrangements and rehearsals for the short tours. On April 13, exactly eight years after our first performance together, Ruth arrived from California, and we shortly set out with the company for the southern shakedown tour.

At its close we had a few free days in New York where I had to give a paid lecture to the Froebel League which met at the home of Mrs. John Henry Hammond, a longtime

friend, generous to me and to the dance. After I spoke, Mrs.
Goddard Dubois, another old friend, took me aside and said,
"Ted, if you want to go on looking as if you were wearing
a younger brother's castoff Sunday suit, all right. But I do wish
that you would put your mind on your clothes while you are
in England. Get yourself outfitted by a good London tailor."

I wasn't the least offended by the advice from Josephine
Dubois. It was well meant and well taken. Like Ruth, I had
always given more thought and attention to stage costumes
than to my personal wardrobe. I insisted on being properly
costumed to the least detail on stage. Off stage I was quite
content to appear in a ready-made blue serge kept scrupulously
cleaned and reasonably pressed. In such conservative attire
Mrs. Dubois had seen me at Mrs. Hammond's house and wearing the same suit I stepped aboard the Cunard Line's S.S.
Samaria for my first of many trips across the Atlantic.

As a London sight-seer, I tramped and trammed about
with the increasing joy of recognition. Hundreds of the books
I had read up to that time had been about England and I
roamed around a London town that seemed already familiar.
I kept saying to myself, "This is the Strand," "This is Fleet
Street," "This is Piccadilly," only half-believing that it was
so and fully expecting to wake up at any time to find that I
was doing one-night stands in Nowhereville, U.S.A.

We experienced normal tourist difficulties with accommodations, moving from one impossible rooming house to the
Victoria, a pleasant hotel, and finally to the Regina in Ken-
sington. There we were pampered by the hotel's owner, "Rose"
Majumbdar, a charming little Hindu, who had been with Ruth
for years as foreman of the East Indians in her troupe.

At the Regina I had the inevitable shattering experience
with a London bathroom. I failed to ask "Rose" to explain
a puzzling sign over the tub and I vaguely thought that the
words DO NOT *let water reach the overflow* might have

something to do with water conservation or flooding the bath-room.

Very late one night the meaning was made shockingly clear to me when I stepped into the tub that was filled almost to the upper outlet. Naturally my added bulk made the water level rise above the overflow and the bath water ran out of the side wall and down to the street three stories below. Fully expecting that police would soon be pounding on the door, I half-soaped and hurriedly scrubbed while the water level dropped slowly. I have always believed that I finished my tub undisturbed only because there were no nocturnal passers-by to be drenched by the cascade.

Tales told by traveling friends had prepared us for plumbing vagaries, food that was unpalatable, and a variety of expected minor mishaps. But no one had exploded a myth that I had long accepted as fact. I grew up on the legend that the British were reserved, cold, unfriendly, and conservative to the point of pain, and was unprepared for the gracious hospitality of the people we met, for the reaction of London audiences.

Because of my misconception of the collective British, our debut audience frightened me into a temporary state of the shakes. Our first performance at the Coliseum was a matinee and when I finished my flamenco solos, I thought from the shouting across the footlights that the audience might be going to throw things. Never in the United States had I danced before an audience that so vocally expressed itself. After I had taken four or five trembling bows, sounds became words and I understood gratefully that the ruckus was friendly and enthusiastically hearty. The traditional *Bravo!* rang out along with shouts of "Good boy" and "That's great!" and "Do it again!" That was the beginning of six weeks of personal success in England, a happy time for me as a performer, and the initiation of my career as an internationally acclaimed dancer.

Our engagement at the Coliseum was for four weeks, a month crammed with unforgettable experiences that began with a dinner given in our honor by the Dancing Circle at the Trocadero. As honor guest, I sat transported at the right of the chairman, Madame Adeline Genée, whom I considered to be the most perfect of classic ballet performers. I had seen her in Los Angeles and from the first felt that she had no peer as ballerina, an opinion that I never changed though I sometimes was at variance with those who idolized Pavlova, beloved by balletomanes the world over, and Karsavina, prima ballerina of Diaheleff Ballet Russe. Understandably I was overwhelmed to be welcomed professionally to London by Madame Genée.

After-theater parties, teas, luncheons, and dinners crowded our social schedule. At one party I reported enthusiastically to a typecast Englishman that I had just made an appointment with the one man I most wanted to meet in England, Havelock Ellis. The compatriot of the great author and psychologist reacted with deadpan but unmistakable emphasis, "Ah, so. Yes, I understand that he is well liked—by *Americans!*" Ellis was indeed well liked by me on the several occasions that we talked seriously while I was in London. His conversation made the whole trip forever memorable to me.

Posing for publicity pictures leads to strange adventures in London as elsewhere, everywhere. On a Sunday, early, our *Egyptian Ballet* number was photographed against a background of bronze sphinxes and the obelisk known as Cleopatra's Needle. We chose a Sunday morning for the location shooting in the vain hope that fewer people would be around than on a business day. We danced and posed while cameras rolled and a gathering crowd swelled until extra police had to be called out. Tram passengers, rolling by, gawked in disbelief at the sight of barefoot Egyptians dancing on the side-walks of London. We pretty well retained our composure until our whole routine was nearly broken up by a youth who yelled at Ruth, "Hello theah, Cleo, old gel."

Our barefoot dancing was criticized in London by two people who should have known better: Theodore Kosloff and C. W. Beaumont. Kosloff, with whom I had coached off and on through the years, thought that our *Egyptian Ballet* would have been quite good had we danced it on-the-point instead of barefoot. Mr. Beaumont, author, publisher, and seller of books about the ballet, nearly tore me limb from limb, in print, because I had danced barefoot to the *Seguidillas* of Albeniz.

The stress we placed on authenticity of movement and concept, and our break with the classical was fully understood by a young British fan, Hal Mann, that rare balletomane with a mind and heart big enough to love the dance as a whole. Hal, a delightful host and cicerone then and during our later visits to England, limited his own first trip to the United States to a stay at Jacob's Pillow and three spree days in New York. Pat Barton, son of Sir Dunbar Barton, another enthusiastic and perceptive dance fan, went along with us on many sight-seeing jaunts. He became a good friend to us all and eventually crossed the Atlantic to study dancing with me at Denishawn.

Not all the friends we saw were British. Mrs. Kate Dalliba John, an American patron of Ruth's early career, had a London house that season and she entertained us at a lunch with Lauritz Melchior, who sang for us, and Madame Ethel Leginska, the pianist, later more famous as a symphony conductor. We were frequently entertained by Maud Allen, an American dancer who had been sensationally successful in London where she then lived in semiretirement. We often saw our treasured friend, Marie Dressler.

Years before, Marie had asked us to do our *Egyptian Ballet* at an Egyptian Ball, a social and benefit event to be held at the Ritz-Carlton in New York. Marie planned to do a take-off of our dance with a famous comedian partner who didn't arrive at the ball and couldn't be located at any of the bars he was known to frequent.

Marie asked if I would do the take-off and briefed me on the routine. At the finale Marie regally plopped herself into a dais and, as planned, fell through its fake bottom. But it was not in the script for Marie to be stuck so she could neither bow nor exit. With me hovering over her, we some-how tipped over the dais and before anyone could rush to help us, Marie began to crawl on all fours with the dais upturned on her fanny. She was strong as well as big and went across the little stage and down red-carpeted steps. I trailed behind holding her straight until she suddenly jerked me off balance and, dragging me behind her, continued to crawl the full length of the ballroom for an unprecedented exit.

Marie and Ruth and I were once signed for a quite different benefit at the Philharmonic Auditorium in Los Angeles. Every luminary of Hollywood was to appear on the same fund-raising program but only the three of us turned up for morn-ing rehearsals. Marie, with serious expression and tone to match, began to deliver a long monologue on how experienced vaudeville and tour performers like us needed rehearsals but, of course, the great movie stars knew all about stage exits and entrances without rehearsing. "We've only been in this business a thousand years," Marie concluded, "so we need rehearsal and the newcomers don't. That's obvious."

On the benefit program, that started late and dragged on as unrehearsed shows do, Marie gave a performance hilarious and warm, and then, after her last bow, fainted. I'll never know how, but I managed to carry her across the stage to her dressing room where we learned that she had been in constant pain from a back injury suffered on a movie set. Marie, who had complained to no one about the excruciating agony she was suffering, was the grandest and greatest of troopers, and an enchanting human being.

At London parties we ran into actor Richard Dix and director Maurice Tourneur, and we were taken out to late supper by publisher Condé Nast and editor Frank Crowninshield. Wherever we went we were surrounded by prominent people with headline names and professional standing to match.

One night when my dressing room was jammed as usual with a throng of admirers, I was quite overwhelmed by the extravagant compliments of a young man identified as Muk de Jari, popular star of musical comedy.

From pictorial magazines I learned that De Jari, a Serbian tenor, was recognized as the best-dressed man in London, the very expert for whom I had been searching. After we had lunched several times at Simpson's on the Strand, I asked De Jari the name of his tailor. Even he couldn't hide his moment of inward struggle at the thought of sharing the treasured expert but his friendship for me stood the strain and he took me to Anderson and Shephards in Savile Row. What De Jari advised me to have tailored was hardly what Josephine Dubois had in mind. In time I was perfectly turned out in morning coat, striped trousers, sand-colored vest, top hat and cane, an ensemble so resplendent that I wore it only three times. Years later Jess Meeker, accompanist of my men's group, dressed in the coat and striped trousers for matinees.

I myself wore the morning coat on only one quite proper occasion, the Denishawn House wedding of Margaret Eddy whom I gave away because her father, Sherwood Eddy, was in Russia on a writing assignment.

After our London engagement we went on a tour of the provinces that Mayer had booked. At Bristol, Sir Henry and Lady Whyte-Smith asked us for tea and I decided to dress up for the occasion in my Savile Row cutaway. If my formal attire startled our hosts neither of them gave a sign. Sir Henry, straight from his airplane factory, appeared at tea in thick rumpled tweeds, a homespun figure indeed.

Between the Bristol engagement and our sailing there were three days which we spent dashing about in Paris where none of us but Ruth had ever been. For me the trip was disillusioning. I tried to do three months of sight-seeing in seventy-two hours, a frustrating attempt, and took a dislike to Parisians that subsequent experience has not changed.

We returned on the S.S. *Majestic* and I slept through the voyage, a shipboard pattern I have since followed for years. I always sail from home exhausted from the effort of getting ready for the trip, and I sail back to the United States worn out by sight-seeing and performances and parties wherever I've been. On that first trip home, I emerged from a state of semi-coma only long enough to take part in the ship's concert. From a program of the event I know the names of others who appeared: Mistinguette, Maurice Chevalier, Dr. Walter Damrosch, and Irving Berlin. What they did or what we danced is a complete blank in my memory.

When the New York customs inspector of our theatrical luggage asked, "Where's your outgoing declaration?" I looked at him blankly. I didn't know that I should have made a triplicate list with full details of every single item shipped out of the United States. Before sailing, our theatrical baggage should have been examined and checked against my list, with one copy signed by the inspecting officer.

Since I had not complied with a ruling about which I hadn't known, the incoming inspector had no choice but to seize our baggage and throw it into "public stores." To regain possession of my own belongings I had to retain a customs broker who bid for them. The procedure took two weeks and $95, and I never made that customs mistake again. Whenever I have left the country with theatrical costumes, scenery, and props, I have made the outgoing declaration, which is a laborious chore. Each item must be listed not only by name but location: "Wardrobe trunk, No. 7, top drawer, 1 tin cup, 1 can resin, 20 make-up cloths, 4 wigs," and so on through each drawer and all the hangers of every trunk.

I developed quite a technique for giving costume descriptions that, while literally correct, would be puzzling to customs inspectors. I once listed "12 goldcloth jockstraps for archangels" and a customs inspector asked to see them. He listened to the story of the ballet, looked at the pictures of the archangel ensemble, nodded approval and checked the listed item without changing expression. Other similar experiences have made me wonder whether customs inspectors really are devoid of a sense of humor or whether they deliberately develop the most perfect of poker faces.

There have been many times in my professional life when only words like "hectic," "mad," "frantic" were quite applicable to the crowding and confusion of schedules and activities. The events of the summer that followed my return from England fully justified qualification by the timeworn adjectives.

With Denishawn summer classes too large to handle in the Chatsworth studio, where assistant teachers had carried on in my absence, I had to search Manhattan for a larger studio. I was looking for lots of space and a good floor, and found both in the gymnasium of a church centrally located on Broadway. I must have rented the gym on the Fourth of July or a Saturday afternoon late, for the neighborhood was very quiet. Too late I discovered that, on normal weekdays, riveters were at work on streetcar tracks outside the gym windows. For the summer I was in competition with the vibrating din and shouted over clangor until fall.

The New York staff remained in town through summer school while Martha and Louis went up to Mrs. Currier's summer theater camp as assistant teacher and pianist. Ruth, though not teaching, stayed for the season at our faculty cottage on the grounds of Mariarden.

I taught New York classes, groups of thirty to forty, on Mondays, Tuesdays and Wednesdays from 8 A.M. until 6 P.M. At midnight Wednesday I took a train for Worcester where, shortly after Thursday's dawn, I boarded the Peterboro train that laid over for an hour at Winchenden, and finally reached its destination at ten in the morning. A beautiful blonde but terrifyingly efficient secretary from Mariarden combined Peterboro marketing with meeting me, and we seldom reached the camp before noon. I taught at Mariarden on Thursday afternoon, all day Friday and Saturday, and then on Sunday returned by way of a succession of local trains to New York.

The schedule when stripped to the bone sounds grueling but I remember that Mariarden summer with pleasure. I headed the dance department; Tony Sarg taught puppet theater; and the director of the dramatic faculty was Adrienne Morrison, wife of Richard Bennett and mother of Constance, Joan, and Barbara.

Barbara Bennett had been studying with me for some time on the advice of her doctor. He explained to me that she had an ailment in which the bones were becoming brittle, and he believed that dance training would benefit her. She took private lessons and I was careful not to let her leap or make a violent movement lest bones disintegrate into bits that looked like blackboard chalk, that being the term used by the doctor. He was right about the effect of exercise on Barbara and pronounced her cured after several months of dance training.

Joan Bennett, shy and demure, looked like a beautiful little boy as the tiny page in the summer's production of *As You Like It*. I played Charles the Wrestler in that same production and arranged its dances to some deadly English folk dance tunes.

Berthe and Francesca Braggiotti, students of mine at Mariarden, later opened a Boston dancing school called a branch of Denishawn. In subsequent years at the end of each tour, I spent a week at the Braggiotti home in Brookline, taught a master class at Braggiotti-Denishawn, and helped with the school's final program on which I was guest artist.

During the Mariarden summer, hours of teaching and miles of traveling occupied only part of my attention. I was very much involved with expanding the company and organizing the program for the fall tour booked by Mr. Mayer.

Daniel Mayer was a real impresario, one of the last of a profession that no longer exists. He was a sophisticate in the finest sense and in manner an *élégant*, wearing white tie and tails and top hat for the concert of any of his contract artists. In winter he wore an overcoat fur-collared, and the year round swung a cane with silver head. When he came backstage before a performance, he made you feel that you were the most wonderful artist born. No matter what the actual circumstance he had you believing that your appearance was awaited with bated breath by the audience in the full house beyond the curtain. Under the management of this suave and ever-courteous gentleman we began the first tour of our record-breaking series.

10

●●●

Dance by the Mile

We had been on the road for only three days of our fall tour when I ran afoul of a board of education at Sunbury, Pennsylvania, where our advance press agent, J. Francis Smith, had arranged for me to give a talk on the dance at an assembly program of the local high school. My foot had no more than touched the Sunbury station platform when the principal of the high school had me on the phone. My talk was canceled.

The principal explained with much uhming and ahing that the board of education "and I have decided that it would be dangerous for our students to listen to a dancer." The school authorities felt that it also would be ill-advised for them to give official approval to the dance by sanctioning a lecture on the subject at an educational institution.

Such reasoning, incredible as it seems now when the dance has a recognized place in American education, was not then limited to educators at the secondary school level. By telegram I was invited to talk at Washburn College in Topeka, Kansas, and, in spite of previous experiences, accepted with no foreboding. At the Topeka station I was met by Washburn's director of physical education, who whisked me straight to the college, and dragged me, train-grimy and somewhat breathless, onto the chapel platform.

An assembly was already under way with the faculty on platform staring out at the student body that glared back while all voices chorused a hymn. Followed by me, the phys. ed. director edged along into two empty seats near center stage. She hastily scribbled a note that was passed to the hymn leader, dean of the college, I learned later. He looked at the note first through his glasses, then having snatched them off, registered increasing incredulity with a second reading. As the "Amen" faded in the air, the dean made the following introduction which I quote in full: "We will now hear a talk by Mr. Shann [sic]—a talk on [dramatic pause] *dancing*, a subject in which *he* is interested."

"Dedicated" might have been a better word since I willingly, even eagerly traveled fifty thousand miles annually giving dance performances, lectures, and lessons, a routine I followed for thirty years. Beginning with the tour of 1922–23, our company rolled up impressive statistics. Pavlova's company was the only one which approximated anything like our tour mileage on the map of the United States, and that company alternated American tours with seasons in other countries. We were the first truly American dance group and were the only major dance attraction ever to play the United States for twenty-eight consecutive weeks of three successive years. In a six-year period, we set a tour record that still stands.

We pioneered for the dance in America, pushing on against

jibes and setbacks, making progress slowly, and advances little by little. Today pupils trained by us teach in colleges and high schools, both private and public. Degrees in dancing are offered by some universities, and credits for off-campus dance courses are given by others. I have taught both at colleges and universities and, for achievement in the dance, was awarded an honorary master's degree by Springfield College in 1940.

In 1922 we had a long way to go on the road to recognition as responsible artists. Dancers were not universally accepted as respectable, and we were uncertain of our reception, particularly in a city or town where we had never before danced. There was no way to know in advance whether we would be feted or swindled, ridiculed or lionized, eulogized or ostracized.

On that tour of suspense we crisscrossed the United States from ocean to ocean, often playing six communities a week, always giving eight or nine performances from Sunday to Sunday. We had a big company that included Martha Graham, Pearl Wheeler, Betty May, Lenore Scheffer, Julia Bennett, May Lynn, Louise Brooks, Charles Weidman, and Paul Mathis, who was replaced along the way by Robert Gorham.

In addition to Louis Horst, we took along three instrumentalists and for the first time were not dependent on local pickup orchestras. With Walter Burke, company treasurer; Sid Winton, stage manager; Ruth's maid; and a two-man backstage crew required by the stagehands' union, the touring troupe numbered twenty.

Our company's size gave us one distinct travel advantage. The number of tickets we bought for our private sleeping car entitled us to the luxury of a baggage car of our own. With that assigned car shunted onto the siding with our Pullman, we were spared the endless and vexing efforts of checking in and out of every town, more often without than with porters.

We traveled with formidable amounts of personal luggage, suitcases, cartons, satchels, and costume trunks, props, but practically no scenery.

When planning our production for the first season with Mayer, we were relatively cautious, for us. Atmosphere for the various exotic countries represented by our dances was suggested by changing props, decorative units, furniture, and *objets d'art*. These were rotated against an opulent-looking cyclorama that actually was made of turkish toweling dyed a rich cinnamon brown and then brushed lightly on its surface loops with gold paint. From out front the stage-lit cyclorama shimmered like gold-brocaded silk velvet, an effective delusion that on one occasion was also a snare.

In Altoona, Pennsylvania, I was standing in the wings with Lenore Scheffer waiting to be cued for the Siamese number in which she as Sita and I as Rama wore heavily bejeweled costumes. A second before we were on, Lenore whispered to me, "Look, I'm losing my Sita sparkles." She was indeed. The costume was splashed with empty prong settings but it was too late for repairs or change of costume and Lenore had to go on minus her "diamonds."

The dance ended with me downstage, knees bent, legs widespread, and arms tilted up stiffly. Lenore, after completing a series of turns around the stage circumference, was supposed to leap into my arms while the other two men dancers in the number closed in for a final tableau.

That night in Altoona, I took the waiting position and suddenly realized that the music had passed the bars for Lenore's leap. No Lenore. Several more bars, and no Lenore. When finally I stole a glance over my shoulder, my Sita was so cocooned in the cyclorama that I could see only the peak of her royal crown and the soles of her bare feet. She had turned too close to the cyclorama and the prongs of her costume had caught in the loops of the turkish toweling.

The musicians stalled for as long as they could while the boys and I quivered with ill-controlled laughter. When Lenore finally struggled free and ran toward me, I put out my arms to keep her from jumping, for I was much too weak ever to have caught her. The Siamese Sita, deadpan and dead serious, looking straight out into the packed auditorium said, in the flat monotone which was Lenore's very own, "I thought I never was going to get loose." The curtain came down to separate an audience roaring with laughter on one side from a cast collapsed in hysterics on the other.

A few days later we learned that certain members of a Baltimore audience were far from amused by the sight of our dirty feet when we were performing at the Lyric Theatre, an old opera house-type of building, hoary with tradition and the accumulation of theatrical years. Our feet stamping on the stage raised layers of dust that may well have dated from the performing days of my ancestor Edwin Booth. Our insteps, soles, and ankles soon were filthy but with Baltimore dirt, a fact that someone should have passed along to those Baltimoreans revolted by our grimy feet.

Soot, dirt, dust, however offensive to audiences, at least did not hurt or injure us as more serious stage hazards quite often did. For years I suffered twinges from a painful injury sustained on stage at the Hill Auditorium of the University of Michigan in Ann Arbor. That hall presented problems both aesthetic and physical. Entrances and exits had to be made through conventional doors that had to be opened with regulation knobs. The doors flanked the stage on either side with an area between them and the edge of our performing groundcloth that seemed to us to be about the size of the Michigan football field. It was exceedingly difficult to maintain theatrical illusion while marathoning from dancing space to the haven of exit doors, from entrance doors to position in the dancing space.

The forty-five hundred people who paid to see us at the Hill deserved more than we were able to give them because of the various handicaps of that stage including trap doors that had brass handles sticking up above the floor. I warned our dancers about tripping over the lethal protuberances and we danced with eyes cast down like so many demure Chinese or shy Siamese or timid Toltecs. I forgot my own advice and just once leaped without looking and landed squarely on a brass handle, hurting my right foot that bothered me for a long time afterward.

I was the only casualty at Ann Arbor but the Denishawn Company suffered more sprained ankles and broken toes in a single performance at the Boston Opera House than in the rest of the twenty-eight weeks of touring. The opera house was a horror for performers, many of whom complained about backstage conditions, and about the cold and unresponsive audiences across the footlights. We never had audience trouble in Boston but the opera house stage played no favorites. It was studded with trap doors that rattled noisily, and lined with slippery metal grooves designed for sliding and maneuvering old-fashioned theatrical flats. Conditions underfoot were rather like those at so-called fun houses where tricks—unexpected, embarrassing, and sometimes painful—are pulled one after the other on amusement park patrons.

There isn't a theatrical trouper who fails to shudder at the mention of Ryman Auditorium. I am uncertain of the chronology but that weird Nashville building was at various times a religious tabernacle, a wrestling and boxing arena, a six-day bicycle track, a center for food shows and miscellaneous conventions. It became at last concert hall and theater, the only place in Nashville where great artists appeared.

Performers were unanimous in their opinion of the Ryman Auditorium. They hated it. The whole floor backstage was acutely slanted since it was a part of the saucer-shaped track over which the six-day bicyclists had competed. Dressing rooms, looking like individual shower stalls, were simply cubicles made by stringing sheets on rope. The pitch of the floor was so steep that it was necessary to make up with one hand while pushing away from an impromptu dressing table with the other.

The stage was a primitive kind of platform set up in the middle of the arena. The false proscenium, a real fake, was made of stretched canvas and the front curtain, an antique model of the roller type, creaked going up and hit the floor with a bang every time it was lowered.

Old buildings were by no means the only ones which were hard to play. One of the worst theaters we ever danced in was Rochester's Eastman, which we nicknamed the "million dollar abortion" after we learned that no expense had been spared in its planning and construction. George Eastman must have been an expert on cameras, films, and photographic equipment, for he made a fortune in the manufacture and sale of of these things. He surely was no expert at theater design and should have sought advice before he built his theater.

When we arrived at the Eastman we found that the stage was constructed on three levels connected by several steps. The design may have been effective for concerts by glee clubs and choral societies, but it was totally impractical for dancers since no one level was big enough for a whole dance.

Our performance must have looked like something straight out of Mack Sennett. For us the experience was nightmarish. Sooner or later in each number the choreography brought us to the limit of what could be done on the level at which we started, and to finish a sequence we had to go up or down a few steps. That's a fine technique for those experts at step dancing who tap up and down flights of stairs or rungs of ladders, but we had neither experience in the specialty nor music to cover the movements.

It was impossible to complete a leap on any one level so we were forced to spring from terrace to terrace with the agility of so many mountain goats. The completion of an adagio sequence was the real challenge to the male dancer who had the choice of carrying his partner upstairs or of putting her down and then scurrying hurriedly with her to a higher level where the original position could be resumed.

The area immediately off stage was broken up with concrete posts that rose about three feet above stage level. These served no purpose that any of us could discover except to prevent the crew from placing a costume trunk, a crate, or an essential prop close to the performing area. Backstage looked for all the world as if an invasion were imminently expected and tank busters had been placed in readiness for duty.

The last time we played the Eastman Theatre, though its stage had been redesigned as a conventional one-level platform, the concrete posts still stood sentinel beyond the wings. They may still be there for all I know. Those posts contributed to funny scenes when fans came back after a performance. A number of people dodging back and forth gave the impression that a large-scale game of puss-in-the-corner was in progress.

Frequently backstage areas were too small to hold the fans who came calling congratulations and clutching autograph books. Denishawn had by then been in existence for seven years during which we had taught hundreds of dance teachers from all over the country. There was hardly a town without at least one former student of Denishawn and if she continued to teach, she invariably brought all the children from her school to meet us. After the performance each of her pupils had to be presented individually and every program had to be autographed by us.

Autographing cuts into a performer's free time that's all

too short between matinee and evening shows. After one Oklahoma City matinee, Ruth signed and signed for teen-age girls who swarmed around and then, during a welcome lull, she slipped away to get out of make-up in order to have time for a nap before the evening show.

A girl who had gone away to get a program came back, loudly demanding, "Where's Ruth?" "Gone," a voice in the crowd answered. "Gone?" the first one shouted. "Why the lousy bum. She left before she autographed my program!" That ill-mannered miss was not typical of our teen-age fans. Most youngsters who came back to see us wanted to be dancers and were enthusiastic about us and our performances.

Ruth's youthful devotees, like her older admirers, lavished her with flowers but unfortunately she never cared for them and, once inside her dressing room, would carelessly fling away her bouquets. When I could, I rescued the flowers and put them in water, after reading the attached card. If the donor of a bouquet was announced at the dressing-room door, I would whisper to Ruth, "Mrs. Jones—red roses." Ruth then would light up and almost sigh, "Mrs. Jones. Those beautiful red roses. They went right to my heart. Oh, my dear, thank you. Thank you so much." And Mrs. Jones never failed to go away charmed—by an expert.

Fortunately I seldom received flowers but I vividly remember every occasion with total recall of embarrassment. A presentation that completely flustered me was made at the Pabst Theatre in Milwaukee on October 21, 1922, my thirty-first birthday. After my Spanish solos, the city's leading dancing master came on stage and delivered a flowery speech while a bevy of his pupils, with elaborate ceremony, presented me with dozens of huge bouquets of shaggy, long-stemmed chrysanthemums. At the time I was too jittery to think of a frightful possibility that occurred to me long afterward. Perhaps

there were thirty-one bunches of those giant blooms, one sheaf
for every year of my life.

I do not mean to indicate that we were not grateful for
those devoted fans who made possible our history-making tours.
It is just that some things which are part of a performer's
life can be wearisome. It is hard work to endlessly sign autographs, and dull to have to say thank you again and again
for the same banal, oft-repeated compliments.

The joy of backstage encounters was sparked by the few
treasured people who came as strangers and remained as
friends we cherished. Counted among these were several from
Omaha, Nebraska. We always eagerly anticipated our reunions
there with the August Borglums, May and Eva Mahoney, and
Maurice Block, when he was director of the Joslyn Art
Museum. On every count Omaha was a place we loved to
dance. We dreamed for weeks of getting to the Fontenelle
Hotel and to the Brandeis, a first-rate theater. Omaha's audiences loved us, and its press was intelligent and informed.

We rejoiced, too, when we played some of the private theaters like the DuPont-built Playhouse at Wilmington, Delaware.
The superbly designed theater was under one roof with a
large office building and a fine hotel. We luxuriated, too, at
the Murat Theatre in Indianapolis which was elegantly appointed backstage and was kept spotlessly clean.

Only those who have dressed in badly lighted cubbyholes
in dank basements can appreciate what the Murat meant to
us. One really felt like a star instead of something that had
just crawled out from the woodwork. I had a spacious dressing room on stage level, so I didn't have to rush up or down
stairs to change costumes. One wall of the dressing room was
solid mirror, corner to corner, ceiling to floor. There was no
need to twist or turn, to stand on tiptoe or to hunch down
in an effort to get a full figure view of a costume. In the private shower there was hot water to be had for the turn of

the tap at all times. It was good for morale to perform out of such a dressing room.

The exhilaration of performance was extended by those who were appreciative of our art, who understood our approach to the dance. There were many who had no inkling even of our intention. Interviews frequently were stupid because the poor reporter sent to talk with us knew nothing of the dance and cared less.

On one occasion Ruth volunteered a glowing comment on Isadora Duncan's contribution to the American dance. The reporter, chewing and puffing on a fat cigar, strummed on his derby hat while he listened attentively. How little he comprehended was indicated by one line in his interview printed the next day: "Miss St. Denis speaks highly of Isadore and Mrs. Duncan."

Interviews were almost matched by the reviews because there were no dance critics in the United States. In big cities we were reviewed by either the music critic or the drama cirtic, and often suffered from their specialization. The one would judge us by our selection of music and would compare our fine quartet to a full symphony orchestra. The other wrote about us in terms of a show, evaluating us like musical comedy entertainment.

In small towns where there were no full-time critics of the arts, we were reviewed by any staffer who was free on the night of our performance. That might be the financial editor, the mail boy, a sports writer, a police reporter, the sob sister.

We would like to have been treated seriously as befitting the first all-American ballet, but newspapers seemed to try to outdo each other in quipping about us. In Pittsburgh the intelligent and dance-minded Harvey Gaul, after reading the names of the countries represented by dances in our program, linked us and Burton Holmes, the best-known travel lecturer then touring, too. Gaul wrote: "Be it ever so humble in the life of a Denishawn dancer, there's no place like Burton Holmes." Another review was headlined AFTERNOON WITH A SHAWN.

We preferred the headline made in the sky for us in Baltimore when we returned to the second engagement of the season. We were booked for the repeat program by the Flying Club of Baltimore and that group arranged our advance publicity. A skywriter flew low over downtown Baltimore for some days preceding our arrival which he heralded with smoke letters that read "Ruth St. Denis and Ted Shawn—Lyric Theatre."

We considered this event historic, at least for our own personal history, like another first which we experienced in Davenport, Iowa. There we did our first radio broadcast from Station WOC which was owned and operated by B. J. Palmer, picturesque head of the chiropractic college. For that occasion we dressed more elaborately than we did for our television debut thirty years later. Ruth wore a gown of American Beauty velvet, and I put on my London-tailored striped trousers and cutaway.

Full color photographs were made of us as we stood proudly at the microphone. Ah, pride, and the fall which came years later when we visited B. J. Palmer in his fantastic house indiscriminately crammed with curios and miscellaneous memorabilia. Imagine our consternation when we found that our radio debut was preserved for posterity in this collection. Our color portraits, Lumière plates on glass, were mounted on two sides of an illuminated lamppost in the Palmer living room.

When I saw myself silhouetted in my tailored finery, I regretted the invention of the camera which for all its admitted advantages can be a plague. Many times when we were touring I wished that every camera extant could suddenly be obliterated as if by the magic of Aladdin. These thoughts always raced through my mind when we stepped off a Pullman at 7 A.M. to the flash and clicking of news cameras. I knew that one more newspaper morgue would have filed pictures of Shawn at dawn, unshaven and bleary-eyed.

Even when wide awake, we were not photogenic in our traveling clothes. Neither of us would agree to pose in dance positions in our drab street garb but news photographers unfailingly wanted pictures of dancers dancing. The clash between photographers, insisting on action, and us, determined to maintain our dignity as the royal family of the dance, continued from city to city. Our rigidity must have been all too apparent to one cheery photographer who said to us, "Well, it's a funny life I lead. Yuh know, I just photographed a stiff in the morgue—and now *this!*" And there was no indication as to his preference.

We could have assured him that his was not the only life marked by violent contrast. Newspaper photographers and reporters, theaters and dressing rooms, spotlights and applause, backstage crowds and individual friends filled the kaleidoscope of our daily living. Always the final shift of that kaleidoscope brought us to the railroad station, to the train tracks, the Pullman car.

The actual travel I never minded. I have always liked to travel and still do. That year the tour was over in mid-April and I was free to retire for rest at some country retreat, if I wished. That was the last thing I wanted, however, because to me relaxation and vegetation are not synonymous. I chose to vacation with tickets and passports and visas and letters of introduction and guidebooks and suitcases and trunks and assorted impedimenta. In short, I relaxed from that extensive tour by taking an intensive trip to Europe.

11

Olé and Away

N No *mañana* tempo crept into my first twenty-four hours in Barcelona. Arthur Buruel and I checked into the Ritz Hotel at 7:30 P.M., dined at nine, and attended a music hall performance at ten. From midnight until long after dawn, we watched gypsy dancers in cabarets and dives. Still sleepy-eyed we breakfasted at noon and spent the early afternoon seeing city sights. At 3:30 P.M. I took a dancing lesson and before 7:30 P.M. came around again, had changed tickets and hotel reservations to extend our Barcelona stay. An ideal vacation was under way in less than a day.

We made it clear to our first guide that our interest was in dancing, not in wine, women, or whoopee, and he took us to the Eden, a music hall where the equivalent of 16 cents paid for lemonade and the right to stay for a three-hour show.

A couple of boring hours of amateurish young dancers preceded the appearance of the dancing star whose name was bright on the marquee, Carolina la Riva.

I was too fascinated by La Riva's castanets to properly appreciate her considerable talent as dancer. She played her castanets with ever-changing rhythms and volume, and seemed able to make them whisper, chat, laugh, and even to thunder and roar like some jungle beast. My curiosity about La Riva's music, superbly synchronized with her castanets, was a lucky break.

In answer to my question the orchestra leader said that the composition was his own, like all of La Riva's music. He was Joaquin Saval, composer and director of a school of music and dancing, where La Riva was trained. A whispered conference resulted in definite plans. With Saval's address carefully noted and an appointment for me to take an afternoon lesson from his *maestro de baile,* we left the Eden and started through crowded streets to the old walled-town section of Barcelona in search of gypsy dancers.

A cabaret called the Vina P. was featuring a troupe of gypsy dancers, singers, and guitar players, who wouldn't perform until two o'clock or perhaps later. That gave us time to wander in and out of cabarets with the guide who spun lurid tales of crimes committed at various locations along our route. Down a dark and fetid alley, we found the Villa Rosa where a gypsy band was at dinner. These were pure gypsy types, the women dressed in cheap cottons draped with skimpy shawls. There was one man dancer, small and blond, with a face strangely wizened though he looked no more than thirty. It was he who told us that there would be no performance at the Villa Rosa until four o'clock, perhaps later.

We dashed back through twisting streets to the Vina P. where the performance was under way. The impact of the flamencos, the first real Spanish dancing I had seen, was so great that I nearly went out of my mind. After fifteen minutes I knew that if Spain offered me no more than that one performance, it was worth the six-thousand-mile trip. The exciting movement and sound finally came to a halt and there was an announcement that there would be more singing and dancing later in the night.

Breathless we pushed through strolling Spaniards and made our way back to the Villa Rosa, by then jammed to the doors with a motley crowd of simple folk and slumming couples in evening clothes. The gypsies, still eating and drinking, were sitting at tables with patrons. Again we asked the man dancer when the performance would start and he answered vaguely, "Four, five, maybe six o'clock," in a tone that implied there might be no performance at all.

At about 5:00 A.M. for no apparent reason and with no visible signal given, the gypsies from all over the room rose as one, like a flock of birds from a tree. Dancers and musicians moved to the stage, some carrying with them the straightback chairs on which they had been sitting in the cabaret. Glaring footlights threw shadows against the backdrop, producing an effect reminiscent to me of John Singer Sargent's paintings of flamenco groups, especially the one I knew well, "El Jaleo" that hung in Mrs. Jack Gardner's Boston home, now the Gardner Museum.

On stage the gypsies acted with casual informality. One woman blew her nose loudly, a second borrowed and carefully examined a neighbor's fan, and still another nonchalantly adjusted some piece of her underclothes that seemed to be uncomfortable.

After a considerable wait, a woman with a slightly bored air got up and started to beat time with her hands and feet. The others on stage remained seated but picked up her rhythm. The guitar players improvised and at last the woman stepped center stage and danced. The numbers merged into one another and could have gone on forever as far as I was concerned. I was reminded of Carl Van Vechten's observation in *The Music of Spain* that one could never satisfactorily import Spanish dancing to America without shipping a Spanish audience along with musicians and dancers. At the Villa Rosa there was a spiritual oneness of audience and performer, a rapport that I had never sensed elsewhere in the world.

I had thrilled to a lot of Spanish dancing and had missed a night's sleep by the time I climbed the five flights to Joaquin Saval's dance studio later that day. Several girls were dancing, when we arrived puffing, and even at first glance I could tell that at least two of them had exceptional talent. The young *maestro de baile*, Perfecto Perez, was a fine dancer and, from watching the finish of the class in progress, I could see that he was a born teacher.

After a few minutes in the studio, I understood how the Spanish were able to use castanets like a part of the body, as an extra, added mode of speech. Pupils played their castanets constantly, ceaselessly, even when some student was doing a solo, and out on the balcony a toddler, surely no more than three, was getting rhythm and tone from a pair of tiny castanets.

While I listened to castanets, Arthur was following every word Perez said. When my own lesson started, Arthur's fluent Spanish was the invaluable asset we hoped it would be. Arthur, a friend from Los Angeles, was on the trip as interpreter. He was half-French, half-Spanish, and his family's at-home language was Spanish. He was dance-minded and knew dance terminology, having been a summer student at Denishawn for several years, and a member of the *Pyrrhic Dance* ensemble, the first all male group I directed.

With Arthur's rapid and perceptive translation, Perez and I worked without a conscious break in our communication. At first Perez was doubtful that I could learn anything of value in a limited time and I was understanding since, under similar circumstance, I would have felt the same way about a new pupil. At the end of the first lesson Perez had changed his mind about me and I had changed my mind about leaving Barcelona on schedule.

We settled to a routine of two lessons a day with Perez, and I learned a number of dances, though not without strain. I was dreadfully impatient if my body failed to follow perfectly the movement and steps that my mind understood. Perez kept patting me on the shoulder, saying soothingly, "Calma, calma!" but still I was frequently annoyed at myself and never more so than when I took a castanet lesson. I knew how terrible I was, but Perez thought that it was quite remarkable that I could manage to do a creditable *a-ria, a-ria, pi-ta.*

Castanets in tourists' shops sold for less than a dollar but I paid $4.00 for mine that had been tone-tested and were approved by Perez and Saval, who was most generous to me in the matter of music. He had stacks of manuscript music of his own composition or arrangements and played for hours so that I might select any pieces I wanted. From dozens of numbers I chose ten pieces of music that Saval copied by hand at 80 cents each.

Every night Arthur and I with guide made the rounds of the cabarets seeing flamenco troupes over and over again. Each day we spent several hours sight-seeing in historic Barcelona. I wrote to Ruth about a beautiful mural done by a living Spanish painter named Sert. "His work has majesty, power and deeply moving beauty," I wrote in my letter. "Why haven't I heard of him before?" I know now that few Americans had heard of José Maria Sert until a few years later when he painted the stunning murals in the Waldorf-Astoria room that bears his name.

The climax of our stay in Barcelona was a bullfight which

for me was an epoch-making event, an emotional personal experience that in no way kept my dancer's eye from functioning like a camera on motion, colors, and costumes. Arthur, ashen-faced by the time the sixth bull was killed, assured me that I would go alone to any other bullfight. He had seen quite enough for a lifetime.

A restless night's train ride from Barcelona took us to Madrid and Raquel Meller. Arthur and I, having heard that Meller was a singer with a tremendous local reputation, went to see her on our first night in Madrid. It is now history that she soon after was internationally acclaimed and much-feted in the United States. That night we thrilled to her performance with all the tense excitement of discoverers. We went again to see her the following night and I saw her once again when the American consul invited me to a box party. During our five days in Madrid I saw Meller give three performances, each something to write home about, and I did, saying that there was not one single detail about her or her artistry or her performance that "one wants to criticize."

By day we saw the sights of Madrid and of Toledo, and enjoyed reunions with acquaintances from New England and the Midwest. At night we were disappointed by the lack of dance performances. Ernest Schelling had given me a letter of introduction to Eduardo Granados, son of the composer, and I had hoped that he would know where I could find gypsy groups. Though he was out of town until the day before we left, a friend of his led us at last to a dancing find.

We went to a zarzuela called *Nino de Oro* with a second act given over to a representation of the gypsy life in Granada. The mores and atmosphere of gypsy living were capsuled in a first-class theatrical production that featured real gypsy actors, singers, and dancers. The second scene, a gypsy wedding, was like nothing I had seen on any stage in the United States or Europe. That performance crystallized for me formative thoughts about a Spanish gypsy ballet which I thought I would call *Cuadro Flamenco*. I left Madrid pondering how I would use the source material seen in Spain in a dance interpretation of the true spirit of the Spanish gypsy.

Seville was the Spain of my dreams, a romantic city straight out of storybooks and travelogues. Madrid and Barcelona were modern cities where few people wore colorful native costumes in the bustling busy streets. In the charming thoroughfares of Seville one saw many ladies wearing mantillas, more often of chiffon than of lace, but voluminous and not the handkerchief-sized head coverings then fashionable in Madrid, and one out of ten men wore the broad-brimmed, high-crowned *sombrero sevillano*. The gardens of Seville were more lush even than the southern California ones I loved. Glowing Moorish tiles decorating buildings, wall fountains, walkways, and park benches added to the color and beauty of the city, a place where I could happily have lingered, and hated to leave.

In a dive of Seville, I met a flamenco dancer, Antonio Ramirez, who reminded me of Ortéga with whom I had briefly studied in New York. It cost $1.60, the price of two bottles of wine, to see Ramirez dance in a little private room above the so-called cabaret, front for a brothel. When he and his guitarist and a girl dancer had drained the second bottle, their performance began. Even in a room no more than 10 by 12 feet, Ramirez stood out as a remarkable dancer. He did many tricks that I hadn't seen before and his patterns and rhythms were complicated in old-style flamenco that was said to be dying out. I had noticed that older generation dancers, like Ramirez, maintained a pure tradition, whereas some of the younger dancers were adulterating Spanish tempo with American jazz, and Spanish techniques with Cossack steps.

I ordered a black alpaca flamenco suit from the tailor of a friend, and went to a second tailor who specialized in *torero* uniforms. These proved to be prohibitive in price for me but he had some secondhand ones from which I chose a bright green suit at a bargain price. The matador who had owned the suit was wealthy enough to be able to tire of his costumes and characteristically superstitious about ever wearing a suit in which he had been wounded, if only slightly. The green suit, which had a small rent made by a bull's horn in a pants' leg, was so loaded with gold thread and sequins that I staggered under its weight. After rather loud and lengthy bargaining I got the whole outfit: cape, jacket, vest, pants, hat, girdle, and pigtail complete with rubber band to hold it on. In my costume shopping spree I also visited and bought from a bootmaker and a shirtmaker.

Twice daily for a month I took lessons from Manuel Otero, nephew of a renowned *maestro de baile*, who in his old age was running a saloon, a barbershop, and a lottery. The Otero school, more elegant than Saval's, was attended by young ladies of Seville chaperoned by duennas who sat stiff-backed on benches that lined the studio walls. When the girls changed from practice clothes they looked very patrician wearing high combs and mantillas softly draped. On arrival and again at departure each student kissed Manuel Otero on the cheek, a custom new to me that I decided to introduce at Denishawn.

Denishawn School was written out on the address labels of countless packages and boxes assembled during the last two days in Seville. All purchases made in Spain had to be prepared for shipping with details in triplicate on consular invoices. In Barcelona I had bought a few things: high combs, earrings, copies of art magazines for costume reference, and music, both printed sheets and the manuscripts prepared by Saval. Every place I had carefully chosen personal gifts for Ruth. In Seville I shopped with abandon chiefly for the projected ballet *Cuadro Flamenco*. I selected combs, shawls, mantillas, castanets, and *crotali* by the dozens, all to be sent along with

my own costumes, the flamenco and matador suits, and a
dashing *sombrero sevillano.*

Faced with the last few days in Spain I settled to several
two-hour sessions of post-card writing and had penned personal messages on more than two hundred before time ran
out. Shipping, shopping, and mail were edged into days of
reunion, and lessons, and good talk, and a tour of a *fabrica de
tabaco* where cigarettes were rolled by hundreds of Carmens,
none glamorous but all wearing carnations tucked into
grizzled hair.

We escorted Mrs. Helen Appleton and Mrs. Boylston Beal
of Boston, whom we had also seen in Madrid, to night spots
where they could not have gone alone. We went to lunches
and dinners with Margaret and Troy Kinney who turned up at
Otero's to our mutual surprise. Troy, whose book on the dance
included one chapter on Spanish dancing, was combining
research and art with sight-seeing. We called at their hotel on
our last night in Seville and found Troy sitting in the middle
of the street sketching a donkey, picturesque cart, and driver
to whom he paid one peseta for every ten minutes posed. We
dined that evening at an open-air restaurant in María Luisa
Park where I had the most ambrosial of desserts, tiny wood
strawberries buried in ice shaved fine as snow and drenched
with Marsala wine.

I was beginning to feel rested from the long winter's tour
by the time we left Seville for Africa by way of a day in Madrid
where we went to one last performance by Raquel Meller.

Bertha Damon had given me a letter to a Mr. Zagha, an
art and brass dealer of Algiers, and I found his shop soon
after we docked. Within an hour I had tentatively chosen
props and costumes for an Algerian ballet that Ruth and I
had been discussing for some months. The second day I spent
sight-seeing and at Mr. Zagha's bought a Moorish coat for
Ruth. It was a museum piece, really, made of ruby-red broad-

cloth solidly embroidered in gold that weighted the coat even
more than the encrustations and embroidery weighted my
torero suit.

Mr. Zagha himself, a cultivated gentleman who spoke
better English than I, guided us through the kasbah and into
a native mosque and through the street of whores where we
were solicited at every doorway. We went into native shops
where I made a collection of shoulder shawl pins, bracelets,
and a diadem, all authentic jewelry of the *ouled naïls*, dancing
girls whom I was destined to pursue across North Africa.
These performers were much more elusive than bargains which
I found quite easily with the help of Mr. Zagha. I bought
white wool burnooses, and the makings for many high turbans
that started from a papier-mâché foundation and were built
up of camel's-hair ropes and white wrapping fabric. When
I had indulged my hobby of shopping to the ultimate, Mr.
Zagha took us to the Moorish home of a French lady who had
a remarkable collection of native jewelry, and then on to see
palaces and cathedrals and libraries. On my own I found a
photography studio where I leafed through twenty albums
of photographs of native types, and ordered many prints for
reference during the costuming of the projected Algerian
ballet.

I was fascinated by Algiers with its sounds weird and unfamiliar to Western ears; with its poor beggar types who never
even looked up in curiosity at a Westerner in the streets or
marketplaces; with its handsome men, dressed in rich fabrics bejeweled, who walked with grace and dignity never looking from right to left. Arthur admitted quite frankly at the end
of the third day that the heat and stench and hordes of
Algerians repelled him. He had no desire to see more of North
Africa, no quest like mine to carry him through primitive
communities and strange desert outposts. We agreed to meet
in Italy after I had tracked down my *ouled naïls*, and repacked

our luggage so Arthur could take most of it by ship. With only an overnight bag, a camera, and my portable typewriter, I stepped into a rented Citroën with my interpreter-chauffeur, O'Kelly.

Arthur was waving his last good-by when Mr. Zagha hurried up to the car with a huge bouquet of calla lilies which he placed in my lap. I was touched by the generous thought but I felt ridiculous starting out into the Sahara Desert with a "lily in my hand." O'Kelly had expertly driven us out of the city and through fertile country and over our first mountains when I decided that it was safe to discard my flowers. I heaved the bouquet and the calla lilies landed at the feet of a shuffling Arab who was sufficiently startled to look up in puzzlement as we sped by.

We had been able to find no dancing in Algiers in spite of strenuous efforts by the brothers Zagha and the concierge of my hotel. The explanation given was that this late in the season the dancers had left the coastal cities for their desert homes.

At our first night's stop, Bou Saada, an oasis town, I hoped for better luck. A guide nodded at the term *ouled naïl* and took us to a house where we were served native coffee before the performance started. We sat in European chairs and two musicians squatted on the floor at the far end of the same room. Two women danced several repetitious routines in which they used not more than three distinct steps. Novelties of the evening were produced by a little girl of about six who held an English walking stick over her head while she danced, and the final solo of the leading woman dancer, wearing nothing but a headdress and a pair of slippers.

The woman's control and discipline would have delighted Jaques-Dalcroze. The triceps moved back and forth, firm round breasts rose and fell alternately, abdominal muscles rotated circularly, and the pelvis bumped backward and forward. The woman's face was hard, gaunt, and expressionless, and her lean body was as sexless as any I had ever seen. She had no allure and made no attempt to be alluring. It was quite patent that to her the routine was work, not art, just a job for which she was being paid.

I didn't need O'Kelly's assurance that what we had seen was a pretty poor show but I was encouraged when he promised better farther along our way. We drove on fine highways, French-built, to continuing disappointments in the dancing at Sétif and Biskra. When a performance at a place on Biskra's *rue des Ouled Naïls* proved to be a dud, we gave our guide a severe talking to and he countered by offering to take us to see a dervish.

At ten o'clock at night we went out to a lonely desert spot where there was an isolated hut, a one-room shack bare of furniture. There we saw a performance that was genuine without any question and as stirring as the bullfight.

The performing group included five men: a priest, a tom-tom player, a flute player, an attendant to the dervish, and the dervish himself. The music started and the dervish, a mangy-looking creature, blind in one eye, began to shake all over and violently. He knelt before the attendant who gave him something which he snuffed up each nostril. The guide said later that the substance was nothing but powdered tobacco that had been blessed by the priest, but I was quite convinced that the snuff was a pain-killing drug.

Quickly the dervish worked up to a frenzy that increased as he danced back and forth calling frenetically to tom-tom and flute. On command the attendant handed the dervish two long spikes, like giant hatpins, which he first jabbed through his cheeks and later shoved through the flesh of his throat. Neither time did he draw blood from the holes in his skin nor was there blood on the pins. Throughout the whole time that he went through one self-torture ritual after another, he never ceased the infernal shaking, shouting, and panting like a wounded animal.

The only unexciting feat he performed was a Houdini-like escape from a burnoose wrapped tight around him after his hands were bound behind his back. Whether that simple trick was to give him a rest or to highlight the horrors that preceded and followed it, it was impossible to know.

I had hardly noticed a charcoal fire in a brazier until the attendant began to fan a flame from which he pulled a sickle-shaped instrument translucent with white heat. The dervish licked at the instrument until it was black and cold. No burn appeared on his tongue although steam hissed and puffed each time the tongue and hot metal touched. At one point while he was licking the white-hot sickle he thrust his face close to mine and I was fearful that in his hysteria he might lose his balance and fall on me, hot sickle and all.

After the sickle was cold, the dervish stripped to his waist and lighted bundles of stiff straw at the brazier. With straw bundles in each hand he folded his arms around his bare torso and let the flames cover his flesh. When the straw burned down to his hands, he held them up to his chin and let the last flames lick over his face. Strangely enough, the movements of the flame frenzy took on a form that was definitely choreographic, not just uncontrolled jerks and motions. When the last straw burned out, the dervish dropped onto one knee so close to me that I could feel his body heat, and smell it.

Fixing me with his eyes, he pointed to the inside of his elbow joint and a vein there which he bit viciously. He jerked his teeth away and made sure that I was watching the blood spurt forth in rhythmic beats. This continued until the blood running from the vein had covered his hand and was dripping to the floor. Nauseous and faint, I leaned back against the wall of the hut and gasped for breath. The dervish put his mouth to the severed vein and finally dabbed at the spot with cloth. There was no visible wound and the skin of the arm was smooth and unbroken. I know what I *saw* was a physical impossibility and I have no explanation since I was not under hypnosis. I only know that there was blood on the dervish's hand when he finished the incredible display and fell to the blood-stained floor, moaning and gibbering and twitching convulsively. His attendant and the priest covered him with a burnoose but he sprang up at once and rushed around the room emotionally kissing each of the other black men. I was tense as he approached me and let go with an involuntary shudder of relief when he only shook my hand.

The dervish performance, however exciting and mystifying, was not a satisfactory substitute for the *ouled naïl* dancing that I wanted so desperately to see. At Biskra, the southernmost point in my planned itinerary, I found that the real *ouled naïls* had gone to Touggourt, their permanent residence. The weekly train had gone the day before my arrival. Biskra to Touggourt and return was an eight-day trip by camel caravan, a trek for which I had neither time nor nose.

On a long chance I went to the airfield to talk to the pilot of the regular plane that made a passenger and mail run between Algiers and Biskra where there was a day's layover. I had a lucky break. The plane had just landed and the pilot, Captain Raymond Perrier, was the airline's chief pilot with authority to charter the plane for a trip to Touggourt and back. I asked him the cost and after he had filled two pages of legal-sized paper with figures, wrote off the trip in my mind. Completing lengthy calculations, he finally gave me the price and I signed for my first plane ride, a bargain at $39.

We flew for two hours in a little two-seat, open-cockpit plane that I would be terrified to be airborne in today. But as dawn over the Sahara, spread spectacularly below me, I resolved to travel everywhere by air from then on. My enthusiastic resolution, which has been pushed aside over the years for ocean liners, station wagons, trains, interurban trolleys, and buses, was broken that very day by a two-wheeled cart, drawn by a raw-boned horse teamed with a dainty donkey. That primitive vehicle returned us to our plane at the end of an incredible day in Touggourt.

Outside of town that morning, the plane floated like a feather to a desert landing strip where there was an empty hangar and no sign of either life or the automobile we expected to find waiting. With no other choice, we waded through sand toward town in heat that seemed to strike like a physical blow. We were met at the edge of town by apologies and excuses for the unfortunate breakdown of Touggourt's only automobile. While we cooled off at the hotel, Captain Perrier made inquiries about the dancers, several thousands of whom lived in one quarter of the town. It was explained that the vacationing dancers would be happy to dance for as long as I could watch for 15 cents each, and I promptly asked for a group of twelve.

The call went out and dancers came by the hundreds. Captain Perrier told me to relax while he selected the choice dozen from the throng and, though somewhat dubious about his qualifications, I agreed. Like a housewife buying melons in a marketplace, he felt the breasts of the candidates, hiring only those with firm and round breasts, and waving away those unfortunates who were not developed to his specifications.

I had no time to recover from my astonishment at the unorthodox casting because Captain Perrier nodded toward one of the girls who was beautiful even by Ziegfeld standards and said that we were going with her while she got ready for performance. We accompanied her to an upstairs room where she dressed from the skin out in her dancing finery, a display for which I quite naturally supposed we would be charged an extra fee. Captain Perrier laughed at my mystification and explained that in singling her out we were paying her a high compliment according to local custom, accepted and expected. She acknowledged our presence with drawing-room composure and graciousness, and we, in the spirit of the ritual, were courtly and complimentary.

We three joined the other performers in a café, dark, cool, and, at that time of day, empty. With the usual African accompaniments of tom-toms and ear-splitting flutes, the dancers performed in couples, in groups, or solo. Here were the real *ouled naïls* at last but as source material for dance creations their dancing was sketchy, and their costumes were not nearly so richly adorned as those I had often seen pictured in the *National Geographic*. I learned that the lavishly dressed dancers whose diadems were massed with overlapping gold coins were the *ouled riches*, retired performers who had made enough money to buy a husband and raise more little dancers for the market.

My less prosperous troupe performed for about an hour in the cool café before I suggested that we go to a rooftop where I could take photographs. That innocuous request caused such a clatter that I thought I had run into a taboo or had unwittingly committed a sacrilege. It developed that the girls were in revolt against the suggestion that they expose themselves to the sun at high noon. Grumbling they agreed to pose for double pay and after I had been on the roof for one minute, I marveled that they had demanded so little. An egg would have fried hard almost on contact with that blazing roof which sent up heat that seemed to scorch through the leather soles of my shoes. The dancers, more experienced with the heat of Touggourt, knew better how to protect their feet. In the café they danced barefoot; posing for me on the roof, they wore slippers over bulky wool coverings not unlike ski socks. I had neither the heart nor the fortitude to protest against footwear that was more sensible than aesthetic.

Two days later in the compartment of the train taking me

from Constantine to Tunis, still-jumbled memories of North
African experiences were cut through by voices I recognized
as American. Preceded by Arab porters loaded down with
luggage were Burton Holmes and his wife. I was open-mouthed
with surprise but the Holmeses, world travelers, were quite
accustomed to the sight of old friends in new settings.

After the most intensive sight-seeing in Tunis with the
Holmeses, we sailed on the same ship for Italy where Arthur
was to meet me. I was rested and ready to get back to work
and impatient to be home. I regretted that I still had two
weeks before the sailing date but as it turned out the time
was filled with experiences that I wouldn't have missed for
anything.

I saw Florence under the direction of Berthe and Francesca
Braggiotti and at their villa, where I was house guest, danced
to the piano accompaniment of Papa Braggiotti, and the
spoken accompaniment of Leon Francesco Orvieto, poet son
of a famous poet father. A second evening of our informal
recital resulted in the conversion of a young Florentine who
previously had told me that he did not believe the dance was
an art.

In Paris I was swept off my feet by the Diaghileff company's
performance of *Les Noces* with music by Stravinsky and
choreography by Bronislava Nijinska. I thought that Nijinska herself was not only an important choreographer but a
fine dancer and a magnificent pantomimist.

In London I saw and heard for the first time both Paderewski and Eleonora Duse. I was transported by his playing which
left me emotionally weak and worn. She affected me as few
artists ever have. As a dancer I found her art supreme with
every gesture a spontaneous expression of emotion that seemed
at the moment fresh and new and quite alive. Old friends and
new filled the days of that second stay in London and once
more I boarded ship ready for the refreshment of lots of sleep.

The homecoming was dramatic. Press photographers who had pictured me kissing Ruth's hand in fond farewell on the deck of the *Berengaria*, now piled aboard the *Aquitania* and shot me in broad-brimmed Italian hat doing a tango with Berthe Braggiotti, wearing daringly the latest and most popular fad of that summer: an ankle bracelet. Ruth and the Denishawn staff and about thirty pupils met the ship and with kisses and embraces welcomed me like a returning hero. The moment of glory was but memory twenty-four hours later when I faced the reality of a hard summer of teaching and a short two months in which to prepare for a new season of one-night stands.

12

Tours de Force

We were $30,000 in the red at the end of our second successful season with Daniel Mayer, and owed $60,000 by the time we began our third solidly booked tour. The second season was financially disastrous only to us. We toured for twenty-eight weeks, and almost everywhere played to capacity houses that often had s.r.o. signs out front. We broke box-office records, making money for theater managers and Mr. Mayer, but we couldn't pocket our profits. They were earmarked for running expenses and for past professional extravagances: the staging and producing of the new lavish ballets, four of them, that were costly to cast and to transport. No matter how hard we pinched pennies, we couldn't make our tour ledgers balance.

Ironically we planned the very ballets that were to plunge

us into deep debt while we worked at profitable teaching in town and country.

Somehow in the frantic bustle of choreographing for the second season and teaching in two locations, at New York and Mariarden, I managed to create a sculpture solo, *The Death of Adonis*, that I called a plastic dance and proposed to perform nude except for white body make-up and a white fig leaf. Similar sculpture make-up had been used for brief statue poses in vaudeville acts but no serious dance artist had ever accepted the challenge then inherent in the combination of nudity with movement. It seemed logical that I should try out my new work at the Mariarden art theater, specifically planned by Mrs. Guy Currier as showcase for experimental plays and dances, and production innovations.

It never crossed my mind that I might run into trouble with my new dance until Mr. Currier arrived in haste from Boston the morning after its dress rehearsal. By long distance someone had reported to him that I was about to do an obscene dance for our summer theater subscribers. Mr. Currier asked me to cancel the number. I refused. He countered with the assurance that he knew I wouldn't do an objectionable dance but he was quite certain that an audience of New England "natives" would be offended by the sight of a naked performer.

I stormed and in vain pointed out that Mariarden's art theater should not let its policy be set by rural neighbors. We battled to a deadlock broken by compromise. I agreed to withdraw the solo from the scheduled all-dance program, and Mr. and Mrs. Currier willingly arranged a private première with invitations sent to worldly and sophisticated friends vacationing at summer colonies of the area.

In the meantime, I danced in a ballet based on the legend of Cupid and Psyche, with a cast made up of Mariarden-Denishawn students and members of our professional company. Charles Weidman was a pink-winged and curly-wigged Cupid, and I was Pan, wearing a headdress set tight in my then-luxuriant hair, so the horns of the god seemed actually to sprout from my skull.

I labored over the rest of my costume, designing footgear that looked like hoofs, and sewing black worsted into tights to give the effect of shaggy furred legs. On dress rehearsal night, I decided that the tights of Pan joined my bare torso with an unaesthetic line, and asked one of the dancers to get me fresh leaves from the woods behind the theater. He dashed back to my dressing room with vines that I quickly wound around my middle to conceal the obvious string top of tights. Carried away by the sylvan effect, I even draped some of the leaves over the tops of my ears. The Pan costume was strikingly realistic with the touches of greenery which, unfortunately, no one backstage recognized as poison ivy.

The story of how I had deliberately bedecked my stomach with a poison ivy wreath was elaborated with increasing merriment to all at Mariarden but me. Sick-listed with thick yellow blisters girdling my midriff and scaly lumps swelling behind my ears, I was visited by a succession of callous callers who started to giggle at the sight of me, scratching on my bed of pain.

I was still scabrous on the night of the invitation performance of *The Death of Adonis* but white body make-up, blue stage lights, and the distance between the audience and me combined to keep my shame from showing. My performance was prefaced by Ruth who spoke briefly on the subject of nudity and the dance. Then the sliding doors that served as front curtain on the Mariarden stage opened to reveal me, a white marble figure, seated on a white marble tree stump atop a white marble pedestal. Slowly I began to visibly breathe, to move with the continuing fluidity that I devised, a brand-new dance technique. With slow legato movements, I proceeded through the awakening of Adonis, the hunt, and the goring of the god by a wild boar.

The curtain-doors closed on such an ovation as I had rarely received but which I was to hear again and again as I danced *The Death of Adonis* around the world. That solo never failed to bring down the house whether the audience was Japanese, Hindu, American, French, British, Russian, German, or Dutch. Long after the vindicating première triumph of *The Death of Adonis,* I learned to my rage that the person who labeled it obscene and endangered its birth was none other than the Mariarden cook!

When both summer schools closed, we settled to six weeks of intense and extravagant preparation for the fall tour. Our first season with Mayer had been a success unprecedented in the history of American dance and, with a greater one scheduled ahead, we saw fortune floating like a cloud through our imaginations. Nothing was too good for our public, or for our company productions. Neither Ruth nor I served as a check on the other and, repeating our familiar pattern, we splurged. We spent recklessly on ambitious ballets that required the increased expense of an enlarged company with proportionate payroll. Short of funds, we ran up bills and borrowed cash. We assembled a quality program of four new ballets with original scores, special scenery, fabulous costumes.

The Spirit of the Sea, expanded from a solo of Ruth's, featured her again as the sea, with me as a fisher boy, and several Denishawn girls as my "fish" playmates. Those water nymphs, costumed in thin silk fleshings, had a nude look that was realistic enough to be controversial on tour. Our seaside idyll was danced against a bright blue cyclorama, and in a fairly uncomplicated set dominated by a practical rock that jutted out onto the stage.

Practical, the theatrical term for a piece of scenery that can be used as a real object, was properly applicable to the rock.

Impractical was a better word for the adobe prefabs in the Indian village set of my ballet *Feather of the Dawn*. Those Hopi dwellings that looked quite real on our stage-mesa were burdensome to assemble, to ship, to unpack and repack. They represented a major investment and so did the authentic Hopi costumes worn by several members of the cast. Other Indian costumes were designed by Erle Franke, the artist who did the sets and copied our three-dimensional katcina masks from exhibits at the Smithsonian Institution in Washington. The production cost of *Feather* soared when I commissioned its original score (at $1200) from Charles Wakefield Cadman, the American composer of "From the Land of the Sky-Blue Waters" and other famous songs.

Louis Horst arranged a score from manuscript and folk tunes for *Cuadro Flamenco*, the ballet inspired by my Spanish holiday, and I designed the set with uncommon restraint. We danced on a slightly elevated platform against a brand-new black velvet cyclorama ($1800), and used a wide assortment of mood properties: chairs, tables, big baskets filled with flowers, and Spanish shawls that overflowed from a carved chest.

The most opulent of the ballets was Ruth's *Ishtar of the Seven Gates*, our program finale. Its set was the interior of a Babylonian temple with a shrine reached by seven steps, grooved so a pair of practical gates on each level could be operated to open and close. Before we had traveled far those gates were fourteen pieces of scrap iron.

Final rehearsals with scenery and lights in a dark New York theater were scrambles that should have alerted us to vicissitudes ahead. We set out for our opening date with two baggage cars instead of one; with a company increased by seven dancers; and a traveling crew of so many extra stagehands that the union made us take on fourteen local stagehands at each town. Fortunately for us, Mr. Mayer had booked us first into Nixon's Apollo Theatre at Atlantic City for a full week in which to organize our complicated productions. Our first-night program was too long and the intermissions were interminable. During the week we cut numbers, rearranged music, and rehearsed every revision. We slept little, ate less, and posed for $1200 worth of full stage pictures shot by staff photographers from White's of New York.

The nightmare week in Atlantic City was followed by a similar stretch of one-night stands. From Brooklyn to Maine we had to appease our backstage staff that struggled daily with cumbersome sets and equipment. The property man nearly lost his mind keeping track of chairs, steps, tables, altars, and platforms; the carpenter, frustrated by inexperienced local help, was ever ready to blow up, and often did; the company electrician, coping with portable equipment for the most elaborate lighting effects we had ever devised, threatened to resign at least once every day, sometimes oftener.

Delays and crises behind the curtain generated repercussions out front. Restive audiences in sell-out houses expressed their irritation at being kept waiting by clapping and stomping and chanting for the performance to begin. We managed to win over those audiences but had no intention of dancing through a season for impatient people antagonized by late curtains and lengthy intermissions.

The backstage situation failed to improve as we traveled. In Baltimore, after two weeks on the road, we were forty-five minutes late getting up our first curtain, and took our last bows after midnight. Right then, instead of cutting, we slashed, sacrificing the gates of Ishtar along with lesser offerings from other ballets. Mobile, at last, we settled to our long winter's tour.

We played in regular theaters that booked road attractions, in municipal and college auditoriums, in concert halls, and even, at Richmond, Indiana, in a skating rink. We appeared under the auspices of local concert managers, chambers of commerce, schools and colleges, and service clubs. Capacity audiences cheered us, and the press showered us with superlatives: *Ruth St. Denis and Ted Shawn Thrill Audience* (Ithaca), *The Art of the Denishawns at Its Zenith* (Buffalo), *Denishawn Troupe Scores Triumph* (Ann Arbor), *Denishawn Dancers Again Triumph* (Portland, Me.), *Dance Glorified by Denis-Shawn Interpretations* (Dayton, O.).

Our personal routine was standard: we rode a train every day, sometimes changing connections three times between one-night stands. We exchanged daily greetings with a welcoming committee, or a local sponsor, or a theater manager; gave interviews to reporters and posed for newspaper photographers. We talked at Rotary luncheons, dramatic club meetings, student assemblies, women's club gatherings, state teachers' conventions, dancing schools, colleges and universities. We attended after-theater parties given for us by personal friends or by some leader of the local Four Hundred.

No matter how rushed or weary we were, Ruth and I kept up our own endless conversation. We talked constantly in theater dressing rooms, at our hotel, and on trains. We caught sleep in what we called link sausages: a link sitting up on a daytime train or a link in a Pullman berth, a nap link between the last interview and curtain time, and, when we had a two-day booking, a luxurious link in a comfortable hotel room.

Our tour schedule read like a jumbled gazetteer of the United States. In a typical month (February, 1924) we danced in:

Pittsburgh, Kans.	Des Moines, Ia. (2 days)
Joplin, Mo. (on a Sunday)	Sioux City, Ia.
Tulsa, Okla.	Omaha, Neb. (2 days)
Muskogee, Okla.	Mason City, Ia.
Fort Smith, Ark.	Waterloo, Ia.
McAlester, Okla.	Peoria, Ill.

Okmulgee, Okla.   Fort Dodge, Ia.
Oklahoma City, Okla.   Iowa City, Ia.
Arkansas City, Kans.   Ottumwa, Ia.
Wellington, Kans.   Keokuk, Ia.
Lawrence, Kans.   Dubuque, Ia.
Lincoln, Neb.

Before long the itinerary became a blur of nebulous locations to us all. Ruth, always vague about names and places, would step off the train at Utica saying, "So this is Ithaca." She confused Fort Dodge with Dodge City, and the Springfield of Missouri with the one in Illinois.

Our tour list gave us the date, the name of the town, and the theater where we were to perform, and we depended on its printed word to keep us posted. One day Ruth and I, walking along the main business street of a biggish city, discovered that neither of us knew the name of the place. "That's easy," I said, reaching into my pocket. "We'll find out from the route list." But the list was no help because neither of us knew the date of the month, and without that essential guide we couldn't check the city's name. At the next busy intersection, we approached a policeman, directing traffic, and asked, "Can you tell us the name of this town?" Afterward we wondered how we escaped being run in as lunatics.

Although cities and towns did seem to overlap and blend into one composite American community, each new audience was distinct, with a personality of its own that was an inspiration to us. We were exhilarated by the knowledge that we were pioneering for the art of the dance to which our lives were dedicated. We performed for thousands who had never before seen a dance program, and learned from audience reaction that dance could share the cultural spotlight with drama and music.

Our way was blocked occasionally by those who questioned

our respectability, personal or professional, and we were amused
or irate dependent on the source and result of the censure.
Inwardly I chuckled through a Louisville reunion with my
cousin, Anne Rebecca Booth, who didn't dare be seen in public
with a dancing relative for fear of jeopardizing the position
of her preacher-husband. She set up our meeting in a manner
that can only be described as *sub rosa* and, for the appointment, wore an enveloping black veil that made her look like
a character from a cloak-and-dagger novel.

Ruth and I were less amused when we were refused permission to entertain another cousin who was at a Hopkins-
ville, Kentucky, boarding school. The administration of that
institution flatly stated that dancers, even if family, were "dangerous associates" for a young girl.

We saw nothing funny about an engagement canceled by
the order of the Providence Police Commissioner who, without seeing our company, decided that its nudity was objectionable. We circumvented that official order by playing a
post-season date at Pawtucket, Rhode Island, just outside the
jurisdiction of the strait-laced commissioner and his police
force.

For a few tense hours during that tour I expected to be
visited by police with a warrant for my arrest. Our press agent,
J. Francis Smith, was a real Denishawn fan and he often
watched the show from behind the low partition back of the
last row. One night he noticed a gaunt female, who applauded
nothing and never changed expression at anything that happened on stage. Curious, Smithy opened an intermission conversation with the woman and, when the next ballet started,
she whispered, "Which one is Ted Shawn?" With eager pride,
Smithy pointed me out, and the woman hissed, "He's the
father of my daughter's bastard child!"

At the next intermission, Smithy warned me about the accusation and I panicked. In spite of my innocence, known

definitely to me but unprovable to anyone else, I left the theater in disguise through the scenery loading door, not by the regular stage entrance. Without taking time to remove my make-up, I slipped out of the theater wearing a ragged overcoat borrowed from a stagehand whose battered hat I pulled down over my eyes. By way of shadowy back streets, I returned unaccosted to the hotel but I didn't completely relax until the next day when I was safely on a moving train.

I escaped from responsibilities for one vacation week at the end of the tour, and Ruth went at once to the West Coast to see her ailing mother. All summer we worried about creditors and impending visits from bill collectors. I taught Denishawn summer classes in New York, and for the first few weeks Ruth was at the Los Angeles Denishawn, our main school then operated efficiently by my stepmother, Mabel Shawn. Boston Denishawn, directed by the Braggiottis, was already well established, and we were experimenting with branch schools in Rochester, New York, and Wichita, Kansas. The Lake Placid Club had asked us for a summer teacher and we had sent Charles Weidman up there as Denishawn representative.

Ruth came East in time for us to fill several profitable engagements in August. The first of these was the annual charity benefit at Southampton where we were the house guests of our old friends, the Albert Herters, parents of Secretary of State Christian Herter. At the benefit, which the newspapers called a "swank affair," we played to an audience of celebrities, people prominent in society, business, and the arts. The great financier and industrialist, Clarence Mackay, who hadn't missed a Southampton benefit in years, came back after our performance to tell us with enthusiasm that none had ever been more artistic, or successful.

We gave a duet program at the Lake Placid Club, and another as guest stars at the Mariarden theater. At Portsmouth,

New Hampshire, we appeared at an open-air benefit of the kind that I have always hated like poison. These are the ones run by committees who, though well-meaning, understand none of the technical problems of lighting and performance. Contrary to the opinions of the inexperienced, the natural beauty of a dell does not compensate for lack of proper performing facilities. By performance time in New Hampshire, the makeshift stage was covered with an inch of ice water, resulting from heavy dew that had fallen at sundown. When we tried to come to a full stop on the low platform, water foamed over our bare and freezing feet, like waves over the prow of a boat. In no time at all, costume draperies were sodden, and the dancers soaking wet to the waist. The worthy cause profited from the event, the audience thrilled to the beauty of the performance in its idyllic woodland setting, but we left Portsmouth damp, disheveled, and disgusted with the whole business of dancing in the "romantic" open air.

Back in New York we dripped with perspiration in the late summer heat, and sweated blood trying to produce a new-season program while we still owed $30,000. We were forced to be sensible in our planning but, even with drastic corner-cutting, expenses ran up. We might have been rigidly economical by planning numbers to be given without scenery on a bare stage but we wouldn't do that. And really we couldn't since our public was accustomed to seeing us in elaborate productions. Neither could we just repeat the program of the season before since we were going back to many of the same towns.

We came up with a four-section program that was far from a compromise in content. The only repeat full ballet was *Cuadro Flamenco* which had been unexpectedly popular on tour, and was relatively inexpensive to ship and to set up. We decided to use the black velvet cyclorama, new the year before, for *Cuadro* again, and also for the first section, *Music Visualizations.*

Divertissements, the third section of the program, introduced three novel numbers: *Tragica,* based on Ruth's long-time experiments with unaccompanied dance, was a group number without music. It featured Doris Humphreys, who did the choreography, with Charles Weidman and an ensemble. Ruth and I did a *Balinese Fantasy,* for the first time using a Balinese theme for the Western stage. Incredible as it may now seem, we felt it necessary, in 1924, to have an explanatory program note that read: "Bali is an island off the coast of Java."

I choreographed the third section's *Five American Sketches* that included a double cowboy number I did with different partners; my popular *Invocation to the Thunderbird,* created in 1917; *Crapshooter,* a new solo for Charles Weidman; and *Boston Fancy–1854.*

By the time I choreographed *Crapshooter* for Charles Weidman, he was reconciled to doing comic numbers. When he first came to me as a pupil, at the Ted Shawn Studio in Los Angeles, he had had only a little dance instruction in his home town, Lincoln, Nebraska, and his immature ideas for dances ran to romantic or tragic themes. Both in appearance and by temperament, Charles seemed unsuited for the roles he preferred and, after studying him carefully, I was quite convinced that he was a natural comic. He disagreed with me on that subject through the years, and was almost resentful about having to learn *Danse Américaine* that I created for the second Mayer tour. Then the first time Charles danced *Américaine,* the audience clapped insistently for an encore, and in an about-face, he claimed that he had been in favor of the number all along. *Crapshooter* further developed his talents and helped to establish the reputation as comic interpreter that he has enjoyed in his subsequent professional career.

Charles was equally right for *Boston Fancy–1854*, a stylization of New England square dances. That ballet, performed by four couples, embodied in miniature the atmosphere of a typical New England party in the year my grandmother was married. I copied one costume from a dress in my grandmother's trousseau, and the other three from *Godey's Lady's Book* of 1854. The four men's costumes were tailored by Brooks from styles in the *Gentleman's Magazine of Fashions*. Today the description of *Boston Fancy* rings bells of recognition for dance fans who have seen similar works in musical shows and in the repertoires of American dance companies. In 1924 the dance was a sensational novelty that won wide acclaim and I was heralded as a choreographer of originality. The number, unique because it used its particular regional-folk theme for the first time, was universally popular with American audiences.

The finale of our third season program, *The Vision of the Aissoua*, a ballet I first dreamed about in North Africa, was sumptuously mounted with costume materials, heavily embroidered hangings, and real props that I had shipped home from Algeria. It was a break to be able to stage one big number for little or nothing by using stored treasures that I had bought and paid for when I was in the land of the *ouled naïl*, the dervish, and the sheik.

In spite of program simplifications and pared production costs, we were nearly $60,000 in debt when our season opened in mid-October at Fall River, Massachusetts. We started the tour with a determined resolve to finish it free of debt. To that end we again had a company of only twenty-five, and we shipped lighter baggage and simpler scenery that required one less traveling stagehand.

The third year lacked some of the excitement of the previous two. We were by then accustomed to the unbroken bookings and overcrowded houses that had elated us during

both the first and second seasons, and we were relieved of
the tensions and vexations of the second tour with its elaborate
productions and attendant worries. Once more we were in
the established routine of train to taxi to hotel; hotel to theater
to party to train. Our route list scheduled us to western Canada, down the West Coast to a Christmas layoff at Los Angeles, where we taught at Denishawn School for a few days
and checked on its affairs with the manager. The holidays at
home were heartwarming and the climax of our Los Angeles
stay threw us into a state of excitement. Mr. Mayer, out for
a business conference, told us that A. Strok, the greatest impresario of the Orient, wanted to sign the Denishawn company
for a long tour beginning in Japan and continuing through
China, Burma, India, and Java.

Singapore and Rangoon and Tokyo and Calcutta were the
cities uppermost in our thoughts as we started back on the
road to play in towns named Albuquerque and Tucson and
Colorado Springs. A swing through Colorado ended at another
of my home towns, Denver, where Brother St. Denis was
working as an oil geologist. Ruth and I talked seriously and
persuasively with him about taking a year's leave of absence
to go with us as manager of the Orient tour.

My own fraternity chapter of Sigma Phi Epsilon had me
to a Denver party to meet the members then on campus and
to reunion with the two brothers who had been my closest
friends in undergraduate days. That was a mistake. My old
friends and I had nothing to talk about beyond a few frag-
mentary reminiscences, and to me they both looked gray and
stodgy. I left hoping that I hadn't aged as obviously as my
former classmates.

In the South, West, and East, fraternity brothers buzzed
around me, not from loyalty, but because I was surrounded
by beautiful Denishawn girls. I was invited to stag dinners
and a few luncheons but my Sig Ep hosts always managed

to get backstage later, and one or two chapters even gave parties for the whole Denishawn company. I was an expert on chapter real estate and community standing since I probably visited more S.P.E. houses than any other member with the possible exception of the national executive secretary.

On tour I sometimes felt like a traveling secretary myself because I kept up a running correspondence with the Denishawn Schools. On one of my enforced letter-writing days, Ruth and Pearl Wheeler went off to shop in Savannah, leaving me at the Hotel de Soto. I was pounding away on the typewriter when I surprised myself by spelling out "I smell smoke." I stopped writing, sniffed, and bowed to my subconscious. From the doorway of my fourth-floor room, I could see down a long hallway that was a mass of flames. I slammed the door, thinking, "Pearl will never forgive me if Ruth's things get burned." Haphazardly I shoved Ruth's possessions into suitcases, and with three bags under each arm staggered down three flights of steps. I intended to go back upstairs for my own belongings but after I had deposited Ruth's luggage under a palm tree, firemen were on duty at the hotel doors, and I was not allowed to enter the building.

I stationed myself where I could see the progress of the fire and also watch for Ruth and Pearl whom I greeted with the good news that I had emptied Ruth's room. The fire burned on, and we had to leave for the theater. When we returned after the show, the fire was out but the whole fourth floor was gutted and I had lost everything: clothes, typewriter, valuable records, suitcases, hats, shoes. I was left with only what I was wearing when I typed the words "I smell smoke."

That was the second time I had saved belongings of Ruth's from a fire from which I salvaged nothing. When our home, Tedruth, burned at Eagle Rock near Los Angeles, I was wakened from a deep sleep by Ruth's scream of "Pyrene." I managed to get the fire extinguisher into the bathroom where the

fire was but the Pyrene tank might as well have been a per-
fume atomizer for all the good it did. An explosion sent flames
to the ceiling and back down on me, burning the hair off my
head and the pajamas off my back. I ran from the house and
shoved a garden hose through the bathroom window but the
feeble water spray was no more effective than the Pyrene.
Through French windows, I could see flames licking across
rugs, and I knew that it was hopeless for me to try to combat
the conflagration alone. I rushed to our library where we had
one of the finest privately owned collections of dance books
in America and, by armloads, saved what I could. I also pulled
out the trunkful of photographs of Ruth that I had collected
and laboriously sorted and catalogued. Pearl, living in a guest
house with other members of our entourage, ran across the
lawn and rescued a lot of Ruth's costumes.

Hours later Tedruth was a smoldering ruin, and I had lost
my street clothes and costumes, every piece of dance music,
and all the photographs and mementos of my career. I did
have one suit at the dry cleaners. With Ruth philosophically
observing, "Material loss is spiritual gain," we moved to the
Sixth Street house which I kept as a studio in Los Angeles.

On our honeymoon tour, fire broke out in a hotel where
Mogul Khan was staying, and the small town where we were
playing buzzed with the story of the rescue of the wizened
brown man. The tiny Hindu, cut off from escape through the
hallway, was forced to hang from the primitive safety rope
that was knotted outside his window. Firemen, arriving at the
scene, found a wide-mouthed crowd staring up at a figure swaying below a third-floor window. It was Mogul, clad only in a
billowing, old-fashioned nightshirt, who clung firmly to the
fire rope with one hand and, in the other, held high an open
umbrella.

Like any touring company ours made news along the way,

and the path behind us was strewn with incidents that grew
to major events in the retelling by local raconteurs.

The highlight of the third season for us was that we did
end it completely free of debt. I had been the tour bookkeeper and by squeezing every nickel, cutting down personal
and professional expenditures, we had managed to take care
of running expenses, salaries, transportation, commissions to
agents, production and printing bills, and to pay in full the
$60,000 we owed at the beginning of the season. Years later
I wrote an article, "The Price of Pioneering," in which I gave
a breakdown of the figures of the most successful tours ever
made by an American company:

Average Net Income for each of three years $200,000

Disbursements: average per season:

Commission to Mayer	$ 40,000
Railroads, Pullmans	54,000
Salaries to company	46,000
Production, scenery, props, electrical equip. and costumes	30,000
Printing, billboards, window cards, circulars, photos, mats, cuts	20,000
Hauling of baggage, upkeep, telegrams, postage, telephone and misc.	10,000
	$200,000

The only tours comparable to ours in length of season,
numbers of performances, and gross receipt figures were made
by the Russian ballet companies, which had none of our
budget problems. The Russian ballet groups were endowed

with unlimited funds and their season deficits that ran to a quarter of a million dollars, give or take a few rubles, were underwritten by American millionaires bedazzled by the glamour of foreign attractions. Ruth and I never received a cent in subsidy or financial backing and the money we borrowed was paid back with 6 per cent interest.

It is undeniable that had we been as economical the second tour as we were the third, we would have made a profit. But the fact remains that things did not happen that way. We made ends meet finally but owned none of the luxurious appurtenances, furs or jewels that were the usual trappings of great stars of the stage. At the end of the record-making tours, we owned a lot of bedraggled costumes and tons of worn scenery. Our treasures were scrapbooks filled with glowing press notices. Slim bank balances represented the small amounts of money that we had saved from the weekly salary of $100 allotted for our living expenses on the road.

In the spring of 1925 we made no appraisal or evaluation of the three years of touring that would never be matched by us, nor by any other touring company. Denishawn had made history by being self-supporting and by laying the foundations of an American art of the dance. Without looking back at our accomplishments, we busied ourselves with plans for the future, for our grand tour of the Orient.

13

••

No Noh!

N I was baffled by a Stanley-and-Livingstone incident on our very first evening in Tokyo. My sight-seeing rickshaw, slowed in a Ginza traffic jam, was approached by a young Japanese who bowed low and murmured politely, "You *are* Mr. Ted Shawn, are you not?"

I nodded in speechless bewilderment. We had docked in Yokohama only that morning and though pictures of the company's arrival had appeared in the evening newspapers, it did seem incredible that any man on the street could be sharp-eyed enough to recognize me in the throng bustling through the Great White Way of Tokyo.

The strange greeting of a chance meeting was readily explained by Natsuya Mitsuyoshi who introduced himself as the publicity man for the Imperial Theatre where we were to play a four-week engagement. He was up to date on Denishawn statistics and familiar with Denishawn faces, having spent the previous five months translating our advance press notices and sorting hundreds of glossy photographs of us. We soon learned that Mitsuyoshi had run an extraordinary promotion campaign with the co-operation of the Japanese press which had published innumerable Denishawn pictures, biographies, and anecdotes, as well as descriptions of our dances. We never had more thorough advance coverage than in Tokyo thanks to Mitsuyoshi, guide and friend, who remained with us constantly until we left for the provinces.

If there was a flaw in our first stay in Tokyo it was that we were never alone. Every morning I wakened to find a delegation of dignitaries at my bedside, and through one half-opened eye I saw a blur of top hats, morning coats, and striped trousers. As soon as I could focus, I was presented with the day's schedule which was always too inflexible for us to indulge in spur-of-the moment jaunts that make sight-seeing an adventure.

There was no way to forestall hovering visitors because the Imperial Hotel lacked a system for announcing guests from the front desk. Anyone who wanted to see me just walked into my room, stayed while I bathed, shaved, and dressed, and if they chose, stuck with me until bedtime. Though a little wearing, the system unquestionably made it possible for me, for all of us, to know Tokyo.

Between arrival and our first performance on September 1, 1925, we had ten days free for rehearsal and sight-seeing, for the shopping that to us was ever irresistible. The Baroness Ishimoto, leader of Japan's women's rights movement, whom we had met in New York, took us to Kamakura to see its famous Buddha. We visited the shrine at Nikko, subject of the Japanese axiom, "Don't say *gekko* (magnificent) until you have seen Nikko." Viscount Shibusawa, who had never before entertained people of the theater, honored us with a tea ceremony conducted by the most celebrated mistress of the ancient rite.

Everywhere snapshots were taken of us by Japanese. Villagers popped out of their little houses, sighted us in their cameras, and shyly darted indoors. Even at the Viscount's house we were startled by the frequent clicking of camera shutters. A knowledgeable friend told me that though many Americans were unable to tell a Japanese from a Chinese if both were wearing European clothes, the distinction could easily be made: "The one with the camera is Japanese."

We were honored with a formal dinner party at an exclusive club, the Koyo Kwan, and from that physical ordeal I developed my list of "five positions" for banqueting in Japan: (1) You start by sitting in the accepted style, on your feet, back upright, and determination strong. (2) When your feet become numb and you are certain that your legs never again will function normally, you move, unobserved you hope, by sliding off onto one hip. This makes eating more difficult since you must support yourself with one hand and arm while manipulating chopsticks with the free hand. (3) The pain shortly gets to be unendurable as your buttocks become paralyzed so you swing your legs around and sit tailor-fashioned. (4) That position agonizingly bends your legs around and painfully stretches the inside leg muscles, and in desperation you ease your legs straight out, rudely exposing your stockinged soles to guests on the opposite side of the dining area.

The final position is inevitable. You have sat for more than six hours at a twenty-course dinner. Strange food, mostly unpalatable to you, has been accompanied by warm *sake* with which your tiny wine cup has been constantly filled. At last you give up and (5) flop out full length on the matting-covered floor, mumbling, "Come what may," and fervently hoping for a stretcher with bearers from a waiting ambulance.

The Japanese habit of sitting long hours was difficult for us to acquire and we were worn out after a seven-hour performance of the famous Noh dances that date back to the year 1000 or earlier. As a company we attended the Noh because we felt that all of us should be exposed to every kind of Japanese dancing. We understood none of the five numbers with their typical movements that are snail-paced. The effect was like slow-motion photography or a nightmare in which it's impossible to pull away from a pursuing savage beast. Stanley, our electrician, capsuled the Noh technique with astute accuracy, "A man came rushing on stage, one step every half-hour."

The rest of us were intrigued by the technical aspects of the Noh performance and by the go-down, the storage area where we examined Noh masks and richly colored costumes, some nearly six hundrel years old. Our host at the Noh theater told us the history of the ancient dances and confirmed for us the impression that no country has had more vigorous dance art than Japan.

We found the Japanese extremely open-minded and sensitive to foreign dances, although they were quite mystified by our genre numbers, like *Boston Fancy–1854.* They liked most of our dances and for some inexplicable reason were wildly enthusiastic about my Cretan dance, *Gnossienne.* After I made my stylized bows, I always went down to my knees and gave a formal Japanese bow, forehead to floor. That really brought down the house.

The Japanese do not normally applaud but, in deference to our custom, they patted their hands together at the conclusion of each dance. Performers are accustomed to applause varying in volume and caliber from audience to audience, but we had never heard anything more weird than the sound made by a Japanese audience making noise in a completely artificial manner. Japanese reactions occasionally disconcerted us. When some detail of movement or grouping pleased the spectators we could feel, rather than hear, a light ripple of approval sweep like a breeze through the theater. Laughter naturally puzzled us when we were dancing something that wasn't intended to be humorous. The Japanese roared at the Hopi Indian dance when the girls made a scooping movement while filling baskets with corn, an action not meant to be funny at all. We learned that the scooping movement was identical with one in a popular geisha dance, and the Japanese were as amused to see that gesture in a foreign number as we would have been by a Charleston step incorporated into a Noh.

We gave programs of conventional Western length, two hours, and were able to attend a variety of Japanese performances that started at two in the afternoon and often continued until midnight. In that time the holder of one ticket could see three full-length dramas, a couple of one-act plays, or dances.

In the course of my play-going I saw a Japanese *Othello* that Shakespeare wouldn't have recognized, and went to a little theater where the active repertory included plays by O'Neill, Strindberg, and Lord Dunsany, and the actors talked of art and drama in terms typical of little theater players around the world. I went half a dozen times to see a thrilling dance-drama, *Momiji-Gari*, which I later produced for our company. The star was Koshiro Matsumoto, then the foremost actor-dancer in Japan where the complete theater artist must express himself equally well by word and motion. In a single afternoon I saw Koshiro play a male role in a blood-and-thunder melodrama, and then portray a graceful exquisite female in a dance drama.

Later in Peking we met Mei-Lan Fang, China's outstanding actor whose name is still legend in international theatrical circles. He was not then performing publicly but he graciously brought his whole company to our theater and presented several scenes for us. He played feminine roles always and there never was a more beautiful real woman. The night we saw him, he moved with two flashing swords in the nearest thing to a dance that could be found in the Chinese theater, where professional dancing was as rare as it was prevalent in Japan.

The finest portrayer of feminine roles on the Japanese stage was Onoe Baiko, a great-grandfather, who told me that his favorite roles were "Ghosts, demons, and hysterical females!"

Japanese theaters fascinated me. Stage areas were much larger than those of the West, and productions were more elaborate mechanically, more lavish in scenery, costumes, and effects. Even unpretentious theaters were equipped with revolving stages, if not with automatic mechanisms. Down deep in the understage of one small theater I saw naked coolies, like so many blind Samsons, pushing crossbars to turn the revolving stage above. Their muscled bodies gleamed with sweat in the flickering light of hot oil flares that feebly illuminated the dank, fetid hole.

At stage level and above, Japanese theaters featured comforts for performing artists. The Imperial dressing rooms, charmingly decorated and spotlessly clean, were ranged on five floors each with a full bath, a luxury for grateful dancers slathered with body make-up. The stage-level floor was reserved for props, workrooms, and the bathroom used by stage hands who bathed as soon as the stage was struck.

Frequently as we left the Imperial after a performance, we met naked stagehands coming from their tubs, towels neatly folded over their arms. Instead of covering themselves with the towels, the stagehands, to a man, made wide gestures with open arms, revealing parts of the male anatomy that our Denishawn girls had previously seen only on museum marbles. Hissing politely through their teeth, the stagehands bowed low and moved to one side so we might pass. After the shock of the first such formality, our Denishawn girls accepted the encounters as routine.

Imperturbability was a characteristic the girls needed as we toured the provinces. At Shizuoko most of the company had to use a central public bathroom where their ablutions attracted an audience of hotel servants, male and female. In Kumamoto several of the girls were mid-bath in a large garden room when a janitor burst in on them. Screeching, they gestured for him to leave, but he good-naturedly indicated they wouldn't disturb him a bit and went on with his chores.

None of us cared for Japanese food that was served to us in the provinces where it was often difficult to get any kind of meal. One dish that most of us liked was literally hash, Japanese style: rice, meat, fowl, and vegetables mixed, but even the palatable *hashi* palled after a while. In desperation we equipped ourselves with a food hamper and prepared some meals over sterno, fending off starvation with tea, powdered coffee, Ovaltine, tinned biscuits, and American canned food.

Ordering food in remote places was complicated by language barriers. One midnight when I hadn't eaten since noon, I tried to get food by carefully reading from a phrase book, "Honorable insides have become empty," and patting my stomach vigorously until a little maid nodded, "Ah, so *desuka*," the "all right" of Japan. She disappeared and returned with two hardboiled eggs and a little rice, a snack that was hardly enough to fill the honorable insides. Charles Weidman fared as badly once when he craved a glass of milk. In a final attempt to get his order across, he dropped to all fours and realistically mooed while George Steares went through the motions of milking. The waiter brightened with the usual, "Ah, so *desuka*," and served a beefsteak to Charles.

When shopping for presents and costume materials, we selected the specialties of the town or province. In Shizuoko we bought lacquer; in Nagoya, porcelain; in Kobe and Osaka, a wide variety of objects and fabrics for Christmas presents to be sent home through customs by early October. Individual gifts went to the students, teachers, and other staff members of each Denishawn school, and to families and friends from coast to coast. Later in Shanghai we mailed five hundred Christmas greetings: cards, prints, and autographed photographs, so that everybody Ruth and I knew would hear from us at holiday time.

We continued our buying through the Orient. Ruth in her excitement over the lacquer furniture of Lahore fell out of a bullock-drawn tonga; and I, while bargaining there for chairs and stools, was hit in the rear by a sacred cow that catapulted me into the shop and on top of furniture. The company contracted buying fever in Shanghai. We bought amber, jade, laces, glass snuff bottles, mandarin coats, fans, and many things we didn't know the names of or use for. Before a performance there would be a general unwrapping and steady stream of questions: "Where did you get that?", "Are there any more of those?", "What did that cost?", "What's it for?" I noticed that Stanley seemed immune to the buying bug, and asked, "In all this time of touring, Stanley, haven't you bought anything at all?" "You bet I have," he answered, "today I found something I've been looking for ever since we got to the Orient —an alarm clock!"

The rest of us left every Japanese town loaded with parcels but without a single sen after the hotel bill was settled and the rickshaw boy tipped at the station. If the accumulation of purchases got beyond us, we shipped cartons home, but most of the time we looked like coolies on the move.

Our touring company totaled fifty: the permanent orchestra of the whole Orient tour; A. Strok and his entourage; two Chinese, one a sewing boy, the other a stagehand; and the Denishawn troupe. At every station we counted off and dou-

ble-checked on baggage, belongings, and personnel. Rural
routes were rugged and on a single daytime hop between one-
night stands, we left Hiroshima by train, changed connections
at Shimonoseki, crossed by ferry to Moji, trained to another
connection change at Tosa, and on to our destination, Kumamoto.

Our provincial tour was broken by a ten-day run at Takaradzuka, midway between the industrial cities of Osaka and
Kobe. Shrewd promoters, who owned the connecting interurban line, developed that remarkable resort park with its huge
theater, a city in miniature under one roof. It had three public restaurants that ranged from exclusive to tea-roomy to
the Japanese equivalent of our soda fountain. Actors and stagehands had their own separate restaurant, and management
had set up barber- and tailor-shops, baths and other conven-
iences of daily living for backstage people who spent most
of their waking hours at the theater that was open from noon
until midnight.

Before we opened at Takaradzuka we had to follow a Japanese custom that has no counterpart in our country. We went
in to Osaka to call formally on the editors of the leading
newspaper and to be interviewed on the spot by reporters.
The more experienced of us were amused at the very thought
of what would happen if dancers and musicians invaded the
city room of any American newspaper to pay their respects to
editors.

At Osaka we were entertained by a department store owner
who spoke little English but thoughtfully provided printed
signs that were strategically placed in garden and house. RE-
FRESHMENTS—PLEASE PARTAKE FREELY were the words tacked
up at a garden pavilion, and inside the baronial mansion, a
sign pointing upstairs indicated PRIVY—FOREIGN STYLE.

There was a drama and dance school in the Takaradzuka
theater and we visited its dormitories, costume and property

rooms, and watched classes in progress under teachers of various styles. Hundreds of students performed a Chinese ballet and a geisha dance at a special performance given just for us.

The theater seated five thousand, a thousand more than New York's showplace, the Capitol Theatre, which at that time had the largest seating capacity of any theater in the United States. The audience at Takaradzuka was drawn from Kobe and Osaka, and we played every performance for ten days to more than five thousand people. Our last-day matinee and evening programs were sellouts with a total of well over ten thousand for the two performances.

Excitement ran high backstage after our last show. Fans and friends came with the typical Japanese *presento*, some little remembrance, artistically packaged. We signed and received autographs, and exchanged pictures with members of the theater company, and resident actors called on me formally, leaving towels, not visiting cards. Too late I learned that each actor in Japan has specially designed make-up towels printed and run off by the hundreds. Some he uses in his dressing room; others, wrapped in gay paper, he signs and exchanges with visiting actors. I didn't know about the accepted custom and was in no position to reciprocate because in those days, before the general use of facial tissues, I removed my make-up with lengths of outing flannel, wash-worn and permanently stained.

We went from Takaradzuka to Kyoto, ancient capital of Japan and surely one of its most beautiful cities, where we visited the country's outstanding geisha school. Madame Katayama, octogenarian head teacher, danced at her own birthday party and gave a magnificent performance of the art which she had practiced for more than seventy years. In the course of a twenty-minute solo, she executed many intricate movements none more exacting than a back bend from a kneeling position that required her to touch her head to the floor between her feet. The bend, an integral part of the patterned choreography, didn't seem like a show-off stunt, although it was a remarkable feat for a woman just turned eighty-eight.

Kyoto audiences were more enthusiastic than any we had played to in Japan and the theater was sold out in advance of our arrival. Word had gone around the provinces that we offered remarkable entertainment that shouldn't be missed, and excitement mounted as we completed the tour. At Hiroshima we were met by fifty rickshaws decorated with American flags, and were drawn through streets lined with banners advertising our show. Another fleet of rickshaws met us at Hakata and again we were paraded through the streets before we paid our respects to local newspaper editors.

Hakata was famous for its tied-and-dyed fabrics and its clay dolls designed in thousands of different shapes, sizes, and characters. As an amateur dyer of costume fabrics and teacher of elementary dyeing techniques, I was fascinated by the cottage industry of fabric tying. Whole families from great-grandmothers down to toddlers tied thousands of tiny knots to pattern cotton stuff that was dipped in indigo. I bought dozens of rolls of the sturdy material which I had made up into dressing room robes that survived decades of wear and wash.

Clay dolls representing me in several dance roles were turned out by Hakata artists and the following year I returned to find my Eagle Dance doll a best seller in toy shops. I posed for the doll sketches on our first visit and on my thirty-fourth birthday, October 21.

In the United States my birthdays were dull because they came at the beginning of tours when we were all too busy getting programs into shape to bother about celebrations. A birthday in Japan was something special in itself and offered a good excuse for the company to have a party. My presents were wrapped Japanese-style, even more elaborately than our

Christmas gifts. After opening an array of beautiful things, I had a fixed smile and a set phrase, "Oh, isn't that stunning, just what I wanted," that didn't fit the last gift—a cold, clammy, and very dead small octopus, or squid. There was a big laugh at my reaction to the joke present and then without warning I broke up the party by flipping the thing into the lap of one of the girls. I recovered the horrid object and playfully tossed it at the girls as they ran screaming from the room. Later when they were taking their baths in a sort of cellar dungeon, I slid the door open a crack and threw the squid that landed with a nasty squish on the wet floor. Our Japanese landlady, aroused by the resultant pandemonium, went through the halls knocking together two wooden blocks, a quaint curfew that produced a sound like an angry cricket.

At the end of the Japanese tour, we embarked for Manchuria, which wasn't as simple as it sounds. Everything we owned had to be cleared through customs: theatrical scenery, props and costumes in 132 pieces of big baggage; one trunk for every member of the company, as well as suitcases, hand luggage, and bundles of purchases. During the actual loading, Brother St. Denis, Stanley, and I stood guard dockside checking every trunk and crate that was hoisted by net from dock to ship.

Exhausted by a long tour in a strange country and the wearing hours of boarding, I collapsed in my stateroom aboard the S.S. *Harbin-Maru*, and stayed there sleeping and reading and sorting impressions of the past two months. On trains through Japan I had read a life of Anatole France and the just-published *Arrowsmith* by Sinclair Lewis; on the short sea voyage to Dairen, I finished Walter Pater's *Miscellaneous Studies*.

The trip by ship gave me time to rearrange my personal luggage and to repack mememtos including little envelopes that I still have as reminders of our Imperial Theatre fare-

well. There was a time in the history of the Japanese theater
when managers treated members of a sellout cast to a bowl
of noodles from the theater restaurant, but management eventually found it more convenient to give each player a five-
sen coin for every sellout show. Aboard ship I boxed and sealed
a sizable collection of Imperial envelopes each decorated with
a large red symbol, each containing a Japanese five-sen piece.
We had sold out for almost every Tokyo performance and on
closing night, we collected quite a lot of noodle money.

14

Oriental Swing

Anna George De Mille, mother of Agnes and an old friend of mine, used to say that she and I were charter members of the Hate-to-Miss Club, and I was never more conscious of my eligibility than in the Orient. I would go to bed long after midnight exhausted enough to sleep until noon and then at dawn I would be wide-eyed thinking of some temple or market-place or dance group that I would hate-to-miss. The eager me would drag its carcass out of bed, give it coffee, and send it forth to see whatever mustn't be missed.

I was as avid a collector of places as of sights. Strok quite justly accused me of thinking of Orient bookings only in terms of a new country whose dancing I wanted to study. My persistence, which nettled him, enabled me to see dancing that no longer exists in pure form and to learn dances that few Westerners have seen. Junkets into remote areas developed only as we heard about village troupes and native dance rites in various countries where we were booked.

War was all around us when we left Japan and we had to go from Dairen to Tientsin by ship because the rail lines were either bombed out or under fire. A battle raging close to Peking prevented us from sight-seeing beyond the Great Wall, and at a garden party we were startled by the boom of big guns. Our British hostess, seeing our alarm, pouted toward us, "Oh, yes, that wretched war. It's nothing, really." Minor, or not, the shooting made it necessary for us to go by water to Shanghai because the train tracks had been blown up.

Our sturdy little craft, the S.S. *Shuntien*, made an unscheduled stop at Wei-hei-wei to take on a cargo of peanuts that was dumped on top of Denishawn baggage. The loading delay gave us little leeway before performance time in Shanghai, and Strok urged the skipper to speed up by piling "more coal on the machinery." We finally docked at 7 P.M. with our curtain scheduled for 9:15, and Strok in a shaking dither about the peanuts which had to be unloaded before the Denishawn scenery and costumes could even be started through customs.

Helpfully I suggested that I might repeat a tactic pulled off once in Maine when our baggage car was lost in a blizzard. To a waiting audience of three thousand, I had lectured on the dance from 8:30 until 11 P.M. The Portland review the next day made a big point of the fact that not one person had left the auditorium during either my talk or our program that wasn't over until after 1 A.M.

Strok's face brightened and he shouted, "Good, good! You do that again tonight. Now, go!" In a business suit, I stepped onto the Shanghai stage and once more faced a full house. After explaining the dilemma, I started to lecture on the history of the dance, beginning with the Stone Age and slowly progressing through the centuries to medieval times. When

I was discussing the Dance of Death and feeling the part, I thought I heard welcome sounds of backstage activity but nothing happened. Taking a deep breath, I talked on and was about to conclude modern dance and launch into the Future of Dance when wigwags from the wings caught my eye, and I staggered off stage to change like lightning for my first dance entrance.

On tour I was more than male star of the company. I was also papa and paymaster. The latter was a vexing role in the Orient. The guarantee of American dollars was paid in local currency at the rate of exchange posted on payday, and from the total given to me by Strok, I made up individual salary envelopes. The amounts came out to large denominations and small change that in India included pice, which didn't even exist in actual coinage. I had to pay rupees and annas, adding one anna for the percentage of pice with the result that my books in India were ever out of balance, and I was always out of pocket.

As conscientious papa, I served as moderator, confidant, chaperon, and the health officer who devised a method for guarding against unpleasant tropical diseases that might be contracted while dancing barefoot. After every performance each dancer took a Lysol footbath in my dressing room and I checked a list to insure that no one skipped the *pas de prophylaxis*.

When the company visited Rangoon's Shwe Dagon Pagoda, which everyone had to enter barefoot, I took along a folding footbath that I filled at a horse trough and spiked heavily with Lysol. To the amusement of a throng of natives, the Denishawn company doused its feet before entering the shrine and on leaving it.

This pagoda is to me one of the most fascinating buildings in the world. There is about it a strangeness and a beauty that stirred me to ecstasy. On a night bright with the full moon, Ruth and I slipped off alone and spent hours at the pagoda, one of the perfect occasions in my memory. Just the two of us with a portable footbath and a bottle of disinfectant.

Whenever I went shopping in Rangoon, I was trailed by Abdul, a footman from our hotel, who gradually took over my bargaining. He made a remarkable buy one morning and then paid me the ten rupees which was his own commission for having taken a tourist to the merchant. Such honesty overwhelmed me and later I was equally impressed by Abdul's enterprise.

For me, I dressed rather flashily in the Orient. My white suits, custom-tailored, had detachable buttons of jade, and I wore only green neckties, especially made of fine brocades. Abdul knew that I wanted a pair of cuff links of plain jade, and one day on the street, he tugged at my sleeve, "Look, Sahib! Your cuff links." He pointed to a pair that were exactly what I wanted but they were being worn by a well-tailored Burmese youth. I shrugged and strolled on while Abdul lagged behind and somehow bought the cuff links, each centered with a small ruby, for only $3.35 in American money.

In India we each had to have a bearer to act as personal porter and bellhop, and I asked Abdul to go with me, a prospect that seemed to please him enormously. When our ship was well out in the bay of Bengal, Abdul dropped a ring overboard, saying, "Thank goodness, I'm free of that." "That" was an arranged marriage and I couldn't tell whether Abdul wanted to be my bearer, to see India, or to be free of a fiancée. Whatever his reason for going along, I never for a moment regretted my decision to hire Abdul. Nearly a year later when we were returning to Japan, I bought him a good camera, gave him an extra bonus, and he left us tearfully.

Brother St. Denis decided while we were in India that he wanted to be an oriental importer and started plans that resulted in the St. Denis Asia Bazaar on Sunset Boulevard in Hollywood, with branches in Palm Springs and Santa Barbara. When the bazaars were flourishing, Brother returned to the Orient on a buying trip, and took on Abdul as bearer. He was still the clever and resourceful servant, and as full of droll chatter as when he was with me.

My only difficulty with Abdul was deciphering some of his English. Once when I was too busy with bookkeeping to go to the dining room to eat, Abdul said, "I go get bliffer," and returned to my room with the bill of fare. I could make nothing of his "Excuse me, Sahib, I go doublousie," until the first time I saw him push open a door marked w.c.

Others in the company were less fortunate with their native servants. Brother caught his drunken bearer stealing Ernestine Day's money out of George Steares's pocket where it had been put for safekeeping. Ruth's beautiful, tigerish ayah hired in Calcutta was so moody and unpredictable that she had to be replaced with a stupid but harmless older woman. Over and over again I was reminded of the prize I had in Abdul.

He was bearer, guide, interpreter, and valet, a service I needed because of our continuous social life. No English or American dance company had ever before played throughout the Orient, and we were welcomed by bishops and sultans, ambassadors and maharajahs, artists, authors, and tycoons. Teas, luncheons, formal dinners, receptions, and beach parties kept us entertained and exhausted. We met old friends and made new ones who came to us with letters of introduction from mutual acquaintances.

The parties and our audiences had one thing in common: some were all Western; others were all native. Most audiences of both kinds were generous and enthusiastic; a few were "dumb," which is what one's ego dubs audiences that are restrained in applause and reaction. We encountered one Singapore audience that was boozy and loud, a typical Saturday night crowd in a wide-open town, and week-end audiences in

Ceylon were rowdy because of tea planters on toots. An unruly mob of planters raucously laughed at *Ishtar* until Ruth stopped mid-dance and gave them a tongue-lashing that subdued them for the evening. Doris and Charles suggested that the planters might be appreciative of a Charleston, and they were, not jeering but cheering during that dance the next night.

The dancing we ourselves saw ranged from inferior through eccentric to magnificent. Malay dancers we hired gave a dull performance on the roof garden of our Singapore hotel and then we heard that the only spirited Malay dancing was done by villagers "likkered up" for a feast day.

For a few weeks we could find naught in the way of nautch in India. Nobody we asked had ever seen a nautch and only a few people had even vaguely heard the word. Relentless inquiry led us in Calcutta to a private home performance by two women; one was really a singer, the other was a model of Victorian elegance complete with crimped iron-gray hair, and a dog collar of seed pearls worn with her sari. The aged woman refused to dance barefoot and strapped twenty pounds of ankle bells around men's socks that she wore for her demonstration. The incongruity of her getup was quickly overlooked when she did her bell tricks, playing any number to ten separate from the rest. We requested that she play just three bells and listened incredulous to three separate and distinct bells chiming from ankles loaded with hundreds.

An American friend organized a *tamasha* for us in the Shalimar gardens, world-famed for the "Pale hands I loved" line from the "Kashmiri Song," and he hired as dancers nautch girls who had returned from the coronation of the new Maharajah of Kashmir. With tingling excitement we anticipated the picnic which was a total flop. The performers were mediocre and the once lovely gardens were neither well pruned nor properly cultivated.

We were luckier with nautch lessons we took in Lahore from Pundit Hira Lal, a learned scholar and born teacher. For a week we took rewarding daily lessons from that authority on the traditional nautch of India.

We tried unsuccessfully in Quetta to copy the nautch turns of a bazaar dancer. The tiny performer, wearing a nose ring so heavy that it was partially supported by a chain hooked over the ear, whirled with incredibly fast turns while rapidly oscillating the fanny, a trick none of us could master. When we hired the bazaar dancers to pose for movies, we found that they were boys, not girls, because in that Mohammedan community females were forbidden by law to perform in public. In the crowd, gathered to gape at our movie-making, I saw an old man weighted with two Baluchistan rugs that I coveted. Abdul did my bargaining and as always paid a price that shamed me, though I still enjoy using the rugs.

Twice on the Orient tour I saw authentic and exciting dancing by large groups of aborigines. Each time the tribesmen were called from distant villages to perform for me in a central location; both times I traveled miles to reach the rendezvous. The second gathering, late in the tour when we were playing an engagement at Manila, was arranged on orders from General Leonard Wood, Governor General of the Philippines, who impressed me at public occasions and in private conversations as one of the greatest human beings I have ever met. Because of his understanding and generous co-operation, we saw truly magnificent dances of the Igorot, the Bontok, Ifugao, and the Apayao, the head-hunting tribes of the hill country. Each tribe sent its best dancers who, for one whole day, performed for us at the Officers Club at Baguio. In the evening, the tribesmen, who had somehow found a liquor supply, danced with wild and primitive abandon around a huge bonfire. We had to drive through one night to reach Baguio, and back another to catch our ship from Manila, but the war dances,

hunting dances, courtship and wedding dances that we saw
were worth every minute of lost sleep.

The first aboriginal dances I saw with Boshi Sen, a Calcutta friend. He and I, with Abdul as bearer, went far up-
country to see the Santals, aborigines of the Chota Nagpur
district where the Rajah had ordered the best dancers from
several villages to assemble. From morning straight through
sunset a group of sixty men danced while, on the sidelines,
women rhythmically swayed and chanted. The dances were
stunning and the effect of the unique accompaniment was
hypnotic.

We shook off the trancelike state and left by *gharri* for
the sleeper to Calcutta, where I was scheduled to leave for
another adventure. We wakened the following morning to find
that our sleeper had been shuttled to a spur in the night and
we were at Purulia, two hundrd miles from Calcutta. An en-
terprising friend of Boshi's found us a Model-T Ford and a
driver, and supplied us with tinned gasoline for a wild ride.
We literally took off across country broken by neither road
nor cattle track, and only my strong topee kept my skull
from being cracked by the top of the car which I hit with
regularity throughout the ride over hillock and hummock. At
a wayside junction we boarded the Bombay-to-Calcutta mail
train which took me back only just in time to change stations
and start with Doris Humphreys for Darjeeling.

Leaving behind the overwhelming heat of Calcutta we
rode a train until three in the morning and changed to one
that jerked upward to eight thousand feet, where cold struck
us. The second night in borrowed warmery we rode by horse-
back to see Mt. Kanchenjunga at dawn, an experience of un-
surpassed beauty. We started back through pine forests starred
with pink magnolia trees in full bloom, and then shuddered
over the narrow paths we had nonchalantly crossed in the
dark. Mountain tops were below us. Had the Tibetan boy

leading my horse made one false move, I could have taken tea right off the cultivated plantations that covered plateaus a half mile down, down, down.

Our second reason for going to Darjeeling was to see monastery dances, one of which had been continuously passed from generation to generation for 2700 years. An impressive general of the British border police arranged a sensational exhibition by dozens of dancing lamas of the Bhutan monastery. The intricate and age-old dances were accompanied by gigantic gongs and diverse drums and by bronze horns that were fifteen feet long.

Another group of vigorous and dramatic men dancers performed at a Javanese party given for us by the Sultan of Djok-jakarta. We sat with our host in a semicircle of gilt chairs, and behind us were regal and exquisite women, the ladies of the court, relatives and wives of the Sultan. The performance, in progress when we arrived, continued for ten hours, and I could have stayed on for ten days the dancing was so strong, so beautiful in line and movement, deeply satisfying in every way.

We were then on a ten-day stretch of one-night stands in Java after an opening week in Soerabaya where Ruth contracted a bad case of "parrotinitis." She went off on a bird-buying debauch and at one time had twenty-seven brilliantly colored birds in our bathroom. These were for a dance in which she was to be a birdseller with two ornamental bird cages slung from a yoke across her shoulders, and live birds perched along the yoke and on her wrists. We tried to rehearse the action at the hotel taking the birds from bathroom to garden where in the flash of a wing every bird that could get loose was off toward the blue sky. Ruth gave up the idea after she had spent a flock of money and we had lost every bird but a white cockatoo, Dada, who for twenty-five years afterward lived the life of a pampered parrot as Ruth's prized pet.

In Java I organized a trip to climb the volcano Bromo,
not too active at that time of year. Strok, short and fat and
out of training, agreed to go with us, to our surprise, since
he loudly and frequently proclaimed that his only interests
in life were women, cold cash, and chilled champagne in that
order.

Ten of us drove to Tosari, a hamlet six thousand feet above
sea level, and blessedly cold after the sweltering heat we had
been enduring. From the mountains we descended by horse-
back to a flat sand sea that was the filled crater of an extinct
volcano. The native boys leading our horses spoke no English
and we had no voice in our direction, speed, stops or starts,
but just hung on and prayed. From the edge of the narrow
trail there was a precipitous drop of more than a thousand
feet, and Strok, the color of ripe Roquefort, tried to bribe his
horse boy to turn around and head back to the hotel. The
boy paid no attention and seemed to take fiendish joy in running the horse so near the edge that one foot went over and
started a small landslide which set Strok to cursing in several
of the many languages he spoke.

At the base of Bromo we faced a climb by foot, and Strok
struck. Ruth stayed behind with him and coaxed, physically
pulled and prodded until they finally joined the rest of us
leaning over the rim. Great clouds of smoke shot up from
the inverted cone and I peered down in awe at lava heaving
in ripples. Suddenly above the deafening roar of Bromo, I
was aware of Strok's voice right in my ear as he mouthed, "Do
you consider dis vort while?" He never understood why we
expended time, money, or physical energy for that experience
which fell into none of his three classifications of the de-
sirables of life.

I also thought it was "vort while" to go to Indo-China where
I pushed through some bookings in order that I might see
native dancing and Ankor-Vat. When houses in Saigon were

poor and box offices bad, Strok looked at me with I-told-you-so eyes, but I didn't care. Though the time element prevented us from going to Ankor-Vat, we saw dancing we'll never forget, for which we risked our necks.

We were invited to Pnom-Penh on the birthday of the King of Cambodia whose royal ballet was to appear at the natal celebration. Ruth, Doris, Jeordie Graham, Charles, and I started for the party at four in the morning, and in six hours of driving crossed four rivers on feeble rafts. Ruth, frightened of automobiles anywhere, kept saying, "God is love, God is love," until we reached the far bank each time. Millions of gnats filled the air and it was impossible not to breathe in a few. After sunup we all were queasy from the almost unbearable heat, and Charles got something in his eye that swelled to baseball size. The rest collapsed at a Pnom-Penh hotel while I went through the museum and the bazaar where I bought a Cambodian dancer's mask for a number I was planning for Jeordie. Finally I, too, succumbed to the heat and was violently nauseated at the hotel.

We pulled ourselves together by late afternoon and went to the palace for the anniversary show given in a pavilion open on three sides. Assorted insects attacked us, and to protect ourselves we wrapped blankets around feet and legs, turned collars up, and hat brims down. The enchanting performance was worth the suffering. A continual display of fireworks lighted palace buildings decorated with long silver finials and lacquered pillars, and the dancers were so fascinating that for four hours we sat transfixed, forgetting the fatigue and heat of the day, oblivious to nibbling gnats.

The return to Saigon in the dark was a nightmare during which we ran into chickens and dogs, and killed one small pony. Night birds dashed themselves to death against the windshield, and from the side swooped into our faces. The driver was drowsy, and Ruth and I in the front seat took turns stuffing pieces of chocolate into his mouth each time he seemed to nod.

Few rigors we endured to see dancing were tougher than our own performances in Ceylon when the rains came, in torrents, cascading like Niagara Falls. On the clear fair night of our opening, an enthusiastic audience filled Colombo's Public Hall but by morning the monsoon had started, and our second-night house was only a third full. Business was off for our twelve-day run and we felt terrible about the total receipts until the manager told us that in spite of the weather we had topped the gross done by Pavlova's company.

Pictures had given me the idea that Burmese dances were static, but a group of girls in Rangoon exploded that myth by moving like Russian Cossacks. They performed intricate steps at top speed to the accompaniment of drums and gongs and the patter of two *loobyets* who seemed to be clowns or jesters but were what the name means—"encouragers." Encouragement from the audience sometimes took tangible form and one charming little dancer raised an eyebrow over the denomination of a bill tossed at her. The gay blade who threw the money shouted out, "What do I get for that?" and the dancer, calmly tucking the folded bill in her bodice, called back, "Only a receipt."

We had not intended to program any Indian-theme dances in Burma or India but, in Rangoon, encouraged by Strok, Ruth gave her *Nautch Dance* and *Black and Gold Sari* that were received with wild acclaim. Burma's most celebrated dancer, U Po Sein, took such a fancy to our whole company that he had his own dressmakers and costume people make costumes for our Burmese ballet at his home. He supervised our shopping, danced for us, and volunteered to give us lessons for a fee. He complimented us all and assured Ruth that, except for his own, her hands were the loveliest and most expressive in the world. The rest of us in the company were amused by his exception to which we didn't subscribe since Ruth's famous hands had inspired poets, artists, and sculptors of renown.

Rabindranath Tagore, winner of the Nobel Prize in Literature, talked seriously to Ruth about staying in India to infuse the young people of his following with her vision of the dignity and beauty of their native dances. These had deteriorated, through years of British rule, into the hands of illiterates and moral outcasts. A renaissance of dance in India dated from the Denishawn tour and was largely due to Ruth's performances of East Indian dances that showed what a real artist with culture and spirituality could do with the raw material.

We played for four months in India, giving a hundred performances in sixteen cities. Ruth's *Nautch* and *Sari* numbers were so popular that she did them on every bill and Doris often said, "Why do the rest of us bother to dance in this hot weather? Miss Ruth could do a dozen nautches and a dozen repetitions of *Sari* and fill the time, and that's all the audiences want, anyway."

The thrill of our success in India has not lessened in memory. *The Death of Adonis* was a hit everywhere, and in Bombay we stopped the show with *Xochitl*, the ballet I created for Martha Graham and was doing on tour with her sister, Jeordie. We were a smash in Bombay for seventeen days, on one of which we grossed 6000 rupees. Big box offices and cheering audiences are stimulating anywhere, anytime.

I have been lionized in my time but only once have I been presented with the skin of a leopard, shot by a fan in Bombay. The young hunter, a Parsee, came backstage after a performance to say that his physical culture club members were much impressed with my physique. They asked me to an exhibition in which most of the members of the club went through fairly routine gym stunts, and my leopard-skin friend displayed muscle control, especially of abdominal muscles, that was more fantastic than similar feats I had seen in North Africa. At the conclusion of the meet I was ceremoniously given a silver medal inscribed *Presented to Ted Shawn—by the Bombay Physicalture [sic] Society.* For what, they never specified.

A royal command to go to Hyderabad for five performances followed a sumptuous party given for us at the Bombay palace of the Nizam of Hyderabad. His Exalted Highness had not been at his own party but we looked forward to entertaining for the richest man in the world, owner of all utilities and every square foot of Hyderabad with its mines, gold and diamond. Not unreasonably we figured that five commands for such royalty might result in a sparkling gift to us.

Our expectations of a priceless present from an admiring Nizam rose when a diplomatic attaché told us of the royal treasure house, well surrounded by moat and sentinel. A snake specialist, immune to viper venom, was custodian of the inner chamber where live cobras were let loose among the coffers. Those incorruptible reptile watchmen were caged whenever privileged guests goggled at diamonds and rubies and emeralds which it amused the Nizam to pour from bin to bin with sugar scoops.

The Nizam was the center of babble, not baubles, when I first saw him through a crack of my dressing-room wall at the commercial theater where we gave the five commands. The crude building, hardly what we anticipated as showcase for our talents, was thatch-roofed, and its side walls were corrugated iron.

On opening night, as I was just beginning to make up, I was rocked by a racket: blend of a single hysterical voice, running feet, and thunderous hammering. Abdul, sent to investigate, reported that the voice was that of the Nizam who seemed to be having the theater rebuilt. Abdul wasn't far wrong. Through my peephole I saw carpenters building a framework of two-by-fours as on-stage purdah for members of the harem. When the primitive hencoop was completed we were issued orders to stay in our dressing room until given royal permission to come forth.

My vantage location enabled me to give the company an eyewitness report of the harem's arrival in five Rolls-Royces. The women scuttled from automobiles to stage door through a sort of tunnel of sheets held high by attendants. With the Nizam ceaselessly trumpeting warnings at the women not to look to right, to left, or at a man, they were herded to purdah.

The Pasha Begum, his queen, with her retinue entered the royal box in the theater proper. That box was entirely covered with cheesecloth to make it purdah and a second royal box was occupied by legitimate heirs to the throne and their attendants. The court children, skittish as baby chicks and shabbily dressed, looked like a group from a charity organization.

I was no more shocked by them than by His Exalted Highness, a thin man with a fanatic expression heightened by a stubble of whiskers. He was dressed like the poorest of his subjects in a tight Mohammedan coat with a button missing; flimsy cotton trousers worn with socks which didn't match, and shoes that badly needed a shine. When I was allowed out into the wings, I saw the richest man in the world take his place on a kitchen chair placed stage right. Two rows of chairs, totaling thirty, were set up for his native staff and the British corps, military and diplomatic.

Hastily we revised action because the Nizam had us blocked with his hencoop on one side and by his entourage on the other. We had no way to enter or exit downstage and nothing was left of our stage setting but a backdrop. Under his direction our black velvet side curtains had been drawn up into the flies.

Our young American girls, barefooted and slim-limbed, de-

lighted His Exalted Highness who began to call out "Bravo"
and "Very beautiful" and "Divine!" After a few such excla-
mations, a voice like that of a macaw came from the Begum's
gauze-covered box, and Abdul translated roughly that the
queen was threatening her lord and master with "Wait until
I get you home!"

During a serious and emotional dance, another squawk came
from the Begum's box, and a native dignitary, wearing a white
uniform set off by colossal gold epaulets and a gold sword,
charged across the stage through the dancers. He discreetly
put his ear to the cheesecloth, then bowed toward the box and
made a second stage crossing to the complete confusion of
the Denishawn girls. One minute later the Admiral, as' we
nicknamed him, made his third stage crossing, holding a
bottle of soda pop in each hand. With face averted, he thrust
the bottles through an opening in the cheesecloth, and for
the fourth time crossed the stage to his seat.

Grotesque masks worn in my *Siamese Ballet* perturbed
the Nizam who kept up a loud and rapid fire of "Those
awful creatures. Horrible things! I don't like this, it frightens
me," but he didn't order us to stop as he might have. Later
he was completely routed when I danced with a long sharp
spear that swished too close to his mortal and vulnerable
ankles. Supreme being or not, the Nizam climbed to the back
of his chair and sat feet-in-the-seat until I exited with my
spear.

The royal concubines left the theater with the same warn-
ings from the Nizam that marked their entrance and then
Ruth and I were called out to be presented to His Exalted
Highness.

The second night was wilder than the first because the
women in both purdah boxes chattered constantly like so many
magpies, crows, and jays. The third night was more con-
fusing than the preceding two. The Nizam, in a moment of

excitement, tipped backward in his chair and had to be righted by his knights. The Admiral, serving pop, by then had been on stage so much that we thought of him as a member of our regular cast. The stage squatters, slowly encroaching on our territory, had us vaulting over them to make entrances and excusing ourselves to get past them with rushing exit leaps.

After every performance the Nizam in exaggerated Oxford English was extravagant in his praise of our company. He showered us with compliments but didn't invite us to the treasure chamber to play with scoops of his rubies and pearls. Little by little we learned that the richest man in the world was regarded as the stingiest. We found out that the Grand Vizier had arranged the Bombay palace party of which the Nizam would never have approved.

The parsimonious and greedy nature of the Nizam was perfectly exemplified by the theater arrangement. The most powerful of oriental potentates was actually making money on our command performances. As theater owner with a percentage contract, he had even figured how to take more profit from ticket sales to commoners by arranging stage seating for an entourage of seventy, give or take a wife.

The fourth night of our run was on a Mohammedan holiday and members of the European colony made up a quiet and appreciative audience. The last night was bedlam. The harem, which previously had attended in shifts, arrived en masse for our farewell performance. Their exodus followed two hours of noise and confusion, and again we went on stage for our nightly session with the Nizam. Our eyes gleamed when we saw that his equerry held a package. Perhaps the stories of stinginess were exaggerated. Maybe we were going to receive a jewel, a trinket.

The Nizam outdid himself in saying how wonderful, magnificent, beautiful, and incomparable we were. While he talked we sized up the package. It was more than an inch thick, about eight by ten in width and length, rounded at the edges like the velvet jewel boxes for necklaces.

At the end of the Nizam's lengthy speech of appreciation, he motioned the equerry to step forward and said that here was a small token of esteem, a present for us. We made jack-knife bows and galloped to our dressing room with the prized package, having previously agreed to divide any largesse fifty-fifty. Only the power of the Nizam restrained us from running after him and hurling at his head our gift volume of poems composed by His Exalted Highness, the Nizam of Hyderabad, himself, and inscribed with gratitude to Ruth St. Denis and Ted Shawn.

●●●

15

Out of the East

N I was recovering from dengue fever when the first copy of my book *The American Ballet* turned up in our Singapore mail on June 30, 1926. I ran to my room, shot the bolt, and read the book from cover to cover, shaking whether from excitement or fever weakness, I couldn't tell. I was deeply affected by the book's introduction that Havelock Ellis had written, and found unfamiliar my own words that I hadn't seen or thought about for nearly a year.

The contract had been signed when I expected to have the summer of 1925 for leisurely writing. Then the Orient tour developed and I had to meet the publisher's deadline as best I could with no free time, much less leisure. I dictated the first five chapters in a drawing room of the train that took us from New York to Seattle, using my lecture notes for source

material. Ara Martin, a dancer in the company, took the short-
hand and, while we played the Seattle dates, typed the first
draft, my rewrite, and a final clean copy that I mailed to the
publisher. Aboard ship from Seattle to Yokohama, the book
was finished and I mailed the last chapters from Japan.

"Yes" is a word that has backfired on me many times
when I agreed to a bright idea. Before we left for the Orient
I told *Dance Magazine* editors that I would send an article
a month while we were away. That commitment meant I had
to turn out three thousand words every thirty days, in the
midst of performing, sight-seeing, traveling, studying native
techniques, creating new dances. Many of the articles were
written on small ships: "Dancing in Burma" aboard the S.S.
Ellora from Rangoon to Calcutta; "Dancing in Ceylon"
aboard the S.S. *Adolph von Baeyer* from Colombo to Singapore, and my monthly pieces were mailed from remote ports
for eighteen consecutive months in which I never missed a
deadline or an issue.

As early copies of *Dance Magazine* carrying my series were
delivered to me, I opened wrappers with misgivings because
of a bad experience with the old *Theatre* magazine. The editor
had published "The Power of Beauty" without changing a
word of my text but, without my consent, had headed the
article with "Is Nudity Salacious?" using profuse illustrations of me as Adonis. *Dance Magazine*, happily, used suitable headlines and illustrations, and took no editorial lib-
erties with the written material. The articles, with additional
information that I wrote to amplify the subjects, were assembled and published as a book in 1929 under the title *Gods
Who Dance*.

The writing I did in the Orient was not all sent to editors
and publishers. By December 1925 our bookings ahead were
so solid that we realized we wouldn't be back in the United
States by the summer of '26, and I outlined curricula for sum-

mer courses at the various Denishawn schools, and advised
the managers of our change of plans. Before we left America
I had hired someone to go over our press clipping scrapbooks and alphabetically list the name of every newspaper in
which our names had ever appeared and, where possible, the
names of reviewers. Six envelopes were addressed for each paper or person in readiness for broadsides that I sent from the
Orient. I had no way of knowing then that our tour was
going to be extended into a second year but I was well aware
that the public was fickle and forgetful. A dance company
out of sight of its audience is soon out of mind and I was
determined that we would suffer no such fate. I mailed a bul-
letin for mimeographing from each major country we visited
and kept our names alive through stories that appeared regularly in newspapers across the United States.

We kept our cameras busy in order to supply photographs,
too. I took pictures of Ruth at the glorious Temple of Heaven
in Peking, and while she was posing on the altar of Heaven
she conceived the dance *White Jade* with which she enchanted
audiences for years.

In Singapore we put on newly assembled Malay costumes
and were photographed in them at the palace of the Sultan of
Johore. In Burmese costumes we made an excursion to the
Royal Lakes and were photographed sitting in a primitive
boat with the Shwe Dagon Pagoda reflected in the water.

For our pictures taken at the Taj Mahal, Ruth was costumed as the lady for whom it was built, and I as the Shah.
We posed in broad daylight but Ruth and I in the wee
hours bribed our way into the grounds to see the sun rise over
the historic building. Some miles outside of Jubbulpore the
girls were photographed at a deserted Hindu temple, remark-
ably well preserved for an edifice built in the eleventh century.
At the same location we made movies and atmosphere stills

of the girls filling *lotahs*, washing saris in a stream, and going through the daily routine of village life.

Partly for press pictures and partly for fun—what a mistake that was—we hired eighteen camels to ride at Karachi. The photographs were impressive but a bicycle ride over a stubble field is smoother than a jaunt by camel. The mahout of a herd of work elephants bathing in a Ceylon river accepted a tip and let us pose in rotation on the back of one patient pachyderm.

I started to reread *Kim* in Lahore when I found that my hotel window overlooked the square where the cannon called *Zamzama* stands. Dressed in full Pathan regalia, I had myself photographed astride the cannon. Also I read the rest of *Kim* as nearly as possible on the very sites described in the book because from Lahore our itinerary roughly followed Kim's progress. Throughout the tour I read books by Dhan Gopal Mukerji and other Indian writers, and by Western authors who wrote about the areas in which we were to travel.

Early in the Indian tour I began to prepare myself for the creation of the *Cosmic Dance of Siva*. I read books on the theology of Siva, talked at length about the subject with scholarly men, and studied painting and sculpture representing the deity. The preparation for the final production was long and thorough.

Lily Strickland, whose published music we already had used for dances, was living in Calcutta where we met and discussed the Siva score which I commissioned her to write. I searched everywhere for proper accoutrements. At the Cawnpore bazaar I bought the first silver pieces of a two-hundred-dollar collection of virgin silver that was assembled into the Siva costume I designed. Silver pieces, gathered from dozens of bazaars, were soldered for me by a silversmith at Calcutta. Delhi woodcarvers were noted for their craftsmanship and I went to the best shop and showed pictures of various bronze

natarajas, figures of Siva as King of Dancers. I indicated, quite
clearly I thought, the size wooden ring I wanted for background of the figure. After hours of talk, the carver said he
understood me and then when I went to pick up the ring,
regretted that they couldn't carve a human figure life-size! He
had missed the whole point since I was to be the human figure
and wanted from him only the ring of flames always shown
in the background of the *nataraja* sculptures. I finally had the
ring made at a Calcutta foundry and machine shop. The drum
for the role I bought in a Tibetan bazaar at Darjeeling. It
was typical of those carried by beggars of India, an hour-glass
drum made by joining two human skulls at the top. I used
that macabre drum for every performance of the *Cosmic Dance
of Siva* through the last revival of Jacob's Pillow in the fifties.

Boshi Sen was a disciple of the Vedanta cult and took me
to Allahabad where he asked a swami to tell me about Siva.
The swami spoke lyric English and his words soared and
burst into rockets of glory, sparkled and spouted like fountains in the sky. My previous studies of Siva and the swami's
exposition convinced me that I had taken on quite a nifty
subject for a solo in which I would try to dance the creation,
preservation, destruction, reincarnation, and ultimate salvation
of the universe. I turned to Boshi and said, "What an awful
fool I've been. Who am I that I should dare attempt this task
that's beyond human doing?"

"You don't have to do it," Boshi answered. "Make your
body an instrument and remove your petty self from it, and
Siva will use your body to dance through. You will not be
dancing, you, the little personal Ted Shawn, but Siva will
dance—if you ask him to." And so it was, and I never gave
a performance of that dance without consciously asking Siva
to take possession of my body to use as an expression of the
power and the beauty and rhythm of his being, and the dance
never failed to reach its audience with power.

The picture-taking of me in Siva costume and setting was an ordeal. With the ring, the costume, and performing platforms in a small truck, trailing our car, we drove three hours down the east coast of India, south of Madras. The paraphernalia was reloaded on barges that were poled to a bayou where the Siva temples were located. Hot sun hammered at us and humidity seeped into every pore. Brother St. Denis directed native porters while Ruth found shade of sorts, and I stripped and then stretched the costume over my damp flesh. Brother took movies and stills of me against the real Siva background and the stage set. My head was protected from the sun by a cloth-of-gold turban topped with the silver crown that scorched my hands when I reached up at last to take it off. Brother had to dash cold water on the crown and me while I lay panting as close to heat prostration as I have ever been.

The dance itself I rehearsed at every chance and Mary Hay's mother often came to see the Siva rehearsals in Manila where General Caldwell, Mary's father, was commander of Corregidor. At that time I was trying out dark make-up in humidity so high that I looked like a sundae dripping with chocolate sauce. In spite of the make-up difficulties, Mrs. Caldwell was fascinated by Siva and arrived one day with five officers, saying, "Oh, Ted, I have talked so much about it that I do hope you're going to rehearse your Queen of Sheba dance today." I'll never forget the faces of those officers. They were won over by the dance, however, when they found that Mrs. Caldwell had been just a little off as to its title and subject.

At Kandy in Ceylon's hill country, we arrived at festival time and the pilgrim processions made the place a paradise for dancers. Little troupes danced everywhere, day and night. There I saw a trick which I incorporated into *Momiji-Gari* at the place where the demon breathed fire into the face of the general. Koshiro told me that this was done for hundreds of years in Japan until a later-day demon had his teeth blown out and the fire-breathing was abandoned.

Abdul paid ten rupees to the Kandy festival fire-breather and found out that a cloth with which the man wiped his mouth really concealed the fire-maker, a short piece of bamboo. It was screened at both ends and contained live coal and pith and a certain kind of incense. The bamboo stick was inserted into the mouth, burning coal end first, and the performer breathed on the coal that ignited the pith which made the incense first smoke, then flame. By trial and error and using up hundreds of chunks of bamboo, I mastered the trick reasonably well, but the gadget was unpredictable on tour. I would be able to breathe realistic fire in Chicago and Emporia, and then the trick would fail me in Nashville and New York. Anyway, it was a good idea and I kept my teeth.

We hired the best troupes of festival dancers to give us lessons and Charles and George and I struggled with complicated rhythms that, with authentic costumes bought in Kandy, we used in the *Singhalese Devil Dance* which I choreographed for our American tour. One of the Kandy dancers was Guneya, now acclaimed as the most distinguished dancer of Ceylon where a postage stamp carries his name. When I presented the National Dancers of Ceylon in their American debut in 1958 at Jacob's Pillow, Guneya identified himself in many of the 1926 snapshots we took of Kandyan dancers.

Several new dances were already in the repertoire by the time we arrived in Ceylon and others, like Siva, were being completed. While there, I created *Chouer Danse* for Ernestine Day, Jeordie, and Ann Douglas and the dance came through complete with no need for reworking. So often light works take form effortlessly and effectively. *Chouer* remained in the Music Visualization section of Denishawn and, through the years, was taught to hundreds of Denishawn pupils.

A postponement of a Java engagement gave us a Singapore

layoff, the first full week free in nearly a year. Those seven days were busy ones in which we rehearsed long hours finishing the Burmese ballet and a new dance for Jeordie and me as respective representatives of *Danse Sacre et Danse Profane.* We completed a Chinese number, *General Wu Says Farewell to His Wife,* that later we dared to première in Hong Kong where our courage paid off because the work was an immediate hit.

Clifford Vaughan, our pianist and arranger, sat in on the dance lessons we took in the Orient and attended various dance performances. Everywhere he extracted rhythms and harmonies and melodic themes for his oriental compositions that provided accompaniments for most of the dances we offered in the United States following our tour of the East. Vaughan's music was composed primarily for piano and Western orchestral instruments, but as we traveled we made a collection of oriental instruments: gongs, bells, reed pipes, and drums. In Batavia we bought an *acklung,* a cumbersome thing made of bamboo rods, that when crated looked like a baby grand piano. The *acklung* almost finished off Strok who was already apoplectic about the increased cost of transporting our baggage to which we continually added with props, décor, furniture, and screens.

Fabrics, though they took up less room than many of our purchases, weighed heavily and were expensive to ship. I simply couldn't resist the patterns of fabrics for which Rudyard Kipling's father was responsible. When Mr. Kipling was curator of the Lahore art museum, he encouraged young artists of India to cut new blocks for the old printing that was disappearing, and the art of hand-blocked printing was restored to the Punjab. I ordered whole sets of the prints in portiere-sized curtains, with correlated border stripes, that I expected to hang in a studio at home. Ruth took one look at the curtain stuff and appropriated it as a perfect backdrop for one of the new numbers, but years later I salvaged a few yards for the barn studio at Jacob's Pillow.

Chinese-Spanish shawls were irresistible for Ruth and me. The huge fringed shawls that were introduced into Spain from Manila actually originated in China where, in the twenties, the most lavish ones were still embroidered for the shops of Spain. We bought ours in Hong Kong and couldn't stop ourselves from investing in a dozen. Our twelve fabulous shawls were covered with finely stitched designs in glorious shades that added excitement and color to one scene in *Cuadro Flamenco*.

We returned to Japan in mid-October of 1926 and sandwiched an Imperial Theatre engagement into a provincial tour that in many ways was unsatisfactory. Not the least of our irritations was the sight of local companies trying to copy Denishawn. There *Adonis* had two men, made up like marble statues, and a flashy ensemble that twirled and whirled with a huge mirrored ball lighted by spots. The Japanese stage was "lousy" with Denishawn imitations: music, movements, costumes. But no credit was given to us, much less royalties or copyrights paid.

Strok was a constant source of trouble during the last weeks in Japan. He wanted to cut our guarantee for the tour of the provinces and one night in Tokyo tried to force his terms on me when I was waiting in the wings for a music cue to go back on stage. I hate to have anyone talk to me in my dressing room before a performance, and if anyone not actually working the show speaks to me backstage I am either coldly silent or violently abusive. Strok loosed a rage that took his breath away and, incidentally, calmed him down once and for all.

Friends from the first Tokyo engagement warmly welcomed us on our return. Koshiro graciously watched my rehearsals of the condensed version of *Momiji-Gari*, and himself danced every single role while I took 16-mm. footage that was invaluable as reference when we went into final rehearsals at Denishawn in Los Angeles.

The day of our last Tokyo performance I spent more than eight hours in costume. Early in the day I put on the Lady Sarashima robes, make-up, and high geta, and carrying costume fans went to a commercial photographer where I posed alone and with Koshiro. After a round trip to the Imperial Theatre where I made elaborate and intricate changes of make-up and wardrobe, I was photographed in the Demon costume with its wig that trailed behind me like a black snake. I bolted a quick supper before I had to get into my first costume for our own farewell program.

It thrilled us to see a Tokyo performance of Bugaku, the ancient court dances that had not been given the year before. Then we had had to be content with an invitation to see the costumes and the instruments in the music department of the Imperial household. The costumes, modeled for us by learned professors on the Emperor's music staff, were even more gorgeous than the Noh costumes which had seemed to us to be the ultimate in elegance, in texture and color. Many of the Bugaku costumes were centuries old and a book of costume plates, superbly painted, made it possible to duplicate any costume that was too old to wear longer.

During the thirteen months between our first and second Tokyo engagements, Mrs. Ayukawa, an artist whose husband was a member of the theater staff, went daily to the Imperial household and made the first and only copy of the Bugaku costume volume. That priceless book, presented to us by Mr. Ayukawa when we left the Imperial the second time, is in the Denishawn Collection at the dance archives of the Public Library in New York.

Dozens of friends from the Tokyo dance world joined the throngs that saw us off at Yokohama in mid-November. They

bowed on the dock and we waved from the rail of the S.S.
Korea Maru, and threw bright-colored paper streamers back
and forth from ship to shore. The formalities over, we relaxed
and settled in for a nineteen-day voyage home.

Aboard ship I edited our movies, pasted still pictures in
albums, and prepared the cussed customs declaration with
Brother St. Denis. Tons of things had been shipped ahead
but we had added props, costumes, and instruments for the
numbers we had been premièring as we toured. For some
dances, like *Momiji-Gari*, we had to have duplicate props for
the hundred one-night stands ahead. The fans, for instance,
were so fragile that a dancer often used up two a night and
it was necessary to have replacements literally by the hundreds.

Although I explained the reason for having the hundreds
of identical fans, the United States Customs Inspector insisted on seeing every fan. He took each fan from its box, removed the paper band, unwrapped the tissue paper and opened
the fan wide: then he reversed the process with almost the
precision of the Japanese packager. Through the tedious and
time-consuming examination, I stood by quietly seething.

At San Francisco, Ruth and the others cleared personal luggage and hurried down to Los Angeles to get ready for the
shakedown opening the following week. I was left behind with
more than two hundred pieces of theatrical baggage and the
thorough customs inspector. He and I spent thirty-six hours
toiling over trunks, crates, and lists. At the end of our ordeal,
I pointed out to him that the new things already in use could
be called "tools of our trade" and so were duty-free as I understood the ruling. The little man listened solemnly, and after
two hours of addition, subtraction, and multiplication, he told
me that the total duty was $750, just half of the sum I had
expected to pay. I was so fatigued by the long check and so
relieved by the result that I almost wept and nearly kissed

the quiet inspector but managed to control myself on both counts.

We tried the new program in southern California with new *Music Visualizations*, and a large section called *Gleanings from Buddha Fields:*

Japan	*Momiji-Gari*
	White Jade
China	*General Wu Says Farewell to His wife*
Java	*Serimpi*
	Shadow Puppet Play
India	*Cosmic Dance of Siva*
	Nautch Finale

Heralded through reports of our triumphal Orient tour as exponents of dances of the mysterious East, we started a long pull of one-night stands on January 3, 1927—at Cheyenne, Wyoming.

···

16

Folly and the Follies

N I enrolled for extension courses at the University of Wisconsin while touring with a Ziegfeld Follies company which was an education in itself.

Ruth and I agreed to go off with the Follies for one reason: money. The Ziegfeld New York company, with its stars like Fannie Brice, Eddie Cantor, and W. C. Fields, played only half a dozen big cities, and rights to tour a Follies in other cities and towns had been bought by George Wintz who wanted us as his headliners because of our box-office drawing power built up through seasons of playing in every state. We resisted the offer until Wintz convinced us to change our minds for a weekly salary of $3500.

After a sensational homecoming season with our oriental program from January through May 1927, we had begun to build Denishawn House in New York, and needed cash for the establishment that was to solve many of our school and production problems. By putting all of our projects in one location we provided living quarters for ourselves, studios for teaching, dormitories for students, huge areas for the preparation of productions, and storage space that would eliminate costly warehouse rental.

I had long dreamed of setting up a central headquarters where a Guild of Dancers could practice and experiment at low cost, and hoped Denishawn House would be that place. However, the guild never materialized, and, after using Denishawn House for our own purposes for several years, we lost it by foreclosure in the depression.

Construction of the house was paid for with the money we made on the long Follies tour. Ruth and I, as headlined stars, did not appear in Follies numbers but had six program spots, two solos and an ensemble number each. My ensemble choice was *Allegresse*; my solos were Spanish flamencos and *Cosmic Dance of Siva* that I knew were strong enough and had sufficient punch to stand up even in the Follies.

Allegresse was a sort of bacchanale that already was an audience-success, and had received the final accolade, praise from John Murray Anderson, well-known producer of musicals and revues. He caught the number four times in New York and told me he'd never seen a more beautiful "presentation," the theatrical term for a spectacular number.

Its ensemble group included six girls in extremely transparent violet chiffon; two girls in leopard-printed silk leotards; three men, including me, in the briefest of G strings; and Ernestine Day, swathed in an orange chiffon scarf over bareskin fleshings. In the finale, lighted to look like a pagan fountain group, Ernestine, perched in a flower-ladened basket, was held high by the three men. That number wowed every Follies' audience.

We expected my Spanish dances to be popular but hadn't counted on the reaction to *Siva*. It stopped the show at every performance and the singer-comedienne who followed me always had to wait while I, dramatically enveloped in a cloth-of-gold mantle, took just one more bow. Though the brown *Siva* make-up was laboriously scrubbed at by my dresser in the theater, I never really was quite clean afterward, and my personal laundry turned tattletale greige. Faced with a thirty-eight-week Follies tour of daily *Siva* performances, I went into brown clothes—suits, hats, and topcoats; I had shirts tailored of sepia-colored silk and my underwear dipped in chocolate-colored dye. Throughout the season I was as Siva-smudged as ever but my clothes and I no longer looked unwashed.

I couldn't bear the tedium of our daily train trips through one-night-stand country by then all too familiar to me, and decided to spend my days doing something organized and constructive. I had no college degree because of my junior year illness, and, thinking that I might work toward a B.A. with extension courses, I enrolled for psychology and French at the University of Wisconsin. I chose the former subject because as an experienced teacher, I might sometime want to use the terminology for a talk or a treatise on the *Psychology of the Adolescent Artist*.

French was a challenge I had faced before, several times. As a very young child I had had Berlitz training at Kansas City's *Alliance Française*, and then when I entered high school at eleven, a distinction I made the most of, I was incensed at being forced into a first-year French class. Brattishly I refused to hand in papers or to do homework, and naturally I was failed. In Denver, years later, I spent a few weeks mumbling with French records, and long afterward started first-year French again with a poet friend, Jean Galeron. Of course, I didn't follow through to University of Wisconsin credits but doing my lessons and assignments helped to fill boring hours that might otherwise have been wasted. I still haven't progressed to second-year French, and the only degree I hold is an honorary one conferred on me by Springfield College.

I did increase my vocabulary on the Follies tour with words I never was able to use afterward. I thought that I had heard my share of rough language and foul jokes before I joined the Follies company but that wasn't so. Through paper-thin dressing-room partitions I unavoidably eavesdropped on the chorines, and heard conversations, phrases, and epithets that, for the first month of shock, kept my eyes a-pop, my jaw dropped.

The girls were wined and dined everywhere by local playboys but in Corpus Christi they were engulfed by the legendary hospitality of Texas, and each girl was feted like a star. Oil and cattle millionaires took the company's arrival as a signal for a celebration that would have made a Roman holiday seem like a Sunday school picnic. Businesses were closed and the town went on a binge. Beginning with our arrival at 7 A.M., gin, served by the pitcher, was poured over ice cubes in hundreds of tumblers. Cockeyed chorus girls opened the matinee, and as they kicked across the stage, first one and then another crumbled with a moan and had to be carried to the wings. By the night show only half the chorus was there and they were only "half there." Three girls, missing at the railroad station roll call, never came back to the company but that didn't bother Wintz who had his own unique way of choosing pretty girls when others dropped out. He simply searched towns as we traveled, and picked girls from behind store counters, out of hotel lobbies, and off the streets, by saying, "You look like a Follies girl. Do you want a job?" And they always did.

During the Corpus Christi revels, we quietly swam and sunbathed on the beach at our hotel where we first met Fred Beckman who shortly after joined us as personal manager, an association that lasted three years. On the same beach I saw a girl in a bathing suit who, without an introduction, said to me, "I can stand on my head, can you?" and flipped over on the sand in an expert headstand. That was Fern Helscher, a friend on sight, and from 1935 my press agent, then the booking and personal representative of my men's group, and business manager of Jacob's Pillow until 1946.

Some of the girls in the Follies were simple and charming, though we made no lasting friendships with any of them and kept pretty much to ourselves on tour. The little lyric soprano, wife of a man on the Follies traveling staff, wore slinky gowns at the beginning of the season but her wardrobe was replaced as we went along and she grew obviously pregnant. She finally was singing torch songs in an Empire bodice with a huge hoop, and we were standing in the wings expecting every tense minute that a Follies' baby was going to be born right in a spotlight. Wise child, it arrived in a hotel room, and within a few days our soprano was back performing in skintight sequins.

One break in the monotony of the nine Follies performances a week came in January when we played an engagement in Havana where the Cubans were seething then, as ever, with political unrest. We luxuriated in resort accommodations and didn't even mind the "dumb" audiences which were hard to please with anything, and were particularly cold to my Spanish dances. After every show we managed to see natives dance *la rumba* in the raw. And it was. Long before the dance became popular in American ballrooms and night clubs, I introduced it to audiences in a quite chaste concert version with Ernestine Day as my partner. Even my mild adaptation was reviewed in the student paper at Cornell University as being "so hot it burned the asbestos curtain." Those college students should have seen the Cuban rumba gyrations that left nothing to the erotic imagination.

From Florida on up the coast, we were visited backstage by more than the usual number of "dug ups," which was what Ruth called chance acquaintances, distant relations, and former students who seemed to be forever surrounded by children with promise as dancers. Progressively as we moved north, we became busier with plans for the opening of Denishawn House. In New York State, New England, and Canada, we were within traveling distance of the staff which came for consultations. Our own plans for furnishing the house were expansive and in Montreal we bought English china, table and bath linens at Eaton's, and Sheffield tea sets, platters, and candlesticks in an auction room; in Corning, N.Y., after visiting the glass museum, we selected crystal tableware for Denishawn House.

We lived a semihome life in a Montreal apartment where we were pampered and waited on by Ruth's maid, Mary, and my valet, Douglas. Ruth and I were both suffering with bad colds and one night to add injury to insult, I dislocated my sacroiliac during performance. I could hardly get through *Siva* and expected a rebuke from Douglas who always stood in the wings and told me off if I danced less well than he knew I could.

That night to forestall Douglas, I said, "Don't say a word. I know I was bad, you don't need to rub it in." Knowing the pain I was suffering Douglas said sympathetically, "Well, you fooled 'em, didn't you?"

I had picked Douglas up in Birmingham where he had been "body servant" for an Alabama colonel recently deceased. Mary feuded with Douglas but he was a gentle soul and faithful to me. When I received silk squares from Brother St. Denis then back in the Orient, I gave several to Douglas for pocket handkerchiefs, and, eyes bugged, he exclaimed, "Say! Dat's de best silk they is, it's crepe machine!"

He was watchdog of my weight and, down south, when I

began to bulge over my *Siva* trunks, he told me my fat was showing. I went on orange juice for three days, and lost both weight and my good disposition. After we had treated ourselves to Canadian delicacies, buttered scones and black current tarts with Devonshire clotted cream, Douglas made me step on the scales and then looked at me with reproachful eyes. That time I tried a new diet, scrambled eggs and raw tomatoes for every meal. It made me irritable but the scale indicator dropped far enough to please Douglas.

From our $3500 weekly salary Ruth and I drew the largest personal allowance we had ever taken. Since we were not under contract to a manager, we didn't have to pay out that 20 per cent commission, and funds, left over after we met the company payroll, were banked in a general Denishawn account.

I spent my personal money on a house, a dog, and an automobile. I was building and furnishing a Japanese pavilion at Westport, Connecticut, where I had bought an acre of land with an unexpected $1000 legacy. The place, on the Saugutuck River, was to be a hideaway for me and headquarters for the Denishawn summer camp-school. The dog was a collie I bought in Toronto where it was boarded until I could take it to Westport. The car was a Packard bought even though finances were running low at the end of the tour. Rationalizing that I would need an automobile for summer runs between Westport and New York, I bought the Packard in Ohio for $300 down, and we finished the tour in it. We even took a little detour to my family's old Kentucky home on the Ohio River. Cousins had spoken for most of the fine old Booth furniture still there but, from the treasure trove, I chose three heirlooms: a four-poster bed and two chairs, all now in use at Eustis.

Ruth and I both spent the Follies' money recklessly, and even loaned several thousand dollars to Brother who was buy-

ing in the Orient not only for his own bazaars but for Ruth,
and for the Westport place which was mine, not in our joint
names. Once when the Follies traveled ahead of us, I found
that I had only $5.00 in cash for a short bus hop which was
$3.00 for each of us. I asked Ruth for a dollar and, while a
patient ticket clerk waited, she turned up her purse which contained 95 cents in silver and two cents. I searched through
my pockets and found three pennies, exactly the number
we needed to make up the fare, and we boarded the bus without a cent between us, two stars making $3500 a week.

My career slowly shifted after the Follies tour, and several
events led, however indirectly, to a permanent summer dance
school, Jacob's Pillow; to the organization of an all-male company, the men's group; and to my own interest and participation in international dance affairs and exchanges. I had a long
way to go but the first faint direction indicators were set up.

The Westport studio was opened formally with an all-Jap-
anese program that we gave on two successive nights in late
July. Classes had been under way for two weeks at Westport,
where Hazel Kranz and Ernestine Day taught with me; at our
downtown New York studio where Charles Weidman and
Doris Humphreys were the teachers; and at Denishawn House
where Ruth had students and rehearsed numbers for our August performance at Lewisohn Stadium.

We concentrated on teaching and didn't go on tour in the
season of 1928–29. Ruth spent most of the winter in California, and I gave my first solo performance in New York
at Carnegie Hall against the advice of friends who urged me
to take a smaller theater. It was a good thing that I didn't
listen to the reasonables. I danced for a house that even had
standees, and my program ended with an audience reaction
akin to revival-meeting hysteria. I stood in my dressing room for
two hours while a continuous line passed through. Many dear
friends, too choked to speak, burst into tears, threw themselves

into my arms, and left without saying a word. It was a great night that changed my life because I had a sense of being established as an independent artist.

About that time, I heard of a Russian dancer, fifth-rate and unknown then as now, who was given $25,000 to produce a ballet, and I moaned, "Why doesn't somebody give me that much money for a production?" Friends laughed and said, "Because you are too damned competent and everybody knows it. They feel sorry for poor impractical Jumpupski who must be taken care of but they figure 'Shawn can manage for himself, he's *so* capable.'" I was capable only of knowing how to use the money for creative works, for artistic projects, not how to get it as a no-strings-attached subsidy.

A bitter experience with millionaires followed a harrowing trip that Mary Campbell and I were forced to take that summer when engagements overlapped. Mary, who first joined me as accompanist at Westport, was with me in Pittsburgh where a week of teaching ended on a Saturday morning. That same Saturday night we had to be in Rhode Island where Ruth and I were to dance at a private party, highlight of Tennis Week at Newport.

A chartered plane was waiting for us at the Pittsburgh airport but ceiling was zero when we reached there in torrential rain. The pilot, looking at me as if I were a moron, asked, "Which would you rather do, go on living and dancing or fly in an airplane today?" We went up and the pilot, by dodging his little open cockpit plane in and out of cloud holes, managed to miss the Pennsylvania mountains. Through lightning and blinding rain, we reached Roosevelt Field at 6 P.M., and the pilot frankly said, "This is as far as I go."

Since it was too late to get to Newport by automobile or train, the airport found us another pilot, another plane. We flew through clear weather to New London but its airport was fogged in. The pilot said, "That tears it. We'll turn back to Bridgeport and land." I protested and he said, "Boy, ten to one we're going to crash as it is." He landed on an unlighted field at West Haven and I phoned the party host who said he would have a speedboat pick us up at a landing across from his estate. Going up the Post Road lightning struck so close that the driver of our rented car was flung over the steering wheel, and the smell of scorched rubber filled the air. We turned off the highway onto a country road where a wave of ditch water washed over the car, stalling the engine. It was nearly an hour before the motor turned over, and we drove on, to the wharf. The speedboat man insisted on waiting forty-five more minutes for wind and the rain to abate, and then started off without running lights, explaining, "On the way over I was shot at by revenue men. They thought no one but a rumrunner would be out on a night like this."

Half-frozen, wind-battered, and soggy-wet, Mary and I reached the estate at 3 A.M., just as the last guest's car was pulling away from the mansion. Ruth, without partner or accompanist, had finally danced at midnight. She listened to a few bars played by the band after she asked if they knew something slow and lazy. "That will have to do," she said and, in her gorgeous nautch costume, improvised for the Newport society audience to the low-down notes of the "St. Louis Blues."

Because only one of the two artists contracted for had performed, we received just half of the fee guaranteed by the party hosts whose Dun and Bradstreet listing was $100,000,000! For such people Mary and I had risked life and limb.

They were very different from an old friend, Mrs. John Henry Hammond, for whom I gave a September lecture at the New York Three Arts Club of which she was founder-president. Through the years I had lectured and danced and furnished Denishawn student programs for organizations in which Mrs. Hammond was interested. She was always gracious and most generous with fees, and I was eager to please her with a program that would be new and different. I gave a showing of oriental textiles, describing the circumstances under which they had been purchased, and demonstrating the use of each fabric in its country of origin. The lecture was so popular that I repeated it several times for high fees that fall, and have given it occasionally since. An expanded version, "Costumes and Fabrics of the Orient," given at New York's Town Hall the next February, helped me to finance a trip to Europe. The materials bought so extravagantly have paid for themselves many times over.

Summer engagements whether at private parties or in tremendous amphitheaters seemed always to be eventful for us. Ruth and I, the first dance artists engaged to perform in the Hollywood Bowl, almost didn't make our own first curtain. We set out for the bowl about five o'clock and were trapped in traffic streaming toward it. We drove around and up and down streets until we finally explained our plight to a policeman on duty about a mile from the Bowl. He stood on our running board and cleared traffic ahead, and then had to shepherd us to our dressing rooms through a throng that was estimated at thirty-five thousand. It was a night to remember and not only because of the record-breaking attendance: two men, who carried a drunk right across stage, staggered violently against me while I waited for my first entrance cue; fire flared in a spotlight pylon; and confusion reigned at intermission while a movie crew shot Jean Hersholt going through the motions of an orchestra conductor.

Before the Orient tour we had given well-attended summer programs at the Lewisohn Stadium and, after the Follies closed, we gave three performances there to twenty thousand people each night. Seats were filled by 5 P.M., and at eight-thirty entrances were still jammed with people hoping to get in. The summer of 1929, we again packed the Stadium, and at long last I gave a performance of *Jurgen.*

Originally I had hoped to do a full-length dance drama based on James Branch Cabell's *Jurgen* and had even paid the publisher for rights. While on tour I had conferred with Mr. Cabell who, after our long discussion, said, "Really, Mr. Shawn, you know more about Jurgen than I do." My option ran out before I could find time to work on the ballet, and then my interest took another turn when I heard that Deems Taylor had written a short tone poem on the theme. He graciously agreed that I might use his music for a dance number, and when it was in shape I asked Mr. and Mrs. Taylor to a run-through rehearsal. It made them both weepy and Mr. Taylor said that he thought *Jurgen* had already squeezed every tear out of him but "You have made it all fresh, poignant, and heart-breaking to me again." I was genuinely grateful to the great American composer for his sincere approval of my choreographic efforts.

On the Lewisohn Stadium program I gave two other new ballets, *The Death of a God,* based on the legend of the Minotaur, and *Pacific 231* with powerful locomotive rhythms performed by an all-male group of twenty-one dancers. The latter work was a confirming development in my long-range planning for a men's dance group.

Alfie, Sammie, and Moe came into our lives that fall when Ruth and I began a short tour without the company. With four musicians and no scenery, just a cyclorama, we didn't think we needed traveling stagehands. But the union had a different opinion and, at New Haven, forced us to take on three backstage men: a carpenter at $100 a week, a prop man and an electrician at $85 each.

With the added staff of three, we were short $100 at the New Haven station where we had to buy tickets before the Taft Theatre paid us. The new backstage men, an unfriendly-looking trio, overheard the company manager say that we needed more cash and offered us the $100. Warm hearts beat under the grim exteriors, and we never had a more human or co-operative stage crew. Alfie and Sammie were with me again in 1930 and 1931 when I took the company out alone, without Ruth.

We played The Greenbrier at White Sulphur Springs on the day of the 1929 stock market crash, and our evening audience seemed at best preoccupied. In spite of the financial crisis, the rest of the tour went well and, during the Christmas layoff, I went to Jamaica where for $5.00 a week I rented a cottage at Ocho Rios, which was not yet *mucho fino*.

The last days of the tour were festive. For a benefit we grossed $8150 at the Boston Opera House and a local impresario had a photostat made of the box-office statement as proof of our exceptional drawing power. New England friends entertained us at luncheons and dinners and teas. One supper-party host was a newspaper editor, Max Farber, managing editor of the Hartford *Times*, who greeted us with shouts of "Extra! Extra!" and made us "buy" papers that he pulled out of a newsboy's bag slung over his shoulder. He had had a special Denishawn edition printed with banner headlines, pictures, and even a review of the performance finished less than an hour before.

In early February Ernestine and I gave the first New York performance of a rumba at a private party given by Mrs. Gerrish Milliken at her Park Avenue home. Francesca Braggiotti also danced there, and that night we dined with the beautiful Cesca and John Lodge whom she had married the previous July.

One of the guests at the party was Katherine S. Dreier, herself a pioneer in modern art, and patron of painters, sculptors, and composers. She understood and was enthusiastic about my dancing, choreography, and the principles of dance I originated.

Mid-February I was sailing for my solo debut in Berlin, and we had a gala farewell party at Denishawn House. There were 150 guests and exciting entertainment by peers and pupils.

Miss Dreier, later author of *Shawn the Dancer*; her sister, Mary Dreier; and Mary Campbell sailed with me on the S.S. *America* on February 13, 1930. Our farewell on board was just what I think such things should always be. Thirty people came to see us off, our staterooms overflowed with baskets of fruit and flowers, and I personally received twenty-five *bon voyage* telegrams. I have always liked to give and get gifts, and to make occasions of goings and comings, or anniversaries and birthdays, opening nights and première performances. It takes a point of view and really little effort to make life routinely exciting.

On the voyage to Hamburg, I slept long hours as always. The rest of the time I had my head in another Berlitz book, this one in German.

•••

17

Entr'acte

℣ Three major events highlighted 1930 for me: I gave my first solo program in Europe; performed my third version of *Orpheus;* and bought Jacob's Pillow.

My Berlin debut at the Bachsaal on March 15, 1930, followed several weeks of rehearsal at the Wigman-Schule directed by Margarete Wallmann with whom I got on well from the start. She was an imaginative and creative artist and went on to a distinguished career as choreographer first for the Salzburg Festival, then for the Vienna Opera, and later for the Teatro Colón in Buenos Aires. She is now one of the great opera directors of the world and directed the Chicago Opera's *Carmen* in the season 1959–60.

I recognized Margarete at once as a born teacher, and in time I found her to be a driving ballet mistress. Before I had been long in Germany, I persuaded her to teach at Denishawn the following year. German-modern dancing had no message for me personally but in keeping with Denishawn's clearly stated dedication to every form of dance, I felt that our students should have firsthand knowledge of European dance developments.

Wigman's reputation already was influencing and intriguing dancers in America though neither she nor an authorized Wigman teacher had yet crossed the Atlantic. Wallmann, Wigman-trained and member of the performing company, through our school, would be the first modern dancer of Germany to demonstrate and teach in the United States. Margarete was enthusiastic about the plan, and consent was given by Wigman, then teaching at the original school in Dresden.

Two days before my debut Margarete honored me with a Berlin tea to which she invited critics and feature writers of newspapers and magazines that carried Shawn photographs —several on the covers of illustrated weeklies—Shawn interviews, and quotes from the speech I made at the tea. That was an ordeal because, though I had been taking daily German lessons, I was not proficient enough to use the language. I spoke in English, paragraph by paragraph, and then, like a ventriloquist dummy, stood by while Katherine Dreier translated, segment by segment.

My debut program included the solo *Prometheus Bound* which had as its key prop a large rock to which my left wrist and right ankle were chained throughout the dance. In the United States I had been using a did-it-myself practical rock which had been left at home after I had half-killed myself on it. The prop was crudely made and though slightly padded, quite unsafe, as I found out one night when the ankle manacle tore out of its mooring. Still attached at the wrist, I sailed like a captive airplane across the rock hitting hidden supports with such force that I boomeranged back to center stage. As a

result of that accident my back was scarred for months, and
I was scared to use the rock again.

In Germany I made arrangements for the construction of
a solid rock, and the ever-thorough Germans insisted that I
take a trip to Cologne for a rock fitting. In the scenery studio
I went through my choreography in bits and pieces, being
interrupted every few minutes by a little prop-tailor who, with
tape measure and yardstick, made note of the various levels
at which I stood, sat, or leaned, as well as for placement of the
wrist and ankle manacles. The finished rock, sturdy and de-
pendable, was also Shawn-contoured.

My Berlin opening was marked by an anti-American disturbance by a few young Germans who were put out of the
theater during an intermission. For me the night was a phe-
nomenal success. The ovation after the last curtain went on
for half an hour, and hundreds in the audience surged to the
footlights, applauding and huzzaing. Before the theater could
be cleared I had to step off the stage and shake hands with
fans, ringed below the apron.

The demonstration, a mixed blessing, long delayed my
change into white tie and tails for a party that Katherine Dreier
gave for me at the Adlon. In spite of my tardiness, her distinguished guests greeted me with more cheers and with dizzy-
ing rounds of champagne toasts. In the wee hours we all
seconded someone's suggestion that we send Miss Ruth a cable
signed by everyone present, eighty names of the famed and
fortuned.

Similar memorable nights followed performances in Munich, Düsseldorf, and Cologne where the people, naturally
effervescent and ebullient, responded to my dancing with a
reaction that was electric and thrilling.

Before I had even completed my scheduled German engagements, Margarete talked to me about staying on until June
for the Third German Dance Congress, an event given over

to group dancing. Margarete had gathered together thirty solo dancers who separately would not have been able to perform at the Congress in Munich. She arbitrarily named the group *Tanzer-Collectif-1930*, and planned a dance drama based on the Orpheus legend.

The catch was that she had been unable to find a German man dancer heroic enough in stature and style for the title role. When she saw me dance, she decided that I was the man she had been looking for, the Orpheus for her Congress work. My size, in this instance, was an advantage, and I wanted to do the part because I already had portrayed Orpheus twice, once at the Greek Theatre in Berkeley in 1916 and again at the Hollywood Bowl in 1927. Regretfully, I turned down Margarete's offered honor—that's what it was—since the Congress participants were not to be paid.

As always I was budgeted to the last penny, and my engagements were to end weeks before the Congress started. There was no way for me to finance an extended stay for myself and Mary Campbell, my accompanist, and Fred Beckman, my stage manager and personal representative who had preceded us to Germany, and booked the tour. Happily, Katherine Dreier thought that the Congress opportunity was one I shouldn't pass up, and she supplied funds that made it possible for Mary, Fred, and me to stay in Germany for an additional six weeks.

When we began serious work on *Orpheus-Dionysus*, we moved into a pension within easy walking distance of the Wigman-Schule. The second day, after posing for photographs of my *Japanese Spear Dance*, I walked into the pension wearing the horrendous wig askew, and brandishing the spear. A shy little man in the main hall took one look at me, fell to his hands and knees, and, on all fours, scrambled up the steps, locked himself in his bedroom, and couldn't be persuaded to leave it for two days.

Only then were we told that the pension was a boarding-house for patients in psychoanalysis, and it was also the temporary home of a British spinster-psychoanalyst doing graduate work. She was the only guest with whom I ever had any trouble. After attending one of my solo programs and listening backstage to my fans, she asked me at dinner if I would give her a private interview. I said that I would gladly answer any question right at the table since my life was an open book. Smirking archly, she said, "Oh, I'm sure it hasn't been that uninteresting."

She finally cornered me one evening and probed like a termite, ending our conversation with, "Well, I diagnose your case as one of arrested development at a point of infantile narcissism." I made it clear that I was not a case, and tried to convince her that I did not take to myself, personally, the praise I received as performer. She was certain that when someone said to me, "You are beautiful in such and such a dance," I preened myself and smacked my lips and wallowed in the compliment as if it were intended for me as a private person.

I assured her that a dancer has to consider his body with detachment as a sculptor does clay that he models, or a painter a canvas he brushes. I explained that the dancer, as artist, does not identify with projected creations though both they and he use and inhabit the same body. The distinctions were beyond the lady psychoanalyst who had pegged me her way and did her best to alter my ego.

Margarete gave me my head with the *Orpheus* role. She understood that I was accustomed to choreographing my own dances and performing with my own company, trained by me, and let me work with Mary Campbell on scenario and music to create my own role. When the first of the four acts was completed, I danced for Margarete and gave her my ideas for the group as related to the solo part. She was an expert, and faithfully followed my requirements for all four acts, and at the same time did a magnificent job of original creative choreography for the whole company.

For reasons of diplomacy, I attended every *Orpheus* rehearsal. The thirty German solo dancers were understandably antagonistic to me, the foreigner who had been chosen for the lead role in the ballet that was to climax Congress week. Though I had thoroughly rehearsed my solo parts before general rehearsals were called, I didn't miss a single one. Wallmann, a Prussian drillmaster in the rehearsal hall, kept us for eight hours daily, and I willingly and without complaint went over and over solo and group scenes. My obvious eagerness to contribute to the group as a whole gradually changed the attitude of the other dancers who took me to their hearts. When I returned to Berlin the following year, many of them were at the railroad station to welcome me back. Both years the dancers left every rehearsal with a parting *Auf WiederShawn,* which *to them* seemed a joke that was ever fresh.

Most of the *Collectif* dancers had been influenced by Mary Wigman, and they kept telling me that certain dance developments and principles originated with her or with Rudolph von Laban, her teacher. I often refuted their claims by showing them works in print, programs or pictures that we had done in America, frequently even passing beyond the discoveries attributed to the German-moderns.

We found only two of the Congress programs at all pleasing; most of the groups danced with movements that were stark, ugly, and grotesque. Our own rehearsals made it impossible for us to go to many of the Congress discussion sessions where critic assailed critic, choreographers and dancers violently abused each other. We missed the most dramatic session during which one man attacked an artistic enemy with a straight razor with which he then tried to commit suicide.

All of the proceedings were enlivened by catcalls, hisses, and boos.

Hoots and howls gave way to reverential silence when we did our ballet. The ecstatic applause afterward was matched by press notices which agreed that Margarete's *Orpheus* was the high point of the Congress. I came off well with all but one critic who wrote that I had "a miraculous technique, marvelous rhythm, a body like a god—but no soul!"

The German compliment I most treasured came not from critic or audience but from the revered sculptor, Georg Kolbe, who had startled Margarete Wallmann with an unprecedented request to watch me rehearse. Margarete told me that he was remote, Olympian, unapproachable, and practically worshiped by Germans. She impressed me with the honor he was conferring on me and warned me not to ask to see sketches, if he did any. He sketched through rehearsal, using up page after page of a large sketch pad. Finally he asked me to hold a pose, and then signaled me when to start again. After two hours, he quietly left, taking every sketch with him. He came a second day, and at the end of rehearsal, with Margarete as interpreter, asked if I would pose for a statue. At his stunning modern studio, he did many more sketches before beginning to work with clay. I posed four hours a day for about a month; hard work, especially for a dancer who is accustomed to be on the move every minute. But I was fascinated with Kolbe's work pattern, his concentration, for he never spoke and seemed to keep his mind as busy as his rapidly working fingers.

When the statue was finished he praised what he considered to be my endless vocabulary of movements and postures. Through Margarete, as interpreter, he said that I had been the most wonderful model of his life, adding, "I am so grateful to you, is there anything in the world I can do to express my gratitude?" Intrepidly, I explained that I had been told not to ask to see the sketches but that I would like to look at them. He shouted, "Of course," and spread the hundred or more sketches of me out on the studio floor. I moaned, I agonized, I acted like a cat with catnip. I have never seen such drawings. He choreographed in pencil with power, rhythm, and beauty. When he asked, "Don't you want some of the sketches for yourself?" I was overwhelmed. He insisted, "Take as many of them as you like; all of them, if you wish." I was struck dumb. Original Kolbe drawings of that size sold for $350 in New York art galleries and I was torn between decent restraint and my eagerness to have many of his stunning works. I finally selected half a dozen and one he signed, "To Ted Shawn, von einem gedenkbaren, Georg Kolbe." That one and one other now hang in my Florida home.

I left Berlin just in time to start my summer teaching at Denishawn in New York and at Westport, which was no longer country and gave me neither expansion space nor personal privacy. During a week-end visit at Josephine Dubois's Forest Farm, I discovered that new highways had made the Berkshire Hills area more accessible to New York than when I first had visited there. By luck Josephine knew of a summer place that was for sale and I went to look at the property. Its house, which had been closed for five years, was in disrepair and the grounds were overgrown but on sight I loved the land. I sold my Japanese pavilion at Westport, and bought the place near Lee, Massachusetts, that was to become famous as my summer school and dance theater. In the house I found letterheads that read "Jacob's Pillow, a Mountain Farm—Arthur E. Morgan, Prop." Ted Shawn, Prop., used the farm that fall only for picnics and for planning improvements and for dreaming of the future of Jacob's Pillow.

That next season flashed by. Wigman herself came to America and, at her New York reception, La Argentina and Ruth and I stood at the head of the receiving line. I wrote an article about Margarete Wallmann for *Dance Magazine* and

she began her classes at Denishawn House, giving me personally invaluable critical assistance in the creation of two numbers, *Four Dances Based on American Folk Music*, and *The
Divine Idiot* which stayed for years in my solo repertoire.

Margarete signed me for a Berlin production of *Orpheus*
to be given in the late spring of 1931, and I also was contracted to Dr. Paul Schiff, head of a concert bureau, for a
solo tour of Germany and Switzerland. With spring plans
settled, I went off with the Denishawn company for a fall
tour in 1930 and, after a Christmas layoff, took a quick tour
on which I made enough money to meet the mortgage pay-
ments due on Denishawn House.

When I swung back into rehearsals at Wigman-Schule, it
seemed that I had never left Germany. The Berlin *Orpheus*
was a success but not even the shrewd and persuasive Wallmann
could get the show on the road. The cast and the symphony
orchestra required too big a guarantee to be swung by any
theater manager in Middle Europe, then impoverished.

Switzerland was exciting and I thrilled to its sights and
audiences. At Berne I was given the most sumptuous party of
my life and was ganged up on by three old friends. The hostess
at the party was the rich and scintillating Gina Vandeveer, a
leading soprano of the Berne Opera Company, who once had
studied dancing with me when she was still young Eugenia
Vandeveer of Illinois. Gina lived like a queen and entertained
royally. Her guests were diplomats and stars of stage and
opera, several of whom entertained at the supper.

The following day, Gina with Katherine Dreier and Allene
Seaman, a friend since our student days at the University of
Denver, dropped by my rehearsal studio and one of them
suggested that I end the first half of my solo program with a
number less somber and tragic than *The Divine Idiot*. They
all agreed that the audience would prefer to go out for the
grosse pause in a lighter frame of mind.

Laughing, "I know what you mean, this kind of thing. May-be, Gina, you'll remember it," I swung into *Spring, Beautiful Spring*, a class exercise created years before at my Grand Avenue studio in Los Angeles. The work was designed to give pupils a sense of flow from one phrase to another, to test their endurance in executing consecutive phrases without stopping. Gina and Katherine and Allene reacted in chorus, "That's it. Do that." I objected on the legitimate grounds that *Spring* was not a dance but only a technical exercise taught to a succession of classes as soon as the students were sufficiently advanced to try it. There was another drawback; I had no costume for any such number.

Then the three friends threw me. They liked what I was wearing, a rehearsal suit that I had designed in desperation. The year before, chilled to the marrow in unheated European halls when I wore swim trunks to rehearse, I had designed a coverall that was made of black glove silk and fitted my body like skin. The neck was high, the sleeves were long and tight, the pants flared slightly at the ankles. Again I protested that I was wearing something to keep me warm, not a stage costume. With three determined women arguing against me I hadn't a chance of winning out but about one thing I was adamant: I would not do a dance entitled *Spring, Beautiful Spring.*

Katherine Dreier came up with the title *Frohsinn* which means the essence of joy. I thought I had her when I asked, "How will I explain dancing about joy in all black?" I might have known there would be a good answer to that, and Katherine gave it: "Even in the midst of world depression, the soul of joy is unquenchable, and shines through however grim and black the gloom."

I gave up. I agreed to put *Frohsinn* on the program in the before-intermission spot but, after Switzerland, I was going to Munich, center of the most fanatic modern dance groups, and I predicted dire consequences if I danced a pattern of ballet techniques in a black practice costume. "You win," I told my friends, "but you know where to ship the body after the first German performance of this so-called 'dance.'"

At Munich the full house with two hundred student standees went wild when I did *Frohsinn*. I took seven bows and, though the dance is an endurance test, as I intended it to be for my students, I danced it again and took seven more bows. The press the next day featured *Frohsinn* as "excitingly new and the spirit of coming dance." I could laugh out loud as I read but during the encore the night before I had to suppress my mirth and shook so hard inside that I hardly had the strength to keep going: in Germany, self-acclaimed leader of modern dance, my old ballet class-exercise was laying them in the aisles!

Reprise

I returned to the United States by way of London where many doors were opened for me by Gracie Ansell, an old friend of Fred Beckman's, who had joined us at the Munich Dance Congress just a year before. It was easy to believe that Gracie had been a reigning English beauty in her youth, for she was still lovely-looking in middle age, and her charm was irresistible. In London I let her talk me into sitting for a portrait that she thought would be good publicity for me, and into giving a private performance simply because she wanted to see me dance.

Encouraged by Gracie, I agreed to pay for a pencil portrait to be done by Violet, Dowager Duchess of Rutland, mother of the beautiful Lady Diana Manners. The Duchess, who had sold many lovely sketches of her daughter at charity bazaars, was more talented in portraying women than men, a fact I learned too late. Charles Farrell was sitting for her at the same time I was, but I never saw what she did to him.

Her drawing of me is now at the Eustis house and is ever a reminder of a delightful old lady, a witty raconteur, with whom I spent four or five delightful mornings posing for a portrait that was a shocker. Like Kolbe, in one particular, the Duchess had not let me see the sketch in progress. On the day of my last sitting she asked Mary Campbell to come with me for the "unveiling." Mary and I thought the sketch the Duchess showed us was unfinished. I was then forty years old, and the pretty boy in the drawing looked younger than I had ever been. Mary tactfully told the Duchess that she thought the picture might be aged a little, and I feebly agreed. The Duchess said, "My dear boy, I know from all that you have achieved in your life and career that you must be over twenty—but this is how you look to me." Against her better judgment she did put a touch of gray at my temples, a few lines under my eyes. How little the aging helped was proved by the people who, when they saw the drawing, remarked in surprise, "I didn't know you had a son of high school age!"

Lady Cunard, Emerald to her friends, overheard Gracie say that she and the Duchess of Rutland wanted to see some of my solos, and offered her house for performance. I demurred but Lady Cunard said, "I have an enormous drawing room with one end as big as a regular stage, and I have nine bathrooms in my house." Just what she expected me to do with the latter, I couldn't imagine. Actually I used one for a dressing room that I reached by a servants' stairway along which nine Marie Laurencin paintings were hung.

Lady Cunard was determined to make an event of my program and reeled off a list of people she would ask. I had to be very insistent that, without lights or a proper stage, I would not dance for a crowd. We compromised on an invited group of nine.

Through Gracie, Anton Dolin graciously loaned me his apartment for a rehearsal and while I practiced I saw him peeking at me from a bedroom window opening onto his vaulted studio. When I finished, he called out, "What was that last music? It was fascinating." I went upstairs to change, and Mary Campbell played "Nobody Knows de Trouble I've Seen" for Dolin. It was my turn to spy on him doing double pirouettes, attitudes, jetés, leaps, and arabesques, all pure classic ballet techniques, to the Negro spiritual.

The luminaries at Lady Cunard's included Sir Thomas Beecham, who explained to me before I started to dance that he was due at a rehearsal and I must forgive him if he left after half an hour. When I had finished my nine solos, Sir Thomas rushed into my makeshift dressing room and said, "I have kept the whole opera and ballet company waiting for more than an hour but I just couldn't leave." He and the others present knew their ballet, Russian and British, but the diversity of styles and techniques I used was a new experience for them. Above all, they were impressed with the rugged masculinity and dramatic power of my work.

It had not been my intention to pose or to perform in England at all and I didn't let my London social life interfere with my objective, which was to confer with Vaughan Williams. He had just composed a new orchestral work, *Job —a Masque for Dancing*, on which I hoped to create a major production for the Lewisohn Stadium. Constant Lambert, then a pupil of Williams and young composer of promise, played the *Job* score for Mary and me and we listened with keen disappointment. On the piano the work seemed incredibly dull, and I left London without committing myself to the composer.

Although I was unhappy about the music, I couldn't resist

the subject of Job, it seemed so right, and I had long wanted to use the William Blake illustrations for the Book of Job as guides for costume and set designs. I cabled Vaughan Williams that I did want to do a production of *Job—a Masque for Dancing*, a happy decision since we found the music as exciting in orchestration as it had been thin on the piano that let us hear only a simple rhythmic structure and melodic line.

It has always been a satisfaction to me that I did the world première dance production of the Williams' work, later choreographed by Ninette de Valois for Britain's Royal Ballet, with Dolin as Satan. Our *Job* was such a success at the stadium that we tried for long afterward to get financial backing for a production at a downtown theater but the plan came to nothing.

Job was a challenge in many ways, and we worked through a summer, hot as hades, producing the ballet scored for nine scenes, a couple of them set in Hell. At my studio on Fifty-fifth Street, we sewed and dyed material and made props and rehearsed solos; ensemble rehearsals were held at Deni-shawn House.

My patience was tried by *Job* casting, make-up, and scenic problems, in that order. I needed more than fifty men for the cast and managed to get together a troupe of forty by recruiting students from the summer school at New York University. The female roles were Mrs. Job, six daughters-in-law, a few shepherdesses, and of necessity, the demons of Hell. I received an unsigned letter expressing bitter resentment that all the *Job* angels were men, all the devils, women; I had no way to reply to *Anon.* with the explanation that I had no other choice, no more available men.

Scholarly Arthur Moor with his long gaunt frame and sad face was practically typecast as *Job*. His seventh son was danced by Paul Haakon who was not working at that time and offered to do the bit part. Jack Cole I cast as Elihu; one of the Three Comforters was Barton Mumaw, who had just become my dresser in return for room, board, and lessons with me. I danced Satan.

I didn't want my Satan to look like a grand opera Mephistopheles or the red devil on an Underwood ham can, but I did want him to stand out from human beings in the cast. Blake's black and white drawings gave me no color clue, so I made a trip to Boston where the Public Library had some original Blake water colors. It turned out to be a remarkable collection that included a whole set of *Job* illustrations. It was thrilling to touch the very paper handled and worked on by a master draftsman, a great artist. More exciting yet was the discovery that Blake had conceived and painted Satan as a reptilian green figure with scales.

My make-up color decided, I was faced with the necessity of finding a green that wouldn't come off. I had once used poster paints to make myself a blue-bodied Krishna and the effect was good, but after contact with other dancers they were streaked with blue, and I was pocked with white splotches where the blue had rubbed off. For Satan, I used green Thespaint that I applied in small patches and rubbed by hand until each skin area was dry. The foundation finished, I applied black liner for the exaggerated musculature as shown in Blake's drawings, and by blacking out my second toe, achieved the effect of hoofs. My wig was green rope, and for costume I made the irreducible minimum covered with huge green sequins as scales; with black pencil I sketched a design of scales down onto my legs. It took exactly one hour and ten minutes to get into that make-up.

Not counting dress rehearsals I put on the make-up five times to dance three. Our stadium contract was for three performances on any nights that it didn't rain. Monday and Wednesday were clear; Friday it was cloudy but the rain held off until after intermission. But on Tuesday and Thursday I was in complete make-up when heavy rain automatically canceled the show.

Near the climax of the ballet, I, Satan, had a fight with the archangels who chased me up steps and closed in on me in front of the throne of God. Two archangels seized me and hurled me into the pit of Hell where my fall was broken by twelve demons and a couple of soft mattresses. After violent dancing and the fight, my body heat and sweat turned the make-up into green glue that smeared onto the archangels who cast me into Hell. At every performance Archangel George Gloss, years later Dr. Gloss of Louisiana State University, reacted with utter disgust at the green slime on his arms and hands, and his face was so funny that I, out of sight in Hell, broke into diabolic laughter.

Vaughan Williams expected, of course, that *Job* would be given on regular indoor stages with facilities for quick changes covered by a very few bars of connecting music. At Lewisohn Stadium there could be no drops, and any scenery changes were in full view of the audience. I designed a structural set, using one long platform with three steps leading up to it full-length. Dead center there were two sets of steps to a higher platform, Heaven, which could be blanked out by a set of clouds that rolled open or shut. The two stairs to Heaven were on either side of the entrance to the lower region, the Hell hole, into which I was thrown. *Time*'s *Job* review was illustrated by a picture of me with the cutline "SATAN SHAWN . . . was driven into the subway."

That casually written line was all but prophetic. I was nearly pushed underground by a succession of unfortunate circumstances that developed in my professional life, after I had produced *Job*.

....

19

Springfield Springboard

Dancers in my company that performed at the Falmouth, Massachusetts, summer theater in 1932 claimed that they "learned about life from the birds, the bees, the flowers, and the *Lysistrata* ballet." Its theme that stressed the meeting of men and women after a long-enforced sexual drought seemed to call for a torrid ballet, and I made it hot! Too hot for a local woman's club that took a block of matinee seats and played censor.

The Falmouth theater was run by my old friends, Bretaigne Windust, Charlie Leatherbee, and Josh Logan, at whose University Players Guild theater I had given several summer dance programs. Their acting group was lively and, over several years of summer concerts at the theater, I became acquainted with youngsters destined for theatrical fame—Margaret Sullavan,

Henry Fonda, Myron McCormick, Kent Smith, and Mildred Natwick.

At Princeton one year, I staged a ballet number as a favor to Josh, then president of the Princeton Triangle Club and also one of the writers of the book for the production, *The Tiger Smiles*. The *Tiger* cast included another Falmouth player, Princeton student Jimmy Stewart.

Whenever I played at Falmouth, I stayed at Wood's Hole as the guest of Charlie Leatherbee's mother, Madame Jan Masaryk, one of my long-treasured friends. She was the beloved "Miss Frances" of the theater crowd and it was to her that the club women complained after the Wednesday matinee of *Lysistrata*. They thought the play itself was shocking but, since it was a Greek classic, they didn't suppose it was possible to tamper with the words of Aristophanes. However, they made it quite clear that something could and must be done about the movements of "that obscene ballet."

Miss Frances repeated the complaint and told me that, to the ladies of Falmouth, "A man and woman lying on the floor together have only one thing on their minds!"

I said, "They're quite right. The man and woman do have just one thing on their minds, and the problem of the ballet was to show it beautifully, which I think I've done."

"You have," Miss Frances nodded. "I agree with you wholeheartedly but somehow or other, we must pacify the club women, or the boys' box office will be hurt for the rest of the summer."

Time was short between Miss Frances' report of the ultimatum and our first evening curtain, and I had to rush into make-up. I managed to send a warning to the company that the ballet should be cleaned up but I forgot to alert Myrna Pace with whom I had speaking and dancing scenes. In one of those I had been picking Myrna up and placing her gently across a marble bench before swinging into a passionate

sequence. At the performance following the censors' edict, I
engaged in an innocent gambol with Myrna who was no end
puzzled, and finally asked, *sotto voce*, "What's the matter?
Don't you love me any more?" The unrehearsed purifications
seemed to satisfy the woman's club spies and, for the rest of
the week, we played the show at a simmer.

During my two weeks at Falmouth, I lived luxuriously on
the Crane estate in the lodge that was home for Charlie and
his two brothers; for Windust and Logan; and also for the
Falmouth scenic designer, Norris Houghton. Most of the
men on the theater staff seemed about to blow their mental
gaskets that summer, so Miss Frances had imported a psy-
chiatrist-in-residence for the lodge. Every morning he had a
private session with each of the men to listen to their dreams.

Finally, I said to him, "I feel very much left out of things
around here. You seem to be interested in everybody's dreams
but mine."

He answered, very solemnly, "It's my theory that the frus-
trations, inhibitions, and unfinished business of a day become
the subject matter and substance of dreams of the following
night, and that, even in forms not easily recognizable, each
individual goes on trying to work out any problems in dreams.
I can figure out from dreams what is worrying a person and
help him to get straightened out. But," he smiled at me, "if
ever I met an individual who gave me the impression of going
to bed each night with his problems all met, and with no unfinished business on his mind, it's you." How little he knew
me!

I was in the middle of an entanglement that embroiled me
in legal hassles and eventually drove me to forfeit life insurance in order to be free of a monster manager. The fall of
1931, I had set out on tour with my own company called
Ted Shawn and His Dancers, and before we were halfway
through the season, I smelled disaster. The depression forced

the cancellation of many road attractions in the 1931–32
season and we were no exception. Our tour was cut short, and
I, $5000 in the red, was in need of a good forceful manager.
When a new one was highly recommended to me, I signed
a contract without reading it, for the first and certainly for
the last time in my life.

While I struggled for survival I became more determined
that somehow I would form the all-male dance group that
I had been planning toward for many years. My firm belief
that the public, once educated, would be receptive to all-
male programs had been strengthened on the ill-fated tour.
I had given three all-male numbers, *Brahms Rhapsody* (Op.
119, No. 4), *Workers' Songs of Middle Europe*, and *Coolie
Dance*, that featured me with the four other men in the company: Jack Cole, Campbell Griggs, Barton Mumaw, and
Lester Schafer.

Art Moor, then in the music department at an upstate
New York college, was enthusiastic about my experiment with
men dancers, and asked me to come to his summer school to
lecture and give the new numbers. We presented the short
program at several small colleges, and at Springfield College,
Springfield, Massachusetts, only thirty-six miles from Jacob's
Pillow. Dr. L. L. Doggett was so pleased with the program
and with the reaction of his Springfield students to it that he
asked me if I would consider teaching at the college. It was
largely devoted to the training of physical education, recreation and playground directors, and athletic coaches; and, at
that time, more than half of the jobs in those fields were held
by Springfield graduates.

My experiences with the all-male dance demonstration made
me more certain than ever that I wanted to try to sell
the public, the press, and the educators of America on the
legitimacy of dancing as a serious career for men. Though
I, the first American man to make the art of dancing his life-

work, had made good, there still was a prevailing prejudice against dancing for men. It was considered to be an effeminate, trivial, and unworthy occupation for the strapping and well-muscled male.

I knew this to be utterly false but men were in the minority in every company, including Denishawn, and the public eye had not really been focused on the problem of men in dancing. I hoped, by touring with a company of men, to make people think about the subject. I was sure that when people saw young American athletes going through masculine dances, prejudice would be overcome and dancing as a career would take its place with other legitimate professions.

I could make no plans for the men's group, however, until I was free of the manager who said I could buy out of our contract for $5000 I didn't have. My lawyer, who later won my case against the man, said that while the legal wheels turned, I was free to make money by teaching, which wasn't covered by the contract. The big question was, Where could I teach? With Denishawn School and its branches disbanded and closed, I went straight to Dr. Doggett. My timing couldn't have been worse. He wanted me on his staff, as he had often said, but the college budget was made up for the year. Without knowing how I was going to live, without cash, I offered to teach for nothing using the classes as an experimental dance laboratory. It was arranged that, under certain conditions on which I insisted, I would teach during the second semester.

The pot was kept boiling with money from lessons I gave at the Boston school of Miriam Winslow who had been a Braggiotti-Denishawn pupil, and a longtime summer student of mine. One day a week, for ten weeks, I taught at Miriam's newly opened school and, on a percentage basis, made enough money to live modestly at Springfield.

I realized what I faced at the college. I would be up against five hundred young men, all set for careers in physical education and athletics, the hardest, toughest group I could have tackled. Up to that time every man who came to study with me already had made up his own mind that he wanted to dance. At Springfield dancing was being forced on the students. I would have to sell dancing to the student body, and I was determined to try, although friends on the faculties of Amherst and Williams did their best to dissuade me.

Leslie Judd, coach of Springfield's famous gym team, was all for dancing as physical training but frankly admitted that his own efforts had failed. I soon found out why. He had tried to teach the students a Spanish dance called *La Señorita*, and a football dance for which he used mazurka music.

I explained to Judd that the distinctive movements and individual rhythms of a specific sport can be incorporated into dance only by a choreographer with the co-operation of a composer and/or arranger intelligent and interested enough to put the rhythms and patterns into suitable musical form. This held true for all powerful dances for men as I already had proved, and later demonstrated conclusively with Jess Meeker's music and my choreography for the men's group.

Dr. Doggett gave me every possible break, and understood exactly why I wanted my courses to be compulsory, not elective, and why I asked to speak at a general faculty meeting and at the semester's opening convocation. I wanted all students to be compelled to take dance training so no bruisers would be in position to yell "Sissies" at students who elected to take dancing. It was to be all or none for the whole student body. I also wanted to be given assurance that I had the support of the entire teaching staff; one dissenter could undermine the entire experiment. In my convocation talk, later printed in full in the college paper, I set forth my ideals and principles as related to dancing for men. I was not totally convincing as I found out when I met my first classes.

Judd was my right-hand man and, without him, the results at Springfield wouldn't have been achieved. Charles Weckwerth, a young instructor, took most of my dance classes and, by transmitting his enthusiasm to the undergraduates, was an inestimable help to me.

Among the students there was hardly a boy who knew anything about or had ever seen real dancing. Skepticism, indifference, lethargy, and even active antagonism were plainly written on the faces of most students in my first classes. Expressions changed when the students found that fundamental dance exercises, which looked effortless and easy when I did them, were more strenuous than basic training for football, basketball, and wrestling. Their muscles were sore and they had an awakening respect for dance. I gave them my alphabets of indivisible units of movement and then, by combining these, spelled out words in motion, without ever using French ballet terms. In short order, the students of Springfield were doing *pas de basques* and *pas de bourrees* which they would have resented and resisted had they known the proper names and usual milieu of the movements.

These we worked into dances: rowing a boat; working with tools like the ax and the two-man saw; or scything a field. I used simple Negro spirituals for music that the students loved, since every man has a deep religious feeling which seeks expression. With the sympathetic music of spirituals, strong and rhythmic, the students found themselves at home, and danced with gusto and surprising effectiveness.

Only the freshman class was a problem. Like the other classes they had a faculty sponsor but theirs held with the theory, then very much on the upswing, that discipline is old-fashioned. He was not opposed to dancing but believed in free self-expression for any educational process. As a result of his influence the freshman class was unruly, and youngsters, bored by dancing, simply strayed off to climb ladders or play on other gym apparatus. I finally whipped them into some kind of shape by sarcasm, brute force, and a violent clash with the class sponsor.

The sophomores were completely different. Their sponsor was the football coach who smartly marched them into class, deployed them into open formation where they stood relaxed, ready, attentive, and courteous.

Upper classmen were the best of the lot. Any misfits or failures had flunked out by the junior year and students who remained were mature in body and mind, co-ordinated both through physical education and sports training. Juniors and seniors, eager to learn what I could teach, progressed rapidly from elementary dances and music. To Bach Inventions and Fugues, they soon were doing dramatic dances that were close to the real art of dancing.

Marks for the courses were based on class work in the final weeks, and a term paper. I explained that I wouldn't be back so nobody need write anything "to please teacher." I simply wanted to know what they had thought about dancing before they had taken my course, and how they felt about it afterward.

The papers followed a majority theme: The men had thought dancing was for the birds before they started the class which had given them respect for the art of the dance. They were honestly convinced that dancing was a valuable masculine activity and should be included in every phys. ed. curriculum, since dance required a man to use his mind, stimulated his mental powers, and provided complete body culture. Students, the college, and I were pleased with the success of my experiment.

My best Springfield students were recruited for a company made up of girls and men that I assembled for ten performances scheduled for the Repertory Theatre in Boston.

Free of the odious manager, I was my own man again and booked a percentage date at a theater in Springfield for a pre-Boston tryout. And double trouble struck. The most painful and least serious was a sacroiliac dislocation. I was strapped by a doctor who said that I mustn't dance for several weeks. I had to dance and asked him to do what he could to make me comfortable. At dress rehearsal, he said, "Show me the scantiest costume you're going to wear." That was the one for the *Brahms Rhapsody,* and consisted of suntan knitted trunks with a gold G string. The doctor marked me off with a make-up pencil and then taped me with a solid corset in which I danced each performance for two weeks. After every show the adhesive was jerked off and a new corset strapped on with the result that every inch of skin under my trunks was broken out with blisters.

The second trouble was of disaster caliber. The bank holiday had been declared and people, caught even without streetcar fare, had no cash for theater tickets. Business in Springfield was terrible but I was stuck with a lease for the Boston theater and filled the engagement, ending it only $10 in the red which under the circumstance seemed miraculous.

Boston was the scene of a giant step forward. At a special performance, I presented for the first time in modern history, a full two-hour program by a men's group. The cast included the men who had danced with me the season before, and the Springfield College group which augmented several ensemble numbers.

H.T.P., the famous critic of the Boston *Transcript,* who never before had written a kind word about me, came out with a rave notice. He even said that the dancing of the men was far more interesting than any feminine dancing he had ever seen, and he was completely engrossed by the strength, the infinite variety, and the superb techniques of the men.

By winning over H.T.P. and a Boston audience, I was assured that I could win any audience, anywhere. I had been given the final push into the next chapter of my life that was to be devoted to an all-male company.

20

Miracles, Minor and Major

Words of warning failed to discourage the young dancers who joined my men's group as crusaders dedicated to a cause. Each of the youngsters understood that I was operating on a shoestring, without capital or professional management, and could promise no security, only an uncertain future in a company that might be short-lived.

Long before we encountered tour tribulations, I realized how hard-working and earnest a band I had with me. They proved themselves time and again at Jacob's Pillow where we spent a long summer working and living under primitive conditions. We had a main house, two cabins and a barn-studio but were without plumbing, electricity, heat, and cash. Although we had a tight food budget, and a slim bankroll for production of our dance program, the boys studied and trained and rehearsed as if we were set for a long tour with assured bookings. Early in the summer it was far from certain that we would have a tour at all, and bookings were light when we did start out.

Our first lucky break came when my old friend, F. Cowles Strickland, founder-director of the Berkshire Playhouse at Stockbridge, Massachusetts, began to drop in on our practice sessions. He asked many intelligent questions which I answered with words that the boys illustrated in movement, a process that gave Strick a double-edged idea. He took me aside one day, and suggested that the boys and I give a series of weekly lecture-demonstration-teas for the public; he was certain that many people, eager to learn about the technical and creative problems of dance, would pay to attend the sort of semisocial occasions he proposed.

We needed money, as Strick knew full well, but I was skeptical about any potential audience that would have to travel a rutted road to reach us, and about the reaction of the boys for whom the teas would mean additional work. They already were doing their own cooking and household chores but they were keen about Strick's suggestion, and in time became expert caterers of tea-party food.

On the Friday of the first experimental tea, forty-five people sat uncomplaining on benches and chairs in our barn-studio while I talked and four dancers performed in practice clothes without stage lights or make-up. The second Friday, seventy-five people came, and the crowds increased until, on the last Friday of the season, we performed for an audience of two hundred. People who couldn't be seated crowded doorways, stood on sawhorses to peek in windows, but no one asked for his money back.

We made a profit on the modest admission charge and at the last tea I made a farewell speech of thanks before we danced the *Doxology*, which struck one regular in our audience as "cute." Strick was horrified at the adjective but the lady insisted, "Shawn told us he was grateful for our dollars which helped to pay the summer grocery bills, and then danced 'Praise God from whom all blessings flow,' and I think that was really cute of him."

Strick further helped the company coffers by giving us his Berkshire Playhouse for a special matinee on which we realized several hundred dollars, desperately needed to get our show on the road. The informal Friday programs and the performance at Strick's theater gave us audience tryouts, and helped to sharpen our dances in a way that rehearsals couldn't have done. By fall we had a polished tour program but no tour route, just a few scheduled dates.

Our booking was being done by Powers and Willmore, professionals who just threw us a few dates if and when they could, and by two inexperienced friends, Margerie Lyon and George Gloss. Margerie had been with me for about twelve years, first as manager of one or another of the Denishawn schools, and then as my personal representative. She had never booked but believed so fanatically in the value of my proposed project that she was eager to try while she drove across the country to her Los Angeles home.

George, a member of my *Job* company, held a master's degree in physical education, the field in which he was working when he joined us at the Pillow with every intention of dancing in the men's company. After he realized the management problems we faced, he willingly gave up his chance to dance and took over the booking. His lack of experience was overbalanced by his wide knowledge of the educational field and his close friendships with many phys. ed. directors who were potential buyers for the show.

Confirmed dates trickled in for the first tour month, but we had no way of knowing whether there would be more. We had eaten up our summer income; our cash capital was in costumes; and it was touch and go whether box-office receipts would pay our living and traveling expenses. No salary was guaranteed to anybody, and cash from a general fund, if or as we earned it, would pay for lodging, food, and the gas to run a brand-new Ford panel truck and Juno, my aged secondhand Buick.

Acquisition of the truck was another break, one of the many miracles that contributed to the establishment of the men's group. In September, after I spoke at the Pittsfield Rotary Club luncheon, I had cornered a Ford dealer who inexplicably took my personal note in down payment for the truck. Juno, so named because of her opulent rear end, was on her last legs but we just crossed our fingers that she would hold up until we could get a new car by some other miracle.

Eight of us started on the tour with high hopes and little to encourage us about the season ahead. We all were in top physical shape, but before we were through we needed every smidgen of stamina built up in a summer of hard work and outdoor living. Three of the company, Barton Mumaw, Wilbur McCormack, and Frank Overlees, had been studying with me before the group was formed. Barton, onetime piano student at the Conservatory of Music at Rollins College, had been with me as pupil since the Lewisohn Stadium concert in the summer of '31. Wilbur was a junior at Springfield College and captain of its wrestling team the year I taught there. Frank Overlees was well on his way to being a champion swimmer when I first met him at Falmouth, and Springfield had given him special-student status so he could take my courses.

George Horn, a little older than the others, had danced in several musical comedies. He was talented in designing and making costumes but his forte was stage management. He appeared in ensemble numbers of our first program, and stage-managed the tour while he trained Frank, our stage manager for the other six tours. For years afterward, George was of invaluable assistance to me in many capacities. Each fall he came from his home town, Springfield, and stayed at the Pillow working on costumes, props, and electrical equipment for the tour-in-preparation; later he helped with the expansion of facilities at Jacob's Pillow.

Dennis Landers and Jess Meeker both came from Arkansas City where we had met them through Ernestine Day, by then wife of Dr. Armand K. Fischer. Denny, a sketch artist of considerable ability and an athlete whose high school pole vault records of 1930 stood for many years, had studied a little with Tini. Jess, a composer and pianist, had impressed Mary Campbell when we heard him play at Tini's Arkansas City studio. Since Mary sincerely believed that the men's company should have a male pianist-composer, she joined Miriam Winslow as accompanist, and I took on Jess. Ours was a happy creative association which lasted nine years. As a composer he was superb and much more remarkable than even Mary had guessed.

Willard van Simons, who had joined the company late, was primarily interested in ballet and was replaced by Fred Hearn, who auditioned for us when we were playing Asheville. Fred, who held a degree from a business college, was another member of the group who had been an outstanding high school athlete.

Our tour opened on October 23, 1933, at Burlington, Vermont, and we danced our way south, challenged by unpredictable hazards of blizzards, blowouts, and bigots. We played to many pathetically small houses because, we were told, it had been impossible to get people to buy tickets to see an all-men's group. We heard the same story everywhere but the enthusiasm after each performance resulted in promises of a packed house when we returned the next year. Only we questioned that there would be a next year. But, after all, we were the ones who had been eating 15-cent lunches, changing tires blown out in no man's land blizzards, unpacking the show, hanging lights and scenery, then performing and reversing the setting-up process, often starting out at midnight for the next engagement some hundreds of miles away.

We played mostly percentage engagements with profits as low as $22 at Pinehurst, North Carolina, a resort town out of season; $43 at Daytona Beach, its season in full swing; $38 at LaGrange, Georgia, a typical small town. And people talked to us about next year! We had guarantees at few places. The largest, $500, was from Hampton Institute where we had an appreciative audience, and met a faculty that was sympathetic. The director of music, Clarence White, told me that he had made the very arrangement of *Calvary* that I had used for the first all-men's program in Boston; and the physical education director made plans to study with me at the Pillow in preparation for dance classes at Hampton.

We went to Black Mountain College, like us a pioneer group, newly formed. It had opened that fall with the express purpose of proving that art activity was the animating and vitalizing center of true education. We were the guests of Katherine Dreier's nephew, a member of the Black Mountain faculty, and, for our room and board, I lectured, conducted an informal forum, and taught a dance class, a sort of barter for art.

Trouble that I hadn't anticipated first struck us at Columbus, Mississippi, where the college treasurer who gave us our check wouldn't shake hands because I had danced *John Brown Sees the Glory*, for which Jess wrote music, using the theme of the familiar song very sketchily. In Tallahassee our sponsors were afraid to print the John Brown program notes, and the Williamsburg ladies who promoted our performance on the campus of the College of William and Mary wouldn't let the words "John Brown" be printed on the program at all.

There we called the number *The Forerunner* and had one tense moment backstage. When Jess played the identifiable theme in the finale, an old stagehand, tilted back on a rickety chair, sat forward suddenly and straightened like a war horse scenting powder. The theme quickly died, and the old boy relaxed and resumed his snoozing.

Everywhere, deep South or not, audiences were excited by the dance which was appreciatively reviewed in the *Daily Illini* by a member of the faculty of the University of Illinois: "The portrayal of the somber passion of John Brown, danced by Shawn alone, assumed symphonic proportions, a fine dramatic unity being sustained without any necessary reference to literal narrative values. With magnificent economy of means, a single dance here comprehended and made manifest a conception of tremendous sweep and truly epic grandeur. I don't pretend to have an inkling as to how it was done. The achievement was extraordinary and, in the state of my ignorance, an even incredible thing. I don't know why a group of dances at the end of the program should have been singled out for distinction as *religious* dances when the whole program was just 'that.' "

Attachment of property plagued us in the South. A disgruntled manager from Columbia, South Carolina, chased me down at Spartansburg and said that the professional bookers had promised that his would be our only South Carolina date, and he had lost money because we had broken the pledge. We knew nothing about the arrangement but the man claimed $100 for his losses, and, on his heels, came a sheriff with papers for attaching our truck. Luckily it had been unloaded, so we had scenery and costumes for a performance that thrilled the sighing students at Converse College. We took in enough money to get back our truck, and a young lawyer of the town, who had posted bond for me, promised to sue for the return of my forfeited cash.

Our next date was at Athens, Georgia, where I received a letter threatening attachment of scenery and costumes when we reached Atlanta. A promoter there had a grievance which dated back for several years but which I had no way to check. However, the morning after our Athens performance I dashed to Atlanta, and, after dickering with the promoter, paid him $50 to avoid a second attachment.

As long as I was in Atlanta on that unpleasant business, the woman publicizing our performance a few days later kept me busy for the day. I was interviewed by four reporters, photographed by three newspapers, entertained at lunch with several local celebrities; I autographed copies of *Shawn, the Dancer* in Rich's bookshop, and departed breathless for a Gainesville performance. When we got back to Atlanta all was serene. The audience was intelligent and enthusiastic, and our program review written by O. B. Keeler, known as the Boswell of Bobby Jones, appeared smack in the middle of the sports page, a location we heartily approved.

The week before our Christmas layoff, we made enough money to pay for a much-needed rest and holiday. We played to two thousand people at Tallahassee, and to an excited audience in Eustis, Barton's home town. Barton's parents had a reception at their home where I spent two weeks in a great big comfortable room to myself. For three days before Christmas I dieted and did desk work. I lived on orange juice to reduce and to pamper a nervous stomach battered from lunchwagon meals and banquets at which I had talked every minute, eating nothing.

On my days of rest, I plowed through correspondence, answering a hundred routine fan letters, some autograph requests, writing bread-and-butter notes, and letters to young would-be dancers. It was gratifying to go over the account books covering the first nine weeks of the tour: we had been able to pay running expenses and commissions; the first in-

stallment on a $500 note at the bank; all leftover household
bills in Lee; the photographer in full; and the printer more
than half of his bill for promotional material for the whole
tour.

The motif for the men's group programs and other literature
was the reproduction of a drawing of me in *Frohsinn* costume
that Major Felten had made in 1931; that drawing was also
used as the jacket cover of my book *Dance We Must*. Part
of the printing cost for the first tour was for three thousand
reprints of a full-page article about the men's group that appeared in the Boston *Globe* on Sunday, October 22, the very
day before our first performance as a company. Lucien Price,
the *Globe* editor who wrote the article, had visited us in the
spring, and was convinced that the all-men's dance group
would be a history-making contribution to the culture of the
United States.

Mr. Price, editor, author, scholar, and sage, kept in touch
with us by mail through all seven tours. He kept assuring us
that, in spite of setbacks and discouragements, we would win
out because "Every right idea has within itself the power to
enforce its own recognition and eventual success." He sent me
books of philosophy, history, and ideas that I read both to
myself and aloud to the boys as we traveled. A few themes he
proposed were developed into dance numbers, and he was ever
on the alert for interesting music suitable for men dancers.
Lucien Price's spiritual pep talks by mail were a never-ending
source of encouragement to the company; through correspondence he was a sounding board for my own hopes, fears, and
travails.

At the end of our Christmas holiday in Florida, we rehearsed
with Fred Hearn and he caught on quickly to his solos and
the group numbers. I used the spare time to block out a new
number, *The Dance of the Threshing Floor*, before we started
north.

The first weeks of January we danced up toward New York where I spent hours settling our booking arrangements for the rest of that season, and for the next year. We played at Columbia University where three hundred were turned away from the box office but, to our disappointment, no major New York paper reviewed our program.

Spring was a hard push but we began to see results of our pioneering. Juno finally collapsed under us and Pluto, the replacement, was a DeSoto, midnight metallic blue, chromeplated, and so streamlined that in small towns more natives crowded around the automobile than the box office. The car was such a novelty that we had to lock it up tight, even in garages, after we found that mechanics were taking it for a spin while we slept.

Wilbur McCormack had to have several stitches taken in a leg gashed on a swimming pool in Springfield, Missouri, and two nights later by throwing open a dressing-room window when I couldn't turn off the radiator, I brought on a severe shoulder misery and a deep-seated cold. While I was writhing in sleepless pain with the shoulder, I was called into Barton's room where he was having a kidney stone attack. In spite of accident and illness, we were up the following morning at six-thirty, and drove over snowy roads to Kansas City, covering 108 miles in an hour and forty minutes.

I left the boys with instructions to call a doctor for Barton, and went to talk at a chamber of commerce luncheon. I was in agony from shoulder pain, my throat was sore, and I was exhausted from the sleepless night, the fast morning drive. Suffering, I rose to my feet with a result reported the next day in the Kansas City *Journal Post*: "Staid and reserved business men who had been yawning through speeches on business cycles and economic indexes, woke up and listened with admiring amazement as Ted Shawn squared off from the speakers' table and delivered a belligerent defense of male dancing. The speaker was cheered for several minutes after his speech. Conrad H. Mann, president of the Chamber of Commerce, said to him, 'If you're half as good a dancer as you are a speaker, you are certainly great.' "

After the luncheon I gave press interviews before going to the Nelson Gallery of Art where I lectured on "Hindu Art and Religion." I attended a tea given in my honor, and, after that, a dinner party. Barton was better by night but the doctor who attended me said that I should have my tonsils out, the sooner the better. I had had no tonsils for years so I gargled my way to Topeka the next day, and began to improve steadily.

Hundreds were turned away from our Austin performance at the then-new Hogg Memorial Auditorium where an organization of fifty young Texans, professional Wild Westerners, had announced that they were opposed to men dancers on principle and were going to break up the show. Those who came to jeer must have stayed to cheer because there was not a peep of disturbance from the audience which, at the end, gave us a rousing ovation.

We saw Indian dances at Ponca City and Pawhuska and later I used the basic material for a new group dance that was the opening dance of a Primitive suite which we rehearsed and worked on at Jacob's Pillow. Money that I earned giving private lessons through the Southwest, I invested in costume materials available nowhere but in Oklahoma.

Slowly, as we performed, we noticed that more and more men were coming backstage with their wives. At Richmond, Kentucky, for instance, we played to an audience of nine hundred and there were more men than women in the after-show crowd. Those businessmen and others in many towns told us that our program was the finest that had been on their respective concert series for years.

Before our State University of Iowa performance, Charles

H. McCloy, one of the greats in physical education, talked to me for two hours about the possibility of training a man who, in a couple of years, could put in full time teaching dancing. That was the first university to suggest such an idea. Strong Hinman, president-elect of the National Association of Physical Education Directors, was equally sold on our project and so was Editor Mitchell of the *Journal of Health and Physical Education.*

When a professor, whose subject and college shall be nameless, asked me if dancing was my "escape," I nearly laughed in his face. It seemed impossible that any man of intelligence could so misconstrue the efforts which seemed to me like front-line trench fighting.

Our whole company was increasingly proud as we made chips in the rock of resistance, although we all understood why people had not been immediately eager to buy tickets to see men dance. Dr. Joel Hayden of Western Reserve Academy wrote a letter to Lucien Price that perfectly stated the public case: "Ted Shawn and his boys have come and gone. There is no one on the campus that knows just how to describe the total effect of the performance. It was beautiful; it was dignified; it was novel; it had moments of high mystery, and the audience which ranged from nine to 70 years paid its profound respect to the whole event by attention and quiet most unusual for a program of this sort. You see, there is no measuring stick, no familiar ground from which to move toward the new experience. And yet in spite of the greatness of the stride forward demanded of the audience, that stride was taken, and the whole result was a unique experience for youth and age alike."

On May 1, when we finished our tour, I personally had talked to 150 audiences at luncheons, assemblies, and club meetings; I had given 100 newspaper interviews, and 50 radio broadcasts. Strange, that while I never have felt stale doing any dance, no matter how many times before I had performed it, I felt guilty about parroting the same speech, although I believed to my depths in my message and was earnest about our pioneering. It had been worth while, as we all knew from the incredible number of programs given: they totaled for the season to 111 performances!

••

21

No Rest on Jacob's Pillow

We settled into Jacob's Pillow jubilant at the success of the experimental first tour, eager to start on our dances for a forceful new program. I was choreographer and worked with Jess Meeker to produce a program of dances that was essentially masculine in principle and performance.

Dance ideas had simmered as we traveled, and one was sparked at the Pillow by Fred Stone, veteran star of musical comedy, who dropped by with his daughter Carol, a former student of mine. While Mr. Stone was showing the boys his famous Australian whip tricks, it came to me that the raw material would make a stunning solo for Denny. It went into our program as the *Mule Team Driver's Dance* in which Denny effectively used a long Australian whip that frequently lashed right over the footlights, and two small whips rigged to snap and crack explosively.

The *Primitive and Folk Theme* section of our first tour was revised for the second as *Primitive Rhythms* with Maori and Singhalese dances; the *Dyak Spear Dance*, a solo by Barton; a new *Eagle Dance* solo for me; and the Ponca Indian dances worked into an ensemble. Our primitive dances were not presented as authentic, or exact, copies, but rather as creations from my study of original sources. We did a *Labor Symphony* with a final section of mechanized labor representing the spirit of metals and the machine itself; on tour we visited an industrial plant where powerful photographs were taken of us dancing beside machinery, dynamos, and assembly apparatus.

My own major solo for the second tour was one which had been in my mind ever since I had read Francis Thompson's mystic poem "Hound of Heaven" to Ruth and Fred Beckman during a Denishawn tour. In my experience the time involved in producing a dance, and the travail suffered are proportionate to the content: the deeper the content, the longer the time, the greater the travail. Creation of a serious dance is not a brain activity but a conception that must run its time to be full-born. Jess did stirring music for the *Hound of Heaven* which found its place on a dance program after twelve embryonic years.

We rehearsed the second tour program with three new members of the group, Ned Coupland and Bill Howell, and Foster Fitz-Simons who replaced George Horn. Foster, a Carolina Playmaker and University of North Carolina graduate, had earlier been on the fencing and swimming teams of Emory University at Atlanta.

From the beginning of our fall tour we had high hopes that we would end it with an engagement in London. In the early fall we played a matinee at Carnegie Hall to two thousand people, though the bright afternoon was ideal for our box-office competition: four major football games in New York. At Dallas we had an audience of five thousand, and chanted backstage, "This means London, this means London." Our guarantee was for $250 and 50 per cent of the receipts which we prematurely figured at an astronomical sum. Neither we nor Moyer, our booker from the Horner Bureau of Kansas City, understood that the guarantee covered the season tickets, totaling four thousand, and we were dejected by our check that was for only $375.

Our souvenir booklets for the tour were sold for 25 cents, and profits went into our London fund which built up penny by penny. I was determined that we would not go to England without a backlog for our living in London and round-trip transportation. With the accumulation of receipts from good houses, and money I earned giving private lessons in tour towns, it seemed by March that we really might swing the trip to England. Fern went over to explore the situation, and her cable confirming the signing of our London contract reached us in West Virginia on April 17. On May 17 we sailed.

Less than a week after our arrival in England, Gracie Ansell gave a cocktail party to introduce us to London society. More than two hundred of her three hundred guests were titled; the other hundred were celebrities of stage, screen, press, and from London's music and literary circles. I never finished a sentence to anybody but was hauled from here to there to greet guests as they arrived. After three hours, during which liquor flowed like a mountain freshet, the boys were all sober and still young gentlemen, which astounded Mrs. Ansell, who said, "I assure you, Shawn, no other ten boys of my acquaintance would have ended this party in that condition."

London was good to us, and we saw all of its sights; attended every play and revue; went to dozens of parties; and,

best of all, I took the whole company for a visit with Havelock
Ellis. On one day when two ladies with hyphenated names
gave overlapping cocktail parties for us, I met a dowager who
said, "Wherever I go in London, I hear only one name—
Shawn! There has never been such a *succès-fou!*"

We were scheduled for three performances at His Majesty's
Theatre, and were so well received that we were signed for an
unplanned, extra week at the Apollo. Reviews generally were
very good and the London *Dancing Times* critic wrote, "The
performance of *Polonaise* and of a *Brahms Rhapsody* are unforgettable. In the latter number, which I witnessed as performed without costume or stage set, Shawn has surpassed
any current group composition, 'modern' or otherwise. But,
as should be the case when presenting a programme of
dances by men, Shawn has moved away from many of the
softer and more dreamy aspects of Denishawn dancing. Choosing the subjects for his compositions from three sources—
Primitive, Labor and Religious—Shawn has succeeded in
hitting upon a trail-blazing style of dance presentation for
men which is both artistically important and entirely free from
the purple tints which usually hover about male dancing."

For the MacDowell *Polonaise* the boys wore the briefest
of trunks dyed exactly same shade of their body make-up,
and under certain stage lighting they did look quite nude, an
effect that brought a horrified gasp from the opening night
London audience. In the United States reaction usually was
more swoon than shock.

I was personally disappointed that one or two members
of the British press didn't like either of my two big solos, *John
Brown Sees the Glory* and *Hound of Heaven.* However, under
peculiar circumstances in America, one of England's most
renowned actresses gave her approbation to *Hound.* We were
playing a New York engagement and, as I started the *Hound
of Heaven,* the words of the poem came full voice from a

stage box. I was not only shaken with surprise and progressively confused as I continued the dance but I could hardly hear Jess at the piano. My choreography did not follow the sequence of the poem, a fact that seemed of no concern to the reciting female whose voice, rich and round-toned, soared through the theater to the very last line. After the performance, Mrs. Pat Campbell, the distinguished British actress, swept into my dressing room and said, in a voice that I recognized at once from the richness and its round tones, "I did *so* enjoy your *Hound of Heaven.*" Nobly controlling my inflection I answered, "So I gathered."

We returned from England in time for me to meet my first summer class at Jacob's Pillow on July 2, 1935. A month later we incorporated and our first corporate act was to buy fifty-five acres of land adjoining Jacob's Pillow. Four buildings on the property gave us much-needed dormitory space for summer school students.

Shawn Dancers, Inc., had a big third tour which took us for the first time to the Pacific coast. The one-night-stand schedules and the pattern for our touring and for preparing new dances was more or less set for the rest of the men's group years.

Since we traveled twenty-five thousand miles the first season, and as many as forty thousand in some of the subsequent six years on wheels, we encountered certain inevitable motoring hazards: speeding tickets, blowouts, skids, and collisions. Wilbur McCormack's truck seemed to be the target for most of the mishaps, and one night in wild mountain country of West Virginia, it was an actual target. A bullet circled a neat hole in the truck's back door, but Wilbur didn't linger to find out whether the sniper was a moonshiner, a miner, or just some jolly joe.

Once when an old farmer sent us, turned turtle, down a steep embankment, crankcase oil dripped down inside the car and my first reaction was, "Look what that oil's doing to my new suit." Only then did I check for breaks, bruises, or blood. Luckily nobody was hurt but delay in getting our car up the bank left us without costumes at show time. At the last minute we dashed into a small-town store and bought the only costume substitutes available. These were basketball trunks made of gray jersey that was unsightly and, as we found out, undependable. When the dancers were mid-air in their first strong leap, each pair of trunks, simultaneously and as if perfectly timed, split wide across the crotch.

Our only bad motor accident occurred near Chicago when the truck was hit by a speeding car driven by a Saturday night drunk. Denny, riding with Mac, had muscle surgery on an eye that healed perfectly with only a wrinkle-sized scar to remind him of the gory crash. Mac, not so lucky, was out of dancing for a month with arm injuries and a shoulder blood clot.

The Sunday morning after the accident, I got in touch with influential Chicago friends who, in turn, routed well-known attorneys out of bed to advise me. Because of the location of the accident, it was being investigated by police of Chicago, Cicero, and Oak Park, and the lawyers said that if we didn't want to be held up for weeks of legal entanglements, we should leave town right from the theater after our Sunday matinee. If any process servers or police were at our hotel, they waited in vain because we saved our tour by getting out of Illinois and writing back to the hotel for our luggage.

I learned to work as we motored and, after Katherine Dreier gave me a little folding table for the back seat of the car, I kept books and even typed letters and articles in my study-on-wheels.

My articles in the spring of 1936 included twenty-seven in a series for the Boston *Herald*. I had contracted to do three articles a week for nine weeks and deadline came on deadline until I thought the weeks would never end. The editor told me that mail about my dance articles and increased circulation during the run of the series indicated that his newspaper must have a full-time dance writer or columnist. I introduced him *in absentia* to Walter Terry, a youngster whom I considered to be thoroughly capable and a writer who "will develop into a first-rate dance critic."

Walter had studied dancing at the University of North Carolina with Phoebe Barr, a former pupil of mine, and was a friend of the Carolina men who danced in the Shawn group: Foster and Harry Coble and Fred Howard. When Walter decided not to be a dancer himself, he asked my advice about what he might do to stay in the world of dance, and I suggested that he try reviewing. He gained experience by writing reviews of dance events at his university and at other colleges in the area, established his reputation at the Boston *Herald*, and, in 1939, joined the New York *Herald Tribune* as dance critic.

When I finished my Boston *Herald* series, I returned thankfully to my reading, choosing books that challenged my mind and broadened my knowledge; magazines to divert me and to keep me informed on news events. While we drove over highways and along short-cut back roads, I read aloud to the boys, and always I encouraged them to cultivate the habit of reading by passing around the books in my traveling library.

We tried not to miss the natural wonders on our routes and took advantage of cultural opportunities when we could. We lingered in the beautiful Rocky Mountains, saw gold mined near Central City in Colorado, visited the Garden of the Gods, detoured to visit the Indian pueblos at Taos, New Mexico, and stopped off to see the Grand Canyon at dawn. We visited museums and, on free nights, attended plays and concerts.

Jess and I planned new numbers as we drove, and the dancers were consulted about work in progress. Shawn Dancers, Inc., voted on all major decisions and we were as much as possible a unified group. By constantly reviewing and reassessing our program plans and company aims we arrived at majority rule. We discussed a projected schedule for successive seasons in the United States and Europe, 1938–39; Australia Java, India, Egypt, then Europe again, 1939–40; North and South America, Mexico and Cuba, 1940–41. Fern actually went abroad in midseason of the 1937–38 tour but no contract developed, fortunately, or we would have been trapped in Europe in the critical fall of 1938.

Fern, effervescent and hearty, did a thorough job for us as she toured ahead beating the drums for Shawn and his Men's Group, and taking to the soapbox to promote the cause of men in dancing. While Fern was traveling from Billings, Montana, to Casper, Wyoming, her bus stopped at a country store and, like the rest of the passengers, she got out to stretch, and drifted to the back of the store where a turkey shoot was in progress. Some of the spectators curious about Fern, who was wearing "my funny New York hat and typical city get up," asked her who she was. When Fern explained, the shoot was held up, a crowd gathered around, and Fern gave a pep talk about Shawn and his dancers. While the bus was loading, most of the men from Fern's impromptu audience called, "Good-by. We'll see you at Casper." And good as their word, many of them were at our Casper performance.

Fern enjoyed her own professional work but she grew a little weary of being confidante for the girls who mooned over the boys in the company. We had one real Lothario in the group and Fern insisted that in every single town at least one girl claimed to be engaged to the particular heartthrob. During an engagement in Cuba, the hotel phones rang for that dancer all the time, and he was seen on beach and promenade with the type of girls who I thought were never allowed out without duennas. The day before we left Havana, our Romeo held court and said good-by to girls who entered his room through one door and were shown out another, so there would be no embarrassing meetings in the corridor.

All the boys liked to spend long week ends or even a Sunday in a town where there was a girls' finishing school or college. They went canoeing, skating, dancing, dating, picnicking, and enjoyed every minute of the rare free days. A reporter wrote that the "Men's Group is God's gift to the women's colleges of America," but it was not only student-age females who were fans. One local writer said that the Pillow was "the dowagers' burlesque," and we did seem to attract many representatives of an era now past: elderly ladies who were elegantly gowned, elaborately coifed, and much-bejeweled, complete with pearl dog collars.

The boys had little more time to play over Christmas holidays and on summer vacations than they did on tour. Mid-season layoffs were spent at Eustis, Florida, where I bought property and built a studio in 1936. After celebrating Christmas with friends and families, the boys gathered at Eustis for brush-up rehearsals and the blocking out of new numbers.

We were at Lee from late spring through summer and into fall, and life was ever hectic. Most of our costumes were made right at the Pillow and we did the sewing ourselves before we could afford the luxury of a sewing woman. We worked at building up and keeping up the physical plant of Jacob's Pillow; gave tea lecture-performances; rehearsed when we could; had costume fittings; posed for photographs in completed costumes; and then, after supper, settled beside kerosene lamps to stitch or hem or sew on Indian beads until midnight.

Days were always broken by two hours for lunch and relaxation. After we ate, we stretched out on outdoor practice platforms and soaked up sun, while I read aloud. We did take nights off and time out for the Berkshire cultural events, all in important arts allied to our own: drama at the Playhouse, music at the Stockbridge festival, and the quartet concerts sponsored by Mrs. Elizabeth Sprague Coolidge.

The men's group helped to construct the Hill place to house summer students, many of them college phys. ed. directors whose primary objective was to make dancing for men an integral part of physical education curriculums. Forty men students enrolled the first summer we offered courses, and that same summer we began general classes for girls; courses for women teachers and advanced girl-pupils were added in 1938. The girl students, who lived at a local inn, were constantly chaperoned at Jacob's Pillow where they took lessons and used the studio facilities. The classes for girls were organized and supervised by Carol Lynn, now an associate director of the Jacob's Pillow School.

Before the men students arrived for the first summer school, I suddenly realized that our dining room was too small to handle them even at two sittings. The boys and I went out to the lawn and set card tables, side by side, to the length of the dining table we were going to need and then, allowing for adequate floor space, we staked out a new dining room with sticks and strings. I couldn't stay to supervise construction because I was due in Nashville to teach for three weeks at the George Peabody College for Teachers. It was at Peabody, where I taught in successive summers through 1940, that I hoped originally to establish the University of the Dance, a plan that did materialize, but at Jacob's Pillow.

My first summer at Nashville, I was eager to know about the progress of the dining room building, but the boys answered my letter inquiries with vague phrases. After the long drive home, we pulled into the Pillow one night about ten o'clock and found the whole place dark. Electric cables had been run up our road that spring but there wasn't a light to be seen anywhere until we stepped out of the automobile. Then a spotlight was beamed on the dining room that was roofed and finished, at least on the outside. While I stared in astonishment, lights went on inside the building, and the boys came cheering toward me. In little more than three weeks they had completed the room which had a stunning fireplace at one end, and was equipped with an oak refectory table made by Frank Overlees. I was overwhelmed by the results of the boys' labor and choked up by the look of pride in their eyes. The final touch to my welcome home was party food served right then in our new dining room.

The expanding school and increasingly popular lecture-demonstration teas brought throngs of visitors and audience crowds that meant more work for all. Each man had Pillow duties: Fred Hearn was the gardener for several years; Foster, our company clerk, was boss of the Pillow's kitchen crew; the Delmar twins, John and Frank, built many walks and walls of native stone; Wilbur McCormack, capable assistant teacher and chief of carpentry and building, constructed his own cabin; and Frank Overlees also built the cabin he lived in. In addition, everybody was ready at a moment's notice to pinch-hit at parking cars, ushering, taking tickets, digging ditches, washing dishes, or stirring a stew.

New men usually joined the company at the Pillow, and some of them came out of the summer school after we had had the opportunity to watch them work and rehearse. Denny and Foster left us after the 1937–38 season, and Harry Coble took Denny's place. Frank Delmar was already dancing with us and his identical twin, John, once Foster's understudy, gradually worked into the group. Sam Steen, Fred Howard, Horace Jones, and John Schubert were other dancers who joined the men's group after its early tours.

By late October when new men were finding their way through dance program material and we had finished the first push of preparing for the tour, we had six good excuses for a celebration. Six of us in the group had birthdays within eight days. Several of our October birthday parties were memorable, none more so than the progressive dinner that also was a treasure hunt with clues to indicate at which boy's house the next course would be served.

Inevitably we developed a language of our own through many kinds of shared experiences; our group vocabulary was so enriched by incidents and events that often a raised eyebrow and a key word from an inside joke was enough to convey a paragraph of meaning. We were a close-knit family with ties strengthened by camaraderie and *esprit de corps*.

•••

22

Men Do Dance!

N Long before the men's group played its last engagement, we had silenced the skeptics and scoffers who insisted that "men don't dance," the assertion made years before by my fraternity brother in his vain attempt to dissuade me from a dancing career. Season after season we built up a respectful audience by giving programs of original dances created to use and show the power and prowess of men who were both well-muscled athletes and sensitive artists.

How many dances were created for our repertoire is anybody's guess. We experimented with unique short dances and labored over major works, ambitiously produced. Some numbers we danced only a few times; others were hailed by audiences through several seasons and hundreds of performances. One of the most consistently popular of our dances was the

Kinetic Molpai, a suite of eleven kinetic dances devised so that each spectator might make his own poem of every dance. Jess Meeker composed music for the suite which, after its completion, was named for the Molpê of ancient Greece.

An experiment with dance and notes and a picture resulted in *A Lithograph by Katherine S. Dreier,* a distinct innovation in which three artists starting from the same point, created art works in three mediums. Miss Dreier, in a New York exhibit, showed 40 *Variations* on an abstract theme, and Jess and I took one of her lithographs as the basis for music and dance, a pioneer collaboration. He composed the score and I choreographed the dance while keeping in mind the triangles, circles, open spaces, and quality of freedom in the graphic work.

The company's first full evening work was *O! Libertad!,* an American saga in three acts representing the Past, Present, and Future, the last being the *Kinetic Molpai. Sports Dances* in the Present section were choreographed and magnificently performed by the men dancers. Each sport, choreographed by a different dancer, was presented with strength and originality:

1.	Banner Bearer	Barton, solo
2.	The Cheer Leaders	Frank Overlees as a trio for himself, Denny, and Mac
3.	Decathlon	Foster, solo
4.	Fencing	Fred Hearn, duet with Denny
5.	Boxing	Mac, solo
6.	Basketball	Denny for himself, Mac, Barton, Frank, and Fred

The programs of our first four seasons were given at the Majestic Theatre in New York where we were signed for five Sunday evenings. Our fifth season program was not then complete so, on our fifth Sunday evening at the Majestic, we performed all four movements of a Mozart symphony, another innovation previously given only at Jacob's Pillow. Each man in the company danced one line of the nine-line score; two men were violins, one a cello, and so on through the instruments in an experiment which was interesting to the special and knowledgeable audience we danced for at the Majestic.

The second full evening work that went into our touring repertoire was *Dance of the Ages,* an elemental rhythmus in four movements, Fire, Water, Earth, and Air. It was the first dance in symphonic framework to be presented as a full evening's program; the second such work was not premièred until twenty years later when Martha Graham presented her *Clytemnestra* at the Adelphi Theatre in New York.

In the early winter of 1940, we premièred *The Dome* at Miami, Florida, and we thought the work was one of our best artistic efforts. The whole Bach section was well balanced and we were as pleased with it as the audiences were. We performed just the Bach dances for a small group at Rollins College where Barton, a former Rollins student, did the *Bourrée* solo which he had choreographed and performed with brilliant virtuosity beyond his previous best.

Barton, who had a number of stunning solos on the various programs, was not only the most talented but the most experienced of the men dancers. By the time the group started, he had studied with me for two years and had even toured with my company of girls and men in 1931. His performance of *Pierrot in a Dead City,* a solo I choreographed to Korngold music, was a tremendous London hit.

The second section of *The Dome* included *God of Lightning,* again a choreography by Barton; *Bamboula* choreographed by Fred Hearn; a dance about two Greek warrior brothers, choreographed by the Delmar twins; and *Green Imp,* a witty choreography by Sam Steen. Music for *Imp* and for the work by the Delmars was composed by Weldon Wallace, now a feature writer and dance critic of the Baltimore *Sun,* who was an accompanist at the Pillow's men's school for two summers.

At various times on tour we danced with the symphony orchestras of Amarillo and Austin, Texas, and Louisville, Kentucky. The great musical moment came for Jess when he heard his *Hound of Heaven* played by the Philadelphia Symphony Orchestra during our performance with them at Robin Hood Dell.

Laboriously and slowly, but steadily, the men's group reached its goal: establishment of the man dancer in his rightful place as artist. Progress was reflected by box-office receipts, public reaction, and critical comment. By the fall of 1939, we knew that our work was done, our mission accomplished, and I made an October announcement that our seventh tour would be our last. After serious discussions, the boys and I had voted to dissolve in May of 1940, when they would be on their own to seek individual careers like other young men graduating into professions.

I also faced reorganization of my professional life. The pioneering years had cost me money, $25,000 in all, that was not matched by profits. Cash from my lecturing, teaching, and writing had been plowed back into productions, and I had borrowed, using the Pillow as collateral, to keep the Pillow going.

With futures uncertain but enthusiasm high, we went into our final season determined to make the last the best. The seven-year crusade ended appropriately where it began, in Boston. There at the Repertory Theatre, in 1933, I had presented the first full program of men dancers, with soloists and Springfield students; there at Symphony Hall, on May 6 and May 7, 1940, Shawn Dancers, Inc., gave its last two programs. In seven successive years we had built up a group of Boston devotees who attended both farewell nights with almost religious fervor, mingled with grief. Each member of the company danced as if inspired, and brilliant performances were noted by critics who wrote about the unparalleled enthusiasm of the sellout audiences. Intense emotion in the company combined with the charged atmosphere around spectators, all well aware that they were witnessing the last page of a significant chapter in the history of American dance.

We disbanded before mid-May in 1940, and were not to meet again as a group until the Silver Jubilee season at Jacob's Pillow. Homecoming Week in 1957 was attended by all but one of the original members of the men's group. Fern Helscher came up from New York with Fred Hearn, who took one day off from his duties as stage director of *Damn Yankees*. Foster Fitz-Simons and Harry Coble came from North Carolina, where Foster is on the drama department faculty at his alma mater, the University of North Carolina. Harry teaches dancing and currently is choreographer and dance director of Paul Green's outdoor drama, *The Stephen Foster Story*, given at Bardstown, Kentucky. Frank Overlees traveled all the way from California and Wilbur McCormack, an Army major, flew to the Jubilee festivities from Fort Leavenworth, Kansas. Barton took his first vacation in a year from *My Fair Lady*, and danced on the Homecoming program. Jess Meeker was playing for Pillow classes and performances during the whole Silver Jubilee, and George Horn, who lives in Springfield, was in on all reunion activities. Several of the boys served in various services during World War II and Johnny Schubert was lost on a mission. A new dormitory at the Pillow is named in his memory.

I was very proud of my wonderful "sons," who have grown into fine, solid citizens, every one. I was long Papa Shawn to those men, and to generations of dance students, and I am now Grandpapa Shawn to a host of youngsters, several named for me, including Michael Sean (Shawn) Fitz-Simons and Susan Shawn Overlees.

Since the final performance of my men's group, twenty years ago, I have worked ceaselessly in the field of dance education, a new career, my third, and as challenging to me as the first two.

●●●

23

Choreography for Two Decades

N I finished twenty-seven years of continuous touring in 1940, and since then theoretically have spent summers at Jacob's Pillow and winters in Eustis, Florida. Actually in the past two decades, I have traveled 100,000 miles by plane, train, ocean liner, station wagon, and limousine. I have done hundreds of one-night stands as lecturer and dance soloist, and as adjudicator for regional dance organizations. During one short season, I toured in a chartered bus with my Jacob's Pillow Dance Festival Company that played forty-five engagements in nine and a half weeks. I have been twice to Europe, several times to Canada, and once to South America, ever searching for dance attractions to be presented at Jacob's Pillow. Journeys have sometimes interrupted my stay at Lee, and one winter I was able to spend only six days at my Eustis home.

Jacob's Pillow is now a school which has made an educational dream come true for me; it's a showcase for dance soloists and performing companies, and a mecca for thousands who attend the annual Dance Festivals. It's true that I bought the place near Lee, Massachusetts, believing that I wanted it to be a hideaway where I could rest and do my creative work undisturbed. It's equally a fact that with my eyes wide open and by the efforts of my own two hands, I worked on and directed the projects which brought the world to my doorstep, and completely ruined the place as a cloistered retreat.

The incorporated Jacob's Pillow today spreads over 150 acres and increased facilities include huge parking areas and more than thirty buildings. The Ted Shawn Theatre, opened on July 9, 1942, I myself dedicated on July 8 with *Four Dances Based on American Folk Music* and the *Doxology* performed for an audience made up of members of the board of directors, students, faculty, and the staff of school and theater.

The Jacob's Pillow school is now a University of the Dance with credits, both graduate and undergraduate, granted by Springfield College. My associate directors are John Christian and Carol Lynn, who also is Dance Director of the Preparatory Department, Peabody Institute, in Baltimore. Teachers have included the greats among performers and in the field of dance education. Our registration has increased steadily over the years and students have come to us from every state; from Mexico, Panama, Canada, Europe, Scandinavia, South America, and the Orient. A few scholarships have been made available and, in 1957, the Rockefeller Foundation gave a $5000 grant to the University of the Dance for a scholarship fund.

John Martin, dean of American dance critics, wrote in *The New York Times*, June 12, 1955, "Jacob's Pillow has become not only the largest dance event of the summer season but also one of the most important of our native institutions." Since 1953 Jacob's Pillow has become an international institution by offering in American debuts foreign dance soloists and outstanding foreign companies too numerous to list. We are presenting more and more American civic ballet companies, and our theater programs have listed 150 premières of new dance works, solo and group. We give from fifty to sixty performances during the annual Festival with programs usually combining ballet, modern and ethnic dancing, and mime works.

Every program is planned with full consideration of its educational value to our students and not as entertainment for the public; it is just incidental that the programs are increasingly popular with a widening audience. In pre-performance talks, I always make it clear that the variety and caliber of dance works and dancers presented are specifically to enrich the experience of students, from beginners to professional teachers, who attend the school. Through the Festival performances students have unique opportunities to observe the professional use of many techniques and to see outstanding and successful performers from many countries to which I have traveled to audition solo dancers and dance companies.

I have been away from Jacob's Pillow for only one summer season since I first bought the land. In 1947 I was sick and exhausted from overwork and, to keep from going under mentally and physically, went *down under* for an Australian tour that gave me both a new lease on life and renewed interest in long-range planning for Jacob's Pillow.

From the beginning the sabbatical jaunt gave me a lift. Two hundred old friends and colleagues attended a farewell party for me at Ruth St. Denis's studio at Los Angeles where I was the house guest of Brother St. Denis and his wife. In Honolulu, Kulumanu, former Denishawn dancer and exponent of the true, sacred hula of old Hawaii, gave me a most glamorous party attended by three hundred guests. Entertainment included dances by Hawaii's thrilling performer, Iolani Luahine, and storytelling by Mary Pukui.

By the time I got to Perth I had shaken off a lot of my cares. Australia was restorative but hardly restful, because I gave forty-eight solo performances in five major cities. Government officials set up a *corroboree* of the kind that had been arranged before only for the Duke of Windsor, when he was Prince of Wales, and for King George VI. Delissaville, a community of half a dozen shacks, was the site of the gathering of the Wargaitj, an aboriginal tribe of the Northern Territory to whom word had been sent that they were to perform for the "big boss dance man of the world." The days of dancing were the most sensational choreographic experience of my life, and on the last afternoon I danced, sans costume or music, as a thank-you for the hundreds of tribesmen who had performed during the week-long *corroboree*.

My only trip out of the United States that was pure fun and all vacation was the Christmas holiday of 1949 spent in Haiti with Bertha Damon and John Christian. We saw performances by a native dance company directed by and starring Jean Leon Destiné, who had taught and performed at the Pillow the previous summer. He held company auditions that we attended, though I myself was not auditioning but just plain enjoying the dancing. Through Destiné's efforts we were able to be present at three spine-tingling voodoo ceremonies.

A flying trip to Scotland, England, Denmark, and Sweden in the spring of 1957 was supposed to be a vacation, and we did have glorious times with dancer friends in all those countries. But in England I had a long business talk with Madame Rambert that began negotiations for her company's ultimate appearance at the Pillow in 1959. A return to Europe in the fall of 1958 took us to Denmark, Ireland, Holland,

where I was invited to speak by the Dance Club of Holland
and saw the Ballet of the Lowlands that I hope someday to
have at the Pillow; to Germany, Paris, Italy, and back to England for discussions of definite plans for the Ballet Rambert's
American debut.

John Christian went with me in February of 1960 to see
a Lima, Peru, dance company that may be showcased at some
future Dance Festival. He is an invaluable technical consult-
ant who can decide what numbers from the repertoire of any
given company will be most effective on the Jacob's Pillow
stage, and he helped to make the final decisions about the
Ballet Rambert in 1958.

The highlight of that 1958 trip, and one of the great experiences of my life, was my audience with His Majesty Fred-
erick IX, King of Denmark. The reason for that event dated
back for a full year.

I went to the Pillow in the spring of 1957 stimulated by
an honor I cherish, the coveted annual Capezio Award which
read: *FOR HIS SERVICE TO THE DANCE in making
possible the performances of dancers and dance companies,
both native and imported, both experimental and traditional,
on the Jacob's Pillow Dance Festival, which he founded
25 years ago and which, under his continuing direction has
grown into an annual event of international recognition.* That
award seemed to make my Silver Jubilee year complete and I
was totally unprepared for the next recognition.

On July 10 I received a letter from Denmark's Ambassador
to the United States explaining that "His Majesty, the King
of Denmark, on June 20, conferred upon you the Cross of
the Knight of Dannebrog, as an appreciation of your valuable
work in the cultural field, an achievement that has been very
much appreciated in Denmark." The official envelope contained the Cross itself and the document from the King which
made me a Danish Ridder (knight). The Cross can be worn

only in the presence of the King of Denmark or at state functions where the Danish Ambassador is officially representing the King. There's a miniature cross which I can and do wear with evening clothes on gala occasions, and a rosette for the lapel of my daytime suits. Whatever my title at Jacob's Pillow and in the world of the dance, I am any place now *Ridder of Dannebrog* or *Ted Shawn R. af Dbg*. When I arranged that the ten leading soloists of the Royal Danish Ballet should make their American debut at Jacob's Pillow in 1955, I had no idea that the signed contract would eventually lead me into the royal palace.

I was completely charmed by the monarch, so beloved by the Danes, who is a perceptive balletomane and a fine musician respected by professionals. His usual minute and a half audience was extended to ten minutes while we chatted about Danish dancing and dancers. I almost had a moment of panic when, after repeating my appreciation for the honor of being knighted, I backed toward the door fumbling for the doorknob. The King helpfully said, "The knob is on your left." What he meant was on his left as he faced the door. Finally, I managed to turn the knob but with my right hand, and suddenly understood the slight confusion. The King of Denmark, of course, had never had to back out of that room!

A number of activities which keep me traveling are continuations of lifetime interests: dance as an integral part of religious expression, ethnic dancing, and the education of young dancers.

I gave the first Christian church service in dance forms more than forty years ago, and ever since then religious themes have been recurrent in my choreographic works. Since 1950 I have given a number of religious dance lectures to church groups, and at Boston I taught and conducted roundtable discussions at a three-day meeting of leaders of religious rhythmic choirs from all over New England. From that conference grew an organization designed to correlate the activities of groups interested in sacred dance; to stimulate conventions; to provide a clearing house for information, choreography, and mutual advice. A Rhythmic Choir course, first given at the Pillow in 1958, was attended by leaders of choirs and ministers with their wives, and is now an annual pre-season course.

Talks on ethnic dancing have ranged from the elementary "Costumes and Fabrics of the Orient," which has so long been in my lecture repertoire, to a scholarly series for the Ethnological Dance Center in New York. Ruth St. Denis and I gave joint dance programs at the American Museum of Natural History's series "Around the World in Dance and Song" in both 1950 and 1951.

Ruth has appeared on many Jacob's Pillow Dance Festival programs and, after a long hiatus, we gave a few concert programs together in 1949. I was commentator the next year at her Carnegie Hall solo concert in which she danced more wonderfully than ever before to a sellout house. Our first new duet in more than twenty years was *Quest*, with Ravel music, that we performed at the Pillow in 1951. On August 13, 1957, we celebrated our forty-third wedding anniversary during the Silver Jubilee Festival.

Regional dance festivals are part of an exciting movement that is sweeping across the United States, and I have been delighted to co-operate with those organizing and promoting the significant activities. One of the most taxing tours made for the regional cause followed my return from Europe on Christmas Eve, 1958. I left on an adjudicating trip on January 3 and, by February 1, had motored four thousand miles from New York to Michigan to Florida. There I settled in to evaluate the twenty-eight ballets I had seen; to write a meticulous report with recommendations for a festival program based on eight ballets I had adjudicated. I continue to talk to college groups, and one spring lectured to a series of classes at Springfield though the commitment required me to commute once a week from New York to Massachusetts.

Just after I passed my sixtieth birthday I made my debut as an actor with the Ice House Players at Mount Dora, Florida. In *Death Takes a Holiday* I played Death, a role I repeated at the Berkshire Playhouse in Stockbridge the following summer. Since then I have played lead roles in *The Circle* and *My Three Angels* with the Ice House group. As actor I am not up to playing King Lear straight, but I realized a long-time ambition to portray the role when Myra Kinch created her dance drama *Sundered Majesty* at Jacob's Pillow. She did a strong choreography; Manuel Galea, her husband, composed beautiful music for the dance work and edited the Shakespeare text which was read off stage by Adolph Anderson as The Voice of Lear. I have since appeared in two other Kinch-Galea works, *Bajour* and *Sound of Darkness*.

It may seem from the frequency with which urge, interests, and crises take me away from Eustis that I don't like my home. Nothing could be further from the truth. It is beautiful, quiet, and the place where I can indulge two favorite pastimes: cement mixing and wood carving. When I wanted a quiet room where I could write in peace away from the disturbance of telephone and callers, I dug a foundation, poured a concrete floor for my Pout House, a name borrowed from a dear friend and neighbor, Mary McLeod, who had her hideout garden room first. My Pout House was christened before it was finished when I moved in to complete the manuscript of *Every Little Movement*, my book on Delsarte that I privately printed in 1954.

I tackled bricklaying in 1955 when I topped a cement coping with a nice brick pattern. In 1957 a carport was added to the house, and workmen completed the guest house in February 1960. While the builders worked they could look right across the lawn at me doing every unorthodox thing at the pumphouse, my cement project for the season. It was embarrassing for an amateur like me to be spied on by professionals. I kept at it, however, for I find any leisure period in which I cannot mix cement a dull time. I have never minded the frequent necessity of pouring cement for constructions at the Pillow, and enjoyed every minute spent on construction of the Jacob's Pillow tea garden terrace with its crazy-quilt pattern of multicolored slates.

I was past fifty when I took up wood carving, inspired by a creative urge to combine motion and the human form in wood as I had in dance. Every wood carver understands the pleasure implicit in learning about wood grains and textures; it has given me deep satisfaction to work with many kinds of wood, including the mahoganies of Africa and the Philippines, and I find the challenge of a fine natural wood block absolutely irresistible.

In the past nineteen years I have done about thirty sculptures, one a large garden figure, and the rest small pieces. I've had one-man exhibits at the Ocala Public Library, at the University of Florida at Gainesville, and at the Berkshire Playhouse. I have always thought that Billy Miles, the Playhouse director, evidenced a wry sense of humor when he displayed my sculptures of nudes during weeks when his theater was giving *The Old Maid* and *Reclining Figure*.

When, in 1933, two well-meaning authors asked for permission to write a Shawn biography, I hedged politely. It seemed to me then that their proposed book would indicate the termination of a career which I was in no mood to end. I find myself of the same mind today. It is one thing to write memoirs of experiences and events that have marked a career, and quite another to detail inner thoughts, and complete chronological data with finality. Maybe, and only maybe, after

I have lived and worked for another decade, I will settle quietly to write the complete history of my life, an all-inclusive, definitive autobiography.

For the past sixteen years I have written annual newsletters to "my family," the hundreds of friends, that include associates and students all over the world. In the mimeographed letters I detail the events of the previous year, present my hopes and plans for long-range projects, and outline work in progress. These are lengthy letters—the one telling of the Silver Jubilee year was eighteen typewritten pages—and I send with them one flyer of picture highlights of the year past.

A friend, who has known me since 1911, gently chided me about being too egotistical in the newsletters and pointed out that a man has no right to be proud of his achievements in his main career, but only of his hobbies and sidelines. The interpretation of my enthusiastic reporting of each year was wrong. I try to share with the "family" an account of my doings, the good and the bad, and if I write with ebullience and excitement and pride, it is because those are things of my nature. I am not egoistic about my achievements in the field of the dance, for no one knows better than I how far I have fallen short of my goals, dreams, and standards. I am humbly grateful that God has allowed me so much fulfillment; that at sixty-nine I have the strength and health to do a job that's creative and constructive. All my life for every pat on the head I have had a simultaneous kick in the pants, and if at any time I was about to get a swelled head, my ego was promptly deflated. For the record, I do admit to the allowable vanity in my sculptures in wood, and my constructions in concrete, which give me such joy as I do them.

Life for me has more zest than ever. I only wish that I were quintuplets, for I have enough unfinished projects to keep five busy: one a dancer-actor-lecturer, another an executive, one a writer, one a sculptor, and yet another an expert in the garden—where I spend an increasing amount of time. Perhaps a sixth me could be a contemplative scholar and son of rest. I'd like that. Or would I?

GV
1785
.S5
A3
1979

GV
1785
.S5
A3

1979